Edited by
GESA KIRSCH AND
PATRICIA A. SULLIVAN

Methods and Methodology in Composition Research

Southern Illinois University Press
Carbondale and Edwardsville

Library of Congress Cataloging-in-Publication Data

Methods and methodology in composition research /
edited by Gesa Kirsch and Patricia A. Sullivan.
        p.   cm.
    Includes bibliographical references and index.
        1. English language—Composition and exercises—
    Research—Methodology. 2. English language—
    Rhetoric—Research—Methodology.
    I. Kirsch, Gesa. 1961– II. Sullivan, Patricia A., 1956–
    PE1404.M47   1992   91-20141
    808'.042'072—dc20   CIP
    ISBN 0-8093-1726-5—ISBN 0-8093-1727-3 (pbk.)

The paper used in this publication meets the minimum
requirements of American National Standard for
Information Sciences—Permanence of Paper for Printed
Library Materials, ANSI Z39.48-1984. ∞

Contents

v

PART II.   RESEARCH PROBLEMS AND ISSUES

Acknowledgments

WE WOULD LIKE TO acknowledge all the people
who helped make this book possible. Our thanks go to all the
authors who wrote and rewrote the chapters and who responded
with kindness and patience to our editorial suggestions and dead-
lines.

We are grateful for the support and suggestions from Kenney
Withers; working with him on this project has been a true delight.

We would also like to express thanks to our home institutions—
the University of New Hampshire and Wayne State University—
whose support made the many phone calls and numerous corre-
spondences between authors, editors, and publisher possible.

Special thanks go to close personal friends—Mark Weritz and
Anthony Schreiner.

Methods and Methodology in Composition Research

GESA KIRSCH AND PATRICIA A. SULLIVAN

Introduction

"RESEARCH," ROLAND BARTHES WRITES, is the name we give to "the activity of writing: . . . whatever it searches for, it must not forget its nature as language—and it is this which renders finally inevitable an encounter with writing" (198). Barthes calls attention to the nature of research as language to remind us that research is a discourse, that whatever it searches for, it finally and inevitably entails an act of writing. We encounter writing in the languages with which we conduct our search and in the discourses we compose to convey our findings to others. In composition studies, researchers encounter writing immediately as well as inevitably. Writing is not only the medium we use to make discoveries and impart findings to others but the very "it" we search for. In this respect, writing is what differentiates composition studies from other fields of inquiry and unites its practitioners as a research community.

Within this research community, however, there is little consensus that we are engaged in a common enterprise. Although writing "names" our subject, providing us with a common focus and purpose, there is considerable disagreement about the methods we use to investigate and constitute this subject. Thus, while we might wish to characterize ourselves as a disciplinary community that is uniformly concerned with the study and teaching of writing, we must also acknowledge that our various research practices—our methodological diversity—call this sense of community into question. Linda Flower notes:

> The sudden growth of research, scholarship, and new ideas, as
> well as the sometimes precipitous rush to polemical stands based
> on various moral, teacherly, or political imperatives, makes this a

1

good time to reach for more analytical and balanced visions, for a greater sense of the conditional nature of our various perspectives. It is time for the systematic and self-questioning stance that goes with theoretical explanations—whether we are explaining a historical event, an experimental or observational study, or an approach to teaching. (286)

The purpose of this collection is to contribute to a self-questioning stance, to raise the question of our methodological pluralism, and to cast into relief the issues that unite and separate us. Individual contributors representing a range of research perspectives wade into the methodological crosscurrents of our field, reflecting on the various ways they make knowledge, the various ways, in short, they write about writing.

Individual contributors critically examine their own work and choice of research methodologies, from case studies and ethnographies to cognitive and experimental studies, reflecting on the epistemological assumptions, practical questions, and ideological issues that inform or accompany their respective methods. As the title of our volume suggests, we distinguish between methods and methodology (though the two terms are often used interchangeably) to give equal emphasis to the practical and philosophical issues associated with composition research. Following Sandra Harding, we are defining *method* as a technique or way of proceeding in gathering evidence, and *methodology* as the underlying theory and analysis of how research does or should proceed (3). In each chapter, methods and methodology—the pragmatics and problematics of knowledge making—are intertwined. Contributors address a wide range of questions. What problems emerge in the process of inquiry, and what issues are raised by a particular methodology? What constitutes data? How are data used in producing knowledge, generating theories, and building models? What kinds of questions can and cannot be answered with a given method of research? How does the researcher resolve these problems and issues? In addressing such questions, authors bring to the fore the critical but often tacit assumptions that guide different research approaches in composition, issues that all researchers face when designing, conducting, and reporting research studies but that are rarely reported in the literature because disciplinary conventions and publication requirements do not solicit such discussions.

Qualitative research, for example, presents problematics in the area of researcher-to-subject relations. What degree of objectivity can and should the composition researcher maintain? What information is relevant and what is irrelevant? Who decides on the relevance of data? How should the researcher deal with highly sensitive or personal information provided by an informant? What criteria should a researcher use to resolve ethical problems and potential conflicts of interest? How do assumptions about gender, race, and class inform the observations of the researcher and the perceptions of participants in the study? These are only a few of the questions that practitioners have begun to ask with respect to qualitative research. Similar kinds of questions are now being asked of all research methods. This volume provides a forum in which established researchers address such questions through the lens of their own research experiences; they frequently illustrate their discussions by referring to studies they have conducted or to other published reports. Our hope is that readers will similarly be able to use this forum to reflect critically on their own research approaches, comparing their experiences with those of the contributors and emerging with a deeper understanding of and respect for the problems that engage us all. And like Carol Berkenkotter, we hope that "when we articulate our models of knowing and discuss our differences in good faith, it becomes much easier to stop hurtling epithets (such as 'number-crunchers' and 'storytellers') and engage in the kind of 'multimodal approaches' that Janice Lauer and others have advocated" (70).

This collection is intended for a wide audience, not only experienced scholars and researchers but also teachers and administrators and graduate students entering the field. A growing number of writing teachers are becoming active researchers, and many administrators wish to undertake research projects in their own writing programs and writing centers. We hope this collection will encourage those teachers and administrators to view their own classrooms and writing programs as potential sites of inquiry and that it will prove useful to those who are interested simply in learning more about the nature of composition research. Graduate students interested in embarking on their own research will be introduced to procedural and theoretical issues not readily apparent from reading research reports alone.

Our collection includes chapters on some of the most commonly used research approaches in composition studies, but we also have included perspectives that often have been overlooked in traditional collections on research methods, for example, theoretical, historical, and feminist approaches to research. While the inclusion of such perspectives allows us to expand conventional definitions of methodology, we also have had to limit chapters on more traditional research methods. We do not have chapters solely devoted to quasi-experimental research or survey studies, for example, although several authors discuss these methods when they address epistemological issues that cut across various methodologies. Because this collection aims to expand our understanding of research methodologies, we decided to present reflective essays that examine procedures, assumptions, and issues relevant to a broad range of research methods, and not to only a few well-established methods. Due to space limitations, contributors often had to confine themselves to addressing only one or two of the critical issues associated with any one research methodology. The chapters in this volume, then, do not aim to present a comprehensive view; instead, they focus on one or two pertinent methodological points in order to illustrate the kinds of questions researchers need to ask themselves and to foster a dialogue within and across diverse communities of researchers.

The book is divided into two parts. Chapters in part I represent a spectrum of research methods and methodologies that are commonly used or that are gaining prominence in composition studies; chapters in part II focus on problems and issues that cross or transcend methodological boundaries and are of concern to most composition researchers. Collectively, chapters in the first part reflect both the affinities that diverse research approaches share and the points of contention they harbor; all advance the notion that composition research proceeds not from a preformulated, fixed, or prescriptive research design but from a question or issue that delimits and helps define the options available to a researcher. Chapters in the second part take a metatheoretical approach to composition research, addressing issues that confront researchers across the spectrum inscribed in part I. Boundaries among the methodological perspectives are far from obvious, however, and authors often address issues that are developed more fully in part II. For convenience' sake, we have organized the book into two parts, but we see the methods and issues covered in each part as more fluid and interactive than the visual and physical divisions suggest.

In the first three chapters of part I, authors discuss historical, feminist, and theoretical approaches to composition scholarship. In "Dreams and Play: Historical Method and Methodology," Robert Connors discusses the problems of data collection that historical scholars confront at the outset of inquiry, as well as specific issues that arise during the research process. Noting that "all received wisdom is partial, incomplete," Connors argues that history is the telling of stories, and we will need multiple stories if we are to recover a history that has been lost for 150 years. In "Feminism and Methodology in Composition Studies," Patricia Sullivan reflects on the virtual silence in composition studies on issues of gender relative to feminism's influence in other academic disciplines; then she explores the possibility and conditions of a feminist methodology in composition. Sullivan argues that a fully realized feminist voice in composition studies will entail both reactive and proactive components—feminist rereadings and critiques of androcentric discourse practices in the academy and empirically based studies of the relationships between gender and writing that can transform the social inequities and relations of power they uncover. In "Writing Theory : : Theory Writing," Susan Miller reconfigures Barthes's claim that research is the name we give to the activity of writing, noting that we inscribe our own theories of writing in the very act of writing about theory. Miller distinguishes between "the theory we say we have" and "the theory we actually have." She argues that while the field of composition necessarily constructs theoretical bases for its discourses about writing, such bases have not actually persuaded us to significantly redefine either our assumptions about written discourse or our teaching practices. She sketches the emergence of a "fully theoretical phase," one that draws simultaneously from local and metatheoretical perspectives to theorize both "the text we are in" and the textual practices we teach.

In the next two chapters, authors take texts or transcribed texts as their principal source of data to explore the epistemological and cultural assumptions we bring to our analysis of written and spoken language. Thomas Huckin discusses discourse analysis as a means of studying written communication and its epistemological implications. He argues that after a decade of relative neglect, the linguistic analysis of written texts is reemerging as a major component in composition research because scholars have become sensitive to intertextuality and culturally based discourse conventions as they explore the contextual factors involved in writing. In "Analyzing Talk about Writing," Peter Mortensen examines two approaches to conversation analysis: one emanates from a linguistic tradition and is grounded in a Cartesian philosophy of mind; the other issues from a sociological tradition that contemplates language in phenomenological terms. Mortensen considers the practical difficulties of conducting research on talk about writing and then argues that the socioethnographic approach best serves composition researchers whose goal is to describe the social construction of meaning in talk about writing.

In the next three chapters, individual writers, writing communities, and classrooms form the principal subjects or sources for investigation. In "The Narrative Roots of the Case Study," Thomas Newkirk focuses on the case study and the problem of generalization. Noting that educational researchers have traditionally denounced the case study as unscientific, as useful only for generating hypotheses to be tested scientifically, or as valuable only in its capacity to create a particularized or idiographic portrait of the learner, Newkirk claims that we regularly draw general conclusions from the particular accounts of case studies. Unlike the experimental study, where the methodology supposedly assures generalizability, Newkirk argues, the case study seeks the assent of the reader, primarily through a depiction of the learner that corresponds to individuals the reader has known. In "Ethnography and Composition: Studying Language at Home," Beverly Moss notes that as composition scholars have increasingly come to embrace ethnographic methodology, they have necessarily had to reexamine conventional procedures for data collection and analysis because composition researchers are studying communities with which they have some prior experience or of which they are members. Moss describes her own experience in researching the rhetorical practices of an institution she has belonged to since birth—the African American church—to highlight some of the problems that arise by virtue of the ethnographer's familiarity with his or her own community. She challenges composition researchers to examine their own roles in the communities they study and the ways in which these roles influence how and what they observe in those communities. In "Composition from the Teacher-Research Point of View," Ruth Ray examines the purpose, practice, and politics of teacher research. The distinguishing features of teacher research, she writes, are that it arises out of practice rather than theory, and it is written first and foremost for teachers. Thus, she argues, teacher research is not just a set of methods researchers can use to study writing in the classroom; it is an ideology that determines who and what will be studied, how a study will be conducted, whom the research will affect, how the study will be presented, and where the results will be used. The next two chapters examine more formal research methods in the context of how composition studies has grown and changed as a research discipline. Karen Schriver, in "Connecting Cognition and Context in Composition," explores the nature of cognitive research and its relation to social-constructionist approaches to composition. She urges us to conduct more research on the thinking processes of writers and readers as situated in cultural contexts and to examine the rhetoric of our inquiry in conducting empirical research. In the last chapter in this part, Richard Beach discusses the nature of descriptive and experimental research, its assumptions about studying human activities like composing, and its relation to both qualitative research and content analysis. He distinguishes between various experimental and quasi-experimental procedures, illustrates his discussion with examples of various studies, and explores the benefits and limitations of such research.

In part II, authors deal with issues that cut across many kinds of research and therefore confront many composition researchers today: methodological pluralism, definitions of validity and reliability, collaboration and coauthorship, and the politics of knowledge construction implied in composition research. Gesa Kirsch argues that methodological pluralism is possible if researchers consider several of the important issues raised by feminist scholars. Among these issues are an open discussion of the researcher's agenda (it is never disinterested), the researcher's relation to the subject (the researcher's presence and authority are never neutral), and the purpose of the researcher's questions (they must be grounded in participants' experiences and relevant to participants). Combining multiple methods, Kirsch argues, allows us to see the diversity that accompanies any human behavior as complex as composing and enables us to resist building a single, monolithic theory of composing. Keith Grant-Davie describes the issues involved in defining such terms as validity and reliability as they apply to classifying and coding research data. Using the example of a coding scheme designed to classify readers' and writers' comments from oral protocols, he focuses on the critical decisions necessary to classify and sort research data. Grant-Davie goes on to discuss how coding and classifying data are involved in virtually all research efforts, whether the research is formal or informal in nature. He suggests that classifying data is ultimately an act of interpretation that, nevertheless, can illuminate research findings by functioning as a heuristic for discovering patterns in writers' activities, written texts, or contexts for writing.

Duane Roen and Robert Mittan, in their chapter "Collaborative Scholarship in Composition: Some Issues," directly confront a paradox that currently vexes many composition scholars: as teachers, we encourage collaborative writing on the part of our students, but as scholars, our own collaborative efforts are still infrequent and often undervalued by institutional practices (for example, the evaluation procedures typical of promotion and tenure committees). Roen and Mittan discuss the dynamics and benefits of collaborative research, but they also reveal the institutional prejudices that coauthors face. They argue that we cannot adequately train graduate students to enter the profession unless we collaborate with them in research and publication, and thus, it is important that we challenge the privileged status of single-authored scholarship in the humanities as reflected in the institutional merit and promotion system. In the final chapter, "Methods, Methodologies, and the Politics of Knowledge: Reflections and Speculations," Lisa Ede speculates about the politics inherent in selecting research methodologies. She describes her own experiences as a researcher and her growing awareness of the epistemological questions and political issues associated with the research methods upon which she has relied. Ede explores, among other things, the relationship between "our personal experiences and the work we produce," and she critiques the posture of disinterestedness that is often assumed by literary critics and social scientists alike.

As this brief overview no doubt suggests, our collection does not purport to achieve methodological consensus. We have invited contributors to think critically about their own research practices and hence to reflect on the current state of composition research itself, recognizing that dissent is often the condition of theoretical self-awareness, that self-consciousness emerges, as Gerald Graff notes, "when consensus breaks down" (253). We concur with Anne Herrington, in her review of the first twenty years of publication of *Research in the Teaching of English,* that there remains an

> "abiding uneasiness" within our own research community over research paradigms that differ from our own. It is difficult to accept them as valid given the differences in starting assumptions, methods, and language, and (particularly if one's work is not in the dominant paradigm) the need to make a place for one's own work. Recognizing this difficulty, we still need to continue the process of defining ourselves as a research community through the critical assessment of the nature of our work, its quality, and its guiding theoretical assumptions. (134)

But we believe the very plurality of perspectives represented in this volume may be taken as a sign that we are growing more confident in our identity as a research community and that we are beginning to understand the complexity involved in adapting research methodologies that have their origin in vastly different disciplinary traditions. Composition studies and rhetoric are likely to be shaped by methodological pluralism in the future; we see this collection as a starting point for serious engagement with the methodological issues that face researchers, teachers, scholars, and administrators alike. As we approach the twenty-first century, classroom populations will diversify and so will teaching strategies, research questions, and the methods and methodologies best suited for addressing a range of new research problems. Only by understanding the implicit social, political, and methodological issues involved in our work—the writing about writing we call research—can we partake in self-consciously shaping our growing research community with respect, care, and responsibility for our students, colleagues, and fellow researchers.

Works Cited

Barthes, Roland. "Writers, Intellectuals, Teachers." *Image-Music-Text.* Trans. Stephen Heath. New York: Hill and Wang, 1977.

Berkenkotter, Carol. "The Legacy of Positivism in Empirical Composition Research." *Journal of Advanced Composition* 9 (1989): 69–82.

Flower, Linda. "Cognition, Context, and Theory Building." *College Composition and Communication* 40 (1989): 282–311.

Graff, Gerald. *Professing Literature: An Institutional History.* Chicago: U of Chicago P, 1987.

Harding, Sandra. "Introduction: Is There a Feminist Method?" *Feminism and Methodology.* Ed. Sandra Harding. Bloomington: Indiana UP, 1987. 1–14.

Herrington, Anne. "The First Twenty Years of *Research in the Teaching of English* and the Growth of a Research Community in Composition Studies." *Research in the Teaching of English* 23 (1989): 117–38.

Part I

Research Methods
and Methodology

1   Robert J. Connors

Dreams and Play

Historical Method and Methodology

Historical research, until a decade ago only a minor part of the ongoing activity in composition studies, has recently been evolving into one of the recognized strands in our burgeoning field. Unlike certain other research strands, however, historical research uses methods more closely related to traditional humanities inquiry than to scientific or social-scientific paradigms. What, exactly, does writing composition history presuppose and entail?

What Constitutes Data in Historical Studies?

It has been common until recently to think of data in historical research as composed of historical "facts." These facts would be uncovered by assiduous gleaning of sources, pieced together like a jigsaw puzzle (which has, of course, only one possible correct solution), and presented to readers as "the historical truth." Historians and careful students of history, however, have always known that such an idealized view of their work with data was false. In reality, data in historical studies are made up of at least these three elements: the historian's perceptions of the present, her assemblage of claims based on study of materials from the past, and an ongoing internal dialogue about cultural preconceptions and prejudices and the historian's own. These three elements—present awareness, archival retrieval, and realization of prejudice—are the pieces of information that the historian brings

15

to the attempted solution of the historical problem facing her. Let's look at these elements in more detail.

It may sound strange to say that among the most important data for the historical researcher in composition studies are perceptions of the present day, but every narrator knows it. Until we have some knowledge of the situation a posteriori, our ability to understand the prior situation is hopelessly lacking. Partially, of course, knowledge about the present is central data for the historian because causes can be clearly understood only in the light of their effects; each generation of economic historians since the New Deal has understood and analyzed Roosevelt's policies differently as more and more cause-effect data have come in. But I am also calling perceptions of the present central data because they stimulate questioning, excitement, and curiosity, without which history of any sort is a dead compiling of facts without affect. Without intellectual curiosity, without the wish to discover and explain something about life, history *is* a dust bin.

Knowledge of the present is important data for any historian, but it is particularly fundamental to the history of composition studies, because that history is relatively short. Historians of classical rhetoric, for instance, use their knowledge of the present day primarily in a general way; they examine claims and written sources from ancient Greece with their own perceptions of rhetorical action and their own knowledge of human and institutional behavior in mind. The knowledge of the present they bring to the task is of general human nature and of the slow evolution of large institutions. This is how historians of the remote past must operate, since the "causes" seen at a remove of two millennia must have relatively broad and general effects today. But the historian of composition studies, an essentially modern discipline, sees all around her the direct and specific effects of the activities whose genesis she studies. There, in that classroom next door, is the new edition of the *Heath Handbook;* not even D. C. Heath knows it's really the fourteenth, not the twelfth edition—but the historian knows it was the first handbook, born in 1907. Here, in this curriculum meeting, someone is arguing for the "old four mode from classical rhetoric," and the historian knows that the modes were made up by Alexander Bain in 1866. A news magazine rends the welkin with warnings about "the new illiteracy," and the historian knows this is the fourth great American literacy crisis. All around us are the data of the present, and they constantly press on us the immediate question, "What shall we do?" The historian tries to help answer this by looking into less immediate but essential questions, "What have people done in the past?" and "How did things come to be this way?"

From these observational data we begin. All around the composition historian are phenomena that need to be explained. Why is freshman English the only course required for every student? Where does the paragraph come from? Why do students at many colleges fold their papers in half lengthwise before passing them in, without being instructed to do so? Why are there instructors? Why do many literature specialists despise composition? When did the grading system begin? Is student writing worse now than it was in 1900? In my own case, the vital question often used to be, "How did things get this bad?" History nearly always begins as simple curiosity about how we got here.

The next kind of data must be uncovered by painstaking research. We take our questions and our perceptional data, as all historians must, into the Archive, the storehouse of data about the past. The Archive must be explored, analyzed, cross-checked, deconstructed, reconstructed, made meaning of, be stripped, checked, and polished. Here, for the composition historian, is the world of the written word, the printed word, the picture, the table, the diagram, the voice on the tape. The Archive is where storage meets dreams, and the result is history.

The overwhelming bulk of data from the past that the historian of composition studies must deal with is in written and printed form, and what I am calling the Archive actually consists of two discrete kinds of sources, library and archival. Libraries are repositories for printed and published materials generally, while institutional archives deal in more specific primary sources, many of which exist nowhere else and were never meant to be published. A great deal of the material for composition history is available in good research libraries, since most records having to do with teaching writing in general—as opposed to composition teaching at a specific school—were printed and distributed in either books or journals and magazines. From the 1820s on, rhetoric and writing instruction were important issues in American education, and there is a great deal of information to be sifted through in library sources.

When doing library research, the historian must initially determine whether secondary sources exist, how complete they are, and whether they must be consulted. Only a decade ago, this was much less of an issue, but recently the list of creditable secondary sources in composition history has grown markedly. We now have five or six good short books on composition history, and fifty or sixty respectable journal articles. About even the best of these works, most historians have mixed feelings. On the one hand, it is important to know who has been doing work in the area and what they have found out. No one wants to reinvent the cotton gin. Sharing sources and methods is not just collegial; it is good sense. On the other hand, as the field has grown, so too has a healthy tendency grown to disregard secondary sources, to go directly to the primary sources. Some historians refuse to read secondary sources, especially the better-known works by such authors as Kitzhaber and Berlin, because they want to approach the primary works without preconceptions they could have avoided. Too much reliance on secondary sources may result in historians' efforts being relegated to "normal science," cleaning up small-scale problems within the larger paradigm of the existing source's conception. Perhaps the best answer is to read many secondary sources voraciously, seeking for methods, style, coherence, looking for models to pattern your own history on—in any specific area but your own. There, go to the primary sources. See what *they* say to you.

And what are those primary sources? Composition textbooks

since the beginning of composition history have been obvious sources, able to tell us much about both the theory and the practice of writing pedagogy. From John Walker's *Teacher's Assistant in English Composition* of 1795 onward, they were used as the theoretical matrices of courses. Soon after 1810, questions to be asked in classes became part of textbook apparatus, thus providing classroom organization. Beginning in the 1830s, rhetorics also came to include written exercises, devices which organized homework activities for students. These "do-everything" books could be used by less-experienced teachers as the pedagogical organizing tools for entire courses, and with them the "modern" form of the rhetoric text was set. We can learn about theory, questions, exercises, advice, and assignments from these books. Historians argue about the degree to which we should assume that textbook organization really informed classroom practice, but no one claims that older textbooks do not constitute important data.

Specialized journals and even general magazines also represent important primary sources. From the 1840s onward, education journals like *Barnard's* dealt with pedagogical and even more specialized language and rhetoric issues. With the *Educational Review, PMLA, School Review,* and *Journal of Education* in the late nineteenth century, a recognizably modern literature on educational issues was created, and the researcher can find in them many articles on composition teaching. Finally, in 1912 comes *English Journal,* the first English-pedagogy journal, and throughout the rest of the century this journal and its eventual spinoffs, *College English* and *College Composition and Communication,* constitute the central fora for professional discussion. In addition, there have been periods—especially the late nineteenth and early twentieth centuries—when composition issues have been seen as so important that general-interest magazines such as *Harper's* and *Atlantic Monthly* would discuss them, and so traditional bibliographic tools like the *Poole's Index* of nineteenth-century magazines can be called into play.

The final primary source likely to be found in libraries is the "professional book" written for teachers or practitioners. Professional books about the teaching of writing go back to the 1890s, when the first media-driven literacy crisis had produced the freshman composition course as one of its answers. That course created its own methodological problems for curriculum planners, and specialized books for teachers have existed since then. There are descriptions of programs, tips for teachers, various forms of braggadocio and apologia among these books. Biographies and memoirs of various figures can be helpful, although few full-scale biographies of central figures in composition history have yet been done, and memoirs are about as rare.

With textbooks, journal and magazine articles, and professional books, the primary sources available at general scholarly libraries have probably been covered. Archives are specialized kinds of libraries that usually contain materials specific to one institution or activity. The archival record contains those rarest and most valuable of data, actual student writings, teacher records, unprinted notes and pedagogical materials, and ephemera that writing courses have always generated but rarely kept. Unlike printed sources, by nature meant for distribution and multiple copies, these notes, papers, and ephemera existed in only a single copy (or sometimes carbon-copy form). As a result, such important data are much more difficult for historians to get hold of than are printed sources. Unlike books and journals, which are cataloged by circulation in libraries and can thus be accessed through bibliographic search and interlibrary loan, archival papers and notes tend to be cataloged separately. Usually researchers have no way to know what college archives contain without hands-on examination, and that can be expensive and difficult for many scholars. There is to this point no central clearinghouse or depository for this sort of archival material; Harvard University's collection is the largest and most detailed, but it refers only to one school's work. The Richard S. Beal Collection at the University of New Hampshire was begun in 1989 as a central depository for composition archives, and over the next decade it should develop into a diverse collection in composition studies.

These are, then, what I call the Archive, those written and printed materials that most people think of as the only real historical sources. But finally, along with the historian's current perceptions and the inert archival material that can be worked with or discarded, there is one more source of data that the conscientious historian must keep in mind: his or her own prejudices. No person exists without prejudice. Our entire life experience functions to predispose us favorably toward some ideas or practices and less favorably toward others. Constitutional affinities and ideological positions form what Kenneth Burke calls *terministic screens* through which we view both current reality and archival materials. The question we face is how we work with our prejudices. No historian is free from prejudiced ideas, but no historian wishes to try for anything less than fair presentation of her findings. So the only way of dealing with our always already being prejudiced is to study the prejudices *as data*. Why do we admire Fred N. Scott and despise Adams S. Hill? Why do we dismiss the terms *clearness, force,* and *elegance* while we accept *unity, coherence,* and *emphasis*? Why do we find a sneer in our voices when we say the word "workbook"? We may not always be able to see all of our own terministic screens, certainly, but then again we cannot claim to know all of current reality or to have found all the possible archival sources. We work with what we can find of all three kinds of data.

All of historical work, then, is provisional, partial—fragments we shore against our ruin. We are trying to make sense of things. It is always a construction. It is always tottering.

How Are Data Used in Producing Knowledge, Generating Theories, and Building Models?

We always start with a hypothesis or a question. In some historical research, this question may be abstract, or prompted by other historians' assertions, or based on newly discovered archival material. In composition history, however, it is much more common for the motivating question to arise out of simple curiosity about one or both of two general situations: (1) Why are things around me as they are? or (2) Why do I see and judge things around me as I do?

Why, for instance, does every teacher know the four "modes of discourse" when they are so little treated in modern textbooks? That was the vague curiosity that began the research that ended in my essay "The Rise and Fall of the Modes of Discourse." In another case, the question arose in my mind, "Why do many teachers mark only the mechanical errors in papers?" That was a reasonable perception-data question. If that had been the only question I had considered, the result might have been a straight historical narrative that took no strong position on the phenomenon of journal marking. I had to admit, however, that I found superadded a more complex and interesting corollary question based on my own prejudices: "Why do I condemn formal-criterion grading when I consider it?" With this question, you see, we plunge into the complex world of the historian's own training, context, personality, ideology, and experience. And only from there do we go to the Archive for confirmation or denial.

So how do data first interact in historical research? Most historical writers, if they are honest, will admit that perceptions and prejudices always must come first in shaping a research question. Seldom does anyone plunge cold into the Archive without something to look for, something they're hoping to find, hoping to see proof of. To try to approach the Archive without even a general hypothesis would go against the human instinct to make sense of things. We gravitate toward organizing ideas. Old composition materials are seldom fascinating or enjoyable to read as art-prose, and we enter that jungle because we think something is there for us to track.

So theory generation is never really *ab ovo*. We start from theory, at least from a theory about building challenging, supportable hypotheses, and historians seldom work through serious archival research unless they have a hypothesis that they tacitly think is supportable. My hypothesis about formal-criteria marking went, at the beginning, something like this: "Paper-marking for mechanical correctives began sometime in the middle of the nineteenth century, probably as a result of handbook use, and it's a bad, a-rhetorical way to mark papers, used then, as now, by lazy, untrained teachers." Now I'm not claiming this is a good hypothesis. It's shot through, as early historical hypotheses often are, with vague assumptions, unsupported assertions, huge gaps in knowledge. It is, in fact, largely false. But it was a place to start. From that questionable but real starting place, built on perception and prejudice, I could go to the Archive with the initial distinctions I needed to begin work there.

What do historians do in the Archive, when they confront that inert, dusty mass of past records? Though it would be neat to be able to say that they sift through everything with hypothesis in hand, "keeping up a running fire of exclamations, groans, whistles, and little cries," drawing scientific deductions Holmes-like, t'aint true. What historians really do in the Archive—and really need to do—is play. Search is play.

How can I describe the work of historians in the Archive? It is not, cannot be, a forced march from hypothesis to support to further support to thesis, since more than half of all sources examined with hypothesis in mind turn out to have little or nothing to do with the question at hand. I might leaf through three or four volumes of early *English Journal*, as I did for a recent essay on the status and salaries of composition teachers, without seeing a single article on the topic. But neither is my examination of archival data ever a random stroll, turning pages without purpose. Historians seldom conduct basic research of that sort. Archival reading is, instead, a kind of directed ramble, something like an August mushroom hunt. There are various concurrent intentions in it: I am looking for information on my specific question; I am looking to increase my own general knowledge of various periods and persons; I am seeking to be better acquainted with the sources themselves; I am looking for fascinating anomalies; I am hoping for unexpected treasures; and of course I am seeking those conjunctions of historical evidence with sudden perception or understanding that occasionally light up the skies for the lucky historian and reveal a whole world whose genesis and current realities have been subtly reshaped— the "Ah!" of realization that is always the historian's true payoff.

To shift down a step, what we do is browse with directed intention. There is a track, constraint exercised by the developing hypothesis, but we may and must dart off the track to follow a likely scent, a fascinating claim, a mysterious author, a curious fact. I wander about the library with a stack of five-by-eight notecards and a legal pad—the cards for bibliography and citations, and the legal pad for the slowly accumulating "brainstorming" insights that accrue from gradual mental conjunction of the materials examined. The path is always circuitous. Following up one lead may take all afternoon, forcing me to chase through an early *College English* volume, then to the *National Union Catalog*, then to the library circulation computer and the Online Catalog for the Library of Congress computers, then over to my own office to check my database program, then back to the stacks, and finally—oh, frustration!—to the interlibrary loan office, which means a two-week wait before the chase can be taken up again.

As Nan Johnson once put it at a historians' "octolog," or symposium, we often seem unwilling to admit that our research can be exciting, can satisfy curiosity, can be . . . fun. But it can. Historical research at its best is detective work, with all the intellectual rewards of problem and puzzle solving. Of course, for every moment when "the game is afoot," there will always be hours of careful slogging through quotidian facts, deadly educational statistics, dreadfully written accounts of how writing is taught. But we must come out and say it—much archival research is fascinating, and much of the challenge of history is the challenge of puzzle solving.

What, specifically, do historians do as they read, browse, sift, write notes and cards? There are three primary parts to traditional historical analysis: external criticism, internal criticism, and synthesis of materials. These are not "stages" that must take place only in linear order; they are recursive steps that can take place in various orders. Let me, however, go through them one at a time.

External criticism has primarily to do with the choice of sources the historian will read. Given a hypothesis, she must first establish what sources are available that might support (or disprove) it, and then determine whether those available sources are indeed appropriate to the task or able to handle it effectively. It is here, at this primary stage, that researchers really need to know their Archives. What books, journals, paper, ephemera do they have access to? Which are the most likely to serve the needs of the project? For my recent essay, "The Creation of an Underclass," dealing with the status and labor of writing teachers, I was forced to a whole new level of external criticism, one not demanded by earlier projects. For previous work on textbooks, for instance, I had become familiar and comfortable with the University of New Hampshire Library holdings in old textbooks. But a complex sociocultural inquiry about the conditions surrounding composition teaching required very different sources. I had to acquaint myself with economic studies of college teaching, with educational reports and statistics, with histories of individual colleges and universities, with the few reports English professors ever wrote concerning their own status. I had to go to new journals; I had to explore new sections of the library stacks; I had to examine novel secondary sources; and I had to make extensive use of interlibrary loan. Poring over all this new material was quite a departure from the simpler history-of-ideas research that informed much of my early work, and possible sources seemed to ramify in countless directions. But I had to get as many sources as possible into my hands, and after a search of some months, I was confident that I had at least the rudiments of the map, if not a complete vision of the territory.

At the same time that she searches for and judges sources, the historian must also engage in the next stage of analysis—internal criticism. Internal criticism examines the sources found with the intent of making sure they are judged correctly. Historians check the language and usage of their sources, examine them for obvious or subtle biases, try to eliminate glosses or corruptions. Most importantly, internal criticism implies a search for corroborative support of claims made by sources. If thoughtful, defensible history has a methodological nexus, it must be in this search for corroboration. All records we have are written by human, all-too-human, agents. They are necessarily filled with self-justification, optimistic delusion, pessimistic distortion, partisan argument. Not a one can stand as the complete and trusty truth—not even the statistics. And so a process of comparison and corroboration is central work for the historian.

This internal criticism is especially important when studying the history of composition, because for the last century and a half, teaching writing has been an arena echoing with claims and counterclaims—a genuine rhetorical situation. As I have argued elsewhere, freshman composition is the only college-level course that was instituted to solve a perceived social problem rather than to investigate a branch of knowledge, so claims about its methods, necessity, and usefulness have always been as argumentative as they were expository. Composition historians must dig through this mass of claims and rejoinders. If we cannot always make judgments about whose arguments were right, we can at least try to determine certain factual realities. Barrett Wendell, for example, claims to have invented the "daily theme" at Harvard in the 1880s. Did he? This was the question that my colleague Tom Newkirk faced recently. Was this a claim that Tom, as a historian, wished to endorse? Through a process of internal criticism, he had to test this claim. What did Wendell's students say? What do the Harvard records and memoirs say? What did Wendell's colleagues think? What, if Tom could find evidence in the Harvard archives, do Wendell's teaching notes or student essays show? Only after a thorough cross-check of all these sources could the historian really support the claim.

As you can see, it is never possible to separate internal criticism from external criticism completely, because one often sends a historian out into a round of the other. To understand and accept any claim internal to a document, it must be compared to claims in other documents. When I was searching for information on instructors' salaries in 1920, I could not be certain about the figures I found until I had a second source that gave me approximately the same figures—a second source I had to get from interlibrary loan. Barbara Tuchman, in *Practicing History,* says that she never accepts a single primary source as effective evidence, but always contrasts at least two different accounts. This is not always possible in composition history, but enough different kinds of evidence exist to give a careful historian a sense of whether the archival fact will support a developing hypothesis.

The depth of corroboration needed for a historical claim has a direct relationship to the novelty and current acceptance of that claim. (This is why we cannot completely dispense with reading secondary sources.) What is the researcher's discourse community likely to know already, likely to accept as given? If I claim, for instance, that composition teaching burgeoned after the Civil War because of the growth of universities and the needs of a capitalist economy, I will hardly have to do more than cite one or two secondary sources. No one disagrees with those claims, and they need little corroboration today. But if I claim, as I have been doing lately, that composition burgeoned in America because of the demand of women to be taught rhetoric, the corresponding responses of men, and the general educational changes forced on colleges by coeducation after 1840, I will need to provide considerable evidence and extensive corroboration for that claim. It is a novel claim, and one that must be strenuously supported if it is to be accepted. My internal criticism of sources, given the intensely polemical nature of most of the nineteenth-century debates on coeducation and rhetorical training for women, will need to be deep. That is why I am currently four years into this project and have thus far published little about it.

When external and internal criticism have been brought forcibly to an end—and it is nearly always necessary to bring the research period to an end forcibly, since by its nature research is never "done," and investigation always seems more comfortable than conclusions—the final stage of analysis is synthesis of materials. This step corresponds in some ways to *dispositio* in classical rhetoric. The historian structures the scattered and disparate sources she has located and compared, bringing into play ideas of cause and effect, inductive generalizations, patterns of influence, taxonomic groupings, and all of the other various systems of connection by which we make sense of the world. Of course, since the research has itself been guided by a hypothesis, the synthesis of materials has in a sense been going on since the inception of the project. But even as the index cards mount up, even as the legal pad fills with hastily scrawled connections and insights, the shape of the final thesis-and-support often cannot be seen until the organizing and actual composing begin.

The way this usually happens for me is that the archival sources build up and interinanimate until they produce a subhypothesis that then generates further search. In the case of my "Creation of an Underclass" piece, which had as its general hypothesis the low pay and status of composition teachers, this subhypothesis developed as I struggled to understand why rhetoric came to be so despised at nineteenth-century American universities when it had been so respected at American colleges. What differentiated universities from colleges? Lawrence Veysey's *Emergence of the American University* told me that the answer was specialized schools. What were the most obvious kind? Graduate schools.

What did graduate schools produce? Ph.D.'s. So that was one line of evidence.

Then I turned to biographies of English professors and teachers active from 1880–1900—Adams Hill, Fred Newton Scott, Barrett Wendell, John Genung, Henry Frink. What I found there— what I had always vaguely known but had never really brought together in my mind—was that there *were* no Ph.D.'s in rhetoric. Where Ph.D.'s existed, they were in philology or literature. Except at Michigan between 1896 and 1927, no American university had ever granted rhetoric Ph.D.'s until speech departments took rhetoric over and separated it from written discourse. Why had this been the case? For the answer to that I had to go to the history of international graduate study, especially to the country after whose higher learning nineteenth-century Americans patterned their own: Germany. And there I found my answer, in sources on the German university system that I had never seen before: there was no German intellectual tradition of rhetoric after 1810, and no German rhetoric Ph.D.'s. So by synthesizing my study of American universities and colleges, the development of English departments and their associated literary and compositional luminaries, and the German intellectual condemnation of rhetoric, I was able to come up with a working subhypothesis: that composition teachers were marginalized because they had no Ph.D. licensure and no way to advance in the university hierarchy that licensure had created.

This subhypothesis existed through much of my research, of course, and when time came actually to draft the essay, the synthesis of materials was done on a much smaller scale. The questions involved in *writing* history are stylistic, presentational, small-scale. What order should the stack of note cards take? Which of these juicy quotes must be discarded as redundant? Of the two major modes of presentation available, thematic and chronological, which should be chosen where? How much general explanation does the background of the intended audience require? These are synthetic questions that have more to do with presentation than with research, yet that does not make them unimportant; many times a perceived need for better support during composing has sent me back (grudgingly, and sometimes frantically) to external and internal criticism.

So that is how developing data build theories in historical research. Occasionally a beautiful hypothesis is supported for a while only to be killed by a cruel counterfact, but more often hypotheses start as vague suppositions that are sharpened and directed by accumulating archival evidence.

What Kind of Questions Can and Can't Be Answered by Historical Research?

Obviously historical research can give fairly solid answers to discrete factual questions about the past. I can tell you what the first composition workbook was, and who invented the methods of exposition. David Russell can run down for you the first programs to use writing across the curriculum. Donald Stewart can name all of Fred Newton Scott's publications. And if we don't have the facts at our fingertips, we know where to get them, or at least whether they are likely to be had.

But these discrete historical facts hang in a vacuum, useless, without the interpretations that order them in all historical writing. And so the two questions that are continually argued about in historical writing are these: (1) Does this interpretation of the historical data seem coherent, reliable, interesting, useful? and (2) What can this interpretation of the past show us about the present and the future?

For the first question, there are criteria that can be applied to allow us at least provisional answers. We can make informed judgments about any historian's basic knowledge, depth of research, imaginative facility, ideological predispositions, and writing ability, to determine who writes history we will call "good." How original is the thesis? How broad is the explanatory power?

How many primary sources were consulted? Were any important sources missed or scanted? Are there careless generalizations? Are the assertions backed up with enough proof? Is there any attempt at explaining alternative interpretations, or is it a presentation of only one single strong side? Is the narrative written in a way that draws the reader along? Are the issues explored important or involving to the readership? These and other questions can clarify for us the "quality" of the history being presented.

For the second question, however, the one that historians are always being asked, the answer is much less clear. *Can* we learn about the present or the future from the past? On some levels, obviously, we can be advised by the lessons of the past. But can we learn enough, in enough systematic ways, to make any historian's view of the past an accurate guide to the present and future? The answer to this question must be, sadly, no.

Historical research cannot tell us what we should and should not do in any given set of circumstances. It cannot even give us the plausible "certainties" provided by statistical analysis. History is always written from probabilistic, and therefore rhetorical, points of view. All it can do is tell us stories, stories that may move us to actions but that in themselves cannot guide our actions according to any system. If history were, or could be, systematic, things might be different. But history is not, and never has been, systematic or scientific. Any attempt to make history predictive would have to assume that there are dependable recurring circumstances, which is simply not the case. In fact, history is narrative, and every attempt to create a system to give that narrative a predictive meaning is fraught with peril.

This is not to say that we cannot learn *anything* from history. If history does not allow us to predict or anticipate what is coming on the basis of what has been, it certainly does paint pictures of the past for us from which we can draw lessons. For example, the great literacy crisis of 1885 was followed by fifteen years of frantic attempts to solve it, and these attempts were then followed by thirty years of dogmatic torpor. I would appear foolish if I were to say that the great literacy crisis of 1976 would have to be followed by exactly the same scenario. History has too many cunning passages for that to be simply the case.

But what can I say, with any confidence, on the basis of knowing about the literacy crisis of 1885? Surely I can compare the social and cultural conditions of the time. Surely the economic reasons for and the pedagogic results of the 1885 crisis might tell me something about our own era. Surely the student papers of the time could give me insight into today's basic writing students and their papers. The point is that although what we face as teachers and scholars every day is always new, it is never completely new. Others have been here before, facing similar problems and choices. The story of their hopes, ideas, struggles, disappointments, and triumphs can tell us about our own stories. We may not learn how ours will end from how theirs ended, but we can gain valuable insight into people and their conditions, their motives, and their responses to problems.

So we cannot learn what to do from history. All we can learn is what others have done, perhaps a little about what not to do, and, perhaps, a little about who we are.

What Problems Emerge in the Process of Inquiry, and What Issues Are Raised by Historical Methodology?

The most obvious problem we face as historical researchers and writers is how to make our narratives reliable and persuasive. Practically, this issue comes down to the way in which induction balances deduction during the research process itself. How much do our preexisting ideas about what we will look for in the Archive create the data paths we then actually follow, rendering our narratives self-creating? The Chicago formalist critics used to castigate New Criticism as "a priori" criticism because New Critics would often choose some literary element a priori—an element like irony or ambiguity—and simply chase it down through a text or texts, ignoring other important formal elements at work there. Historians can always be pronounced guilty of this same offense, of course, because we hardly ever step into the archival forest without an existing hypothesis. We are always looking for something. The sticky point remains how the hypothesis we are using may constrain our search and make us less sensitive to other important elements in the historical equation. If an a priori hypothesis is too strong, too neat, it may take over the entire work of seeking archival data. The historian may end up searching through the stacks with blinders on, seeking only confirmation of the hypothesis. Similarly, if a historian depends too much on secondary sources and received wisdom, her hypotheses are apt to be constrained by those sources, and her research is apt to present no threat to standard ideas. That way lies orthodoxy, and bad history.

Again, the case of Barrett Wendell can illustrate this danger. The grandfather of composition history, Albert R. Kitzhaber, pronounced the verdict in his seminal 1953 dissertation, *Rhetoric in American Colleges, 1850–1900:* Barrett Wendell was an interesting eccentric but a dogmatic, retrograde rhetorician whose Harvard department put composition teaching on the road to ruin in the 1890s. Since Kitzhaber's 1953 pronunciamento, nearly all other historians have taken his damnation of Wendell and Harvard as accurate. Donald Stewart and James Berlin in particular, in works they wrote extolling Fred N. Scott and contrasting Scott's University of Michigan department with Harvard, continued Kitzhaber's dismissal of Wendell. The hypotheses historians evolved about Wendell grew out of the Kitzhaber legacy of received wisdom, and the research line followed the hypotheses, which—surprise!—were supported by the research.

Not until 1987, when newer historians such as David Jolliffe and Thomas Newkirk began to investigate the Harvard archives, were a new Barrett Wendell and a new *fin de siècle* Harvard writing program revealed. When historians looked carefully at the heretofore despised Harvard program, they found that under Wendell the Harvard writing courses had been taught almost like contemporary "process writing" courses, with student topic choice, revision, and individual conferences. The myth of the error-obsessed, mechanistic Harvard course that became the freshman composition prototype was exploded.

What's the lesson here? Not, certainly, that all received wisdom is wrong, but that all received wisdom is partial, incomplete. It must be examined again and again, not merely accepted. That, finally, is why there are, and why we need, multiple histories. There can never be any history so magisterial that it precludes the need for other histories. The scholar who claims, as does a classicist I know, that his intention is to write *the* book on Protagoras—one that would render any other book on Protagoras forever unnecessary—is living in an epistemological time warp. We should, of course, always strive to write the most reliable, valid, thorough, coherent, and fair-minded narratives we can, but no one narrative can ever, or should ever, shut down the narrative enterprise. There are too many interesting perspectives for that to be desirable.

This necessity for multiple histories can, of course, be taken on a theoretical level all the way to a claim about the validity of any history—to epistemological atheism, as it were. Victor Vitanza, that loving gadfly of rhetorical historians, is fond of asking "What's the proof for proof? What's the evidence for evidence?" Against so thoroughgoing a critique of any belief system as Victor mounts, historians can only continue to proffer their hard-won narratives and say to readers with A. E. Housman's Terence, "I will friend you, if I may." Simply, we hope to do some good. If we cannot really controvert the deconstruction of all epistemic certainties, we can at least keep the voices going, keep talking to one another, keep telling the stories that finally are all that can ever body us forth one to another.

Because that is what history is: the telling of stories about the tribe that make the tribe real. That is why the recovery of composition history after it had been lost for 150 years is so important. Finally, we are telling the stories of our fathers and our mothers, and we are legitimating ourselves through legitimating them. Yes, the story is sometimes discouraging; yes, many false paths and useless methods were tried; yes, there were long periods of dogma and desuetude. But we in composition studies have a history. It's murky in places so far, and much of it has not been well explored. But it exists. We are part of a discipline that is twenty-five hundred years old, and our continuity from Aristotle and the earliest rhetoricians cannot now be doubted by anyone. Our history is its own justification, and if our methods can grow more solid and sophisticated our motives should not. The methods are not new, nor can they be; the effort there is to wield them with more control, more self-awareness. But our motives for writing our history are what such motives have always been: we write histories to define ourselves on the stage of time.

Works Cited

Bain, Alexander. *English Composition and Rhetoric: A Manual.* New York: D. Appleton, 1866.

Berlin, James. *Rhetoric and Reality: Writing Instruction in American Colleges 1900–1985.* Carbondale: Southern Illinois UP, 1987.

———. *Writing Instruction in Nineteenth-Century American Colleges.* Carbondale: Southern Illinois UP, 1984.

Connors, Robert J. "Rhetoric in the Modern University: The Creation of An Underclass." *The Politics of Writing Instruction: Postsecondary.* Ed. Richard Bullock and John Trimbur. Portsmouth, NH: Boynton/Cook, 1991. 55–84.

———. "The Rhetoric of Mechanical Correctness." *Only Connect: Uniting Reading and Writing.* Ed. Thomas Newkirk. Upper Montclair, NJ: Boynton/Cook, 1986. 27–58.

———. "The Rise and Fall of the Modes of Discourse." *College Composition and Communication* 32 (1981): 444–55.

Horner, Winifred, ed. *Historical Rhetoric: An Annotated Bibliography of Selected Sources in English*. Boston: G. K. Hall, 1980.

———, ed. *The Present State of Scholarship in Historical and Contemporary Rhetoric*. Columbia: U of Missouri P, 1983.

Jolliffe, David. "The Moral Subject in College Composition: A Conceptual Framework and the Case of Harvard, 1865–1900." *College English* 51 (1989): 163–73.

Kitzhaber, Albert R. *Rhetoric in American Colleges 1850–1900*. Dallas: Southern Methodist UP, 1990.

Newkirk, Thomas. "Barrett Wendell and the Birth of Freshman Composition." Paper read at CCCC, Chicago, IL, March 1990.

———. "Octolog: The Politics of Historiography." *Rhetoric Review* 7 (1988): 5–57.

Tuchman, Barbara. *Practicing History: Selected Essays*. New York: Knopf, 1981.

Veysey, Lawrence R. *The Emergence of the American University*. Chicago: U of Chicago P, 1965.

Vitanza, Victor J. "'Notes' Towards Historiographies of Rhetorics." *PRE/TEXT* 8 (1987): 63–125.

Wendell, Barrett. *English Composition*. New York: Scribner's, 1891.

2

PATRICIA A. SULLIVAN

Feminism and Methodology in Composition Studies

THE CONTEMPORARY FEMINIST MOVEMENT and the field of composition studies have, in a sense, grown up together. Both emerged in the sixties, the former as an organized movement to counter large-scale sex discrimination and social inequality in American culture, the latter as an institutional response to a widely perceived literacy crisis. Both came into their own on university campuses in the 1970s, when women's studies programs were developed to research women's issues and concerns long neglected by the traditionally masculinist agendas of the academy, and composition established itself as a research specialization within doctoral programs in education and English. By the late eighties, feminism had made inroads into nearly all academic disciplines and had made a profound impact on literary criticism and the social sciences. Composition studies, too, had expanded its initial focus on freshman composition to include writing across the disciplines and the writing of professionals in both academic and nonacademic settings. While the contemporary feminist movement and the field of composition emerged in the same historical period, however, they developed independently of each other. Feminist research has not made the same inroads in composition studies as it has in other disciplines. Indeed, research on writing has remained silent on issues of gender until quite recently.[1]

Why has composition studies remained virtually unaffected by feminist inquiry and critique until recent years? Feminist critiques of male bias and androcentrism in the academy are usually leveled against established disciplines whose canons, theories, and discourses inscribe patriarchal values and perpetuate sexist and exclusionary practices. When feminist literary scholars in English departments were critiquing sexism in male-authored texts and recovering the work of women writers, composition scholars were engaged in a different kind of political struggle, a struggle for recognition and status in those same departments. Composition itself was marginalized, and composition scholars had to constitute the discipline as a viable field of inquiry and pedagogy. They had to argue the need for scholarship in literacy against the more narrowly defined field of literary studies and clear a space for student writing in a house that was built for canonized authors. Some scholars made the case for composition explicitly, like Maxine Hairston in her address to the 1985 Conference on College Composition and Communication, while others demonstrated the value of composition studies implicitly through their own research, like Mina Shaughnessy in her landmark study of basic writing (*Errors and Expectations*). The fact that women have been at the forefront of composition's struggle for autonomy also has bearing on why composition has thus far been relatively exempt from the kinds of feminist critique leveled at other disciplines: women have been present and influential in the field from the start.

Unlike other, more established disciplines, composition counts a significant number of women among its first and second generations of scholars. Women such as Hairston and Shaughnessy, Janet Emig, Ann Berthoff, Andrea Lunsford, Nancy Sommers, and Linda Flower have played an influential role in defining the field—articulating questions and issues for research, crafting new pedagogies, and overseeing program design and administration. While the ground-breaking work of many of these scholars was not explicitly or self-consciously feminist, the very fact that women helped to chart composition's course over two decades has enabled composition studies to avoid some of the more overtly androcentric practices that inform the research methodologies of other disciplines. Unlike the fields of psychology and medicine, for example, where conclusions about human intellectual development and aging have often been drawn exclusively from studies of male populations, empirical studies of the composing process have always included both male and female subjects, reflecting a more egalitarian ethic. A liberal ethic of equal rights and equal opportunity, in fact, has resided in "the political unconscious" of our discipline from its inception. The emergence of composition was coincident not only with a nationally perceived literacy crisis but with open admission policies that drew a broad and diverse cross section of American culture into college classrooms. Many composition scholars and teachers served as advocates for all students' rights to literacy regardless of a student's age, race, gender, socioeconomic background, or national origin. It is composition's humane disregard for difference under an egalitarian ethic, however, that now renders it pervious to feminist inquiry and critique. For the assumption of equality tends to mask difference, the critical difference it makes, from a feminist perspective, whether a writer, or a researcher for that matter, is a man or a woman.[2]

Some of the earliest and most influential studies of our discipline have forged general propositions about "the way writers write" without considering the influence of gender on the composing process and on the texts and contexts of written communication. We have been slow to take into account either the patriarchal structures and values embedded in our culture that students bring to the classroom or the ways that men's and women's differential relationships to various cultural institutions, including the academy, influence their discursive practices. Women students enter an academic community in which men have largely determined what is important to know, how knowledge is organized, how knowledge is made, and, most importantly for composition scholars and teachers, how knowledge is expressed. The academic discourses that men and women students must "master" in order to succeed in the academy are largely inscriptions of male subjectivities; women have inherited modes of discourse that they have had little voice in shaping.[3]

At issue for feminist composition researchers and teachers is not whether women can accommodate themselves to the knowledge or discourses of academe, for women have proven that they can "cross-dress," that they can master the male idiom, that they can engage in either adversarial or disinterested modes of discourse and succeed by whatever standards we choose to measure success. Rather, feminist scholars take issue with the assumption that discourse is gender neutral, that the literate practices of male and female writers and readers bear no traces of their differential relationships to culture. Feminist scholars emphasize that gender is "basic to all aspects of human experience; it functions as a lens through which all other perceptions pass" (Foss and Foss 67). In composition studies, feminists are concerned with identifying the androcentrism of the academy at large and of our own discipline as it affects research and teaching practices; with uncovering the gendered nature of the written discourses and the writing processes we teach; and with learning what women deem important to know, how women organize and express knowledge, and how women make meaning in a world in which they are differentially situated as subjects. As both an ideology and a praxis, feminism not only reinterprets but seeks to change the dominant, patriarchal structures and categories of experience that have rendered women's activities and social relations analytically invisible. Feminist scholarship in composition thus has both reactive and proactive components: it focuses on received knowledge—on the existing studies, canons, discourses, theories, assumptions, and practices of our discipline—and rexamines them in the light of feminist theory to uncover male bias and androcentrism; and it recuperates and constitutes distinctively feminine modes of thinking and expression by taking gender, and in particular women's experiences, perceptions, and meanings, as the starting point of inquiry or as the key datum for analysis. These two components of feminist scholarship offer the researcher two general strategies or approaches, one derived from the historical, critical, and interpretive practices of humanistic inquiry, the other from experimental and field-research models of the social sciences. While these strategies are not mutually exclusive (both involve theory construction and both draw upon the findings and insights of the other during the research process), I will focus on each of them in turn to foreground some of the procedural and ideological issues germane to each.

Feminist Re-visions: Analysis and Critique

Like feminist literary analysis, feminist critique in composition involves a reinterpretation of the extant literature of our discipline. But since our literature includes empirical studies and textbooks in addition to theoretical and historical scholarship, reinterpretation often involves a metatheoretical critique of methodological assumptions as well as a critical reexamination of a particular study or text. The scholar's purpose may be to expose and deconstruct the latent androcentrism or overt sexism in a text; to pluralize a given perspective by locating an alternate feminist perspective alongside it; to refine or lend an interpretive richness to an existing study by incorporating issues of gender; or to supplant a previous reading or interpretation with a reading grounded in feminist research. In each case, the scholar challenges or problematizes traditional assumptions and theories to help us gain a fuller understanding of the cultural contexts of written communication.

Within this general framework, of course, it would be possible to critique any study that failed to take into account the influence of gender on the rhetorical practices of the writers and readers under study or on the research process. Nearly all of the research that has been conducted in composition studies in the last two decades would fall into this category, rendering feminist critique a formidable if not impossible project. Thus it would be more fruitful at this stage to focus on those cases where a feminist reading or interpretation is clearly at odds with the analysis or interpretation provided by the researcher and/or where considerations of gender might have led the researcher to different results or different conclusions. By implication, I am suggesting that there is a core of knowledge and theory in composition that, if reexamined in light of feminist assumptions, would still elicit our assent, a body of research that does not explicitly take gender into account but that offers no grounds for feminist critique because the conclusions drawn are deemed to be valid across gender categories. I am also implying, however, that the mere inclusion of both men and women subjects at the stage of data collection, either through random sampling or deliberate selection procedures, does not necessarily ensure that a study will be free of androcentric bias. Such inclusiveness, as I suggested earlier, may be a liability in that it may induce a researcher, in some instances, to overlook the potential significance of gender in interpreting her results.

One of my own earlier studies is just such an instance. Several years ago I conducted a study of graduate-student writing that involved case studies of two master's and two doctoral students, each enrolled in a different literature seminar ("From Student to Scholar"). I was careful to include both men and women in my study and, as often as possible, to describe in their own words their writing experiences in their respective courses. But when it came time to analyze the experience of one of the master's students, a woman who found it difficult to meet her professor's expectations about what constituted successful writing in a seminar on Shakespeare, I overlooked connections between gender and composing. In the six position papers the student was required to write, she tended to explore thematic issues she discovered in the plays she was reading rather than argue with critics' assessments of those plays, and she chose to proceed inductively and recursively rather than adopt the "thesis-proof model" her professor specifically asked for. Her term paper similarly reflected exploratory rather than critical modes of discourse. Though she perceived herself as a good writer and had been an *A* student as an undergraduate, in this course she received a grade of only satisfactory on the best of her position papers and a *B* on her term paper. In my analysis of this student's writing, I concurred with her (male) professor and indeed with her own judgment that she had not mastered the standard conventions of literary argumentation, and while I noted that she often expressed a lack of confidence in her own critical authority, I traced both her lack of confidence and her inability to engage in conventional modes of argument to her inexperience in graduate school. In other words, instead of regarding her resistance to these modes as significant in itself and analyzing the modes of thinking and expression with which she did choose to do her intellectual work, I concentrated solely on the disjuncture between her writing performance and her teacher's expectations. Hence, I "saw" deficiency where I might only have seen difference, and I attributed this deficiency to her inexperience as a graduate student rather than to her own sense as a woman "that the terms of academic discourse [were] not her language" (Rich 244). Had I interpreted her experience through the lens of gender, I might not have concluded that I had observed a substandard writing performance born of inexperience, but only a nonstandard performance in a course where male conventions of discourse were allowed to define the standard.

I offer this critique of my own study to illustrate how an analysis of data based on an assumption of gender difference rather than universality can radically alter the conclusions we draw, indeed even the events we observe. To provide a more extensive example of feminist critique in composition and to illustrate the ways that androcentrism can blind an author to the influences of gender not only on composing but on his or her own methodology, I turn to Stephen North's *The Making of Knowledge in Composition: Portrait of an Emerging Field,* where we can find a narrative that has many parallels to my own case study of a graduate-student writer. I could begin by pointing out that nowhere in North's portrait of our field is there any mention of feminism as an ideology or praxis, an omission that says a great deal, depending on a reader's perpective, about composition studies in general or about North's own ideological orientation to the field. But rather than review North's book, I wish to focus on several passages that occur in an early chapter, when North is discussing practitioners as knowledge makers (37–42).

Practice-as-inquiry, North tells us, requires six steps, the first two of which are identifying a problem and searching for causes. When practitioners identify a problem for inquiry, they do so because "routine somehow fails them." "In my own experience," he writes, "this discomfiture has taken the form of a graduate student who, despite serious preparation, had been unable to pass her M.A. comprehensive exam in English in three tries." He then tells the following story to offer his readers a "typical account" of the practitioner's search for causes:

> The graduate student I described above as preparing for her M.A. comprehensive exam worked with me for nearly 1½ years. To prepare her, we studied her failing exams, compared them to passing exams written by other people, had her write (and re-write) literally hundreds of practice exam questions, reviewed the material—in short, we tried every approach I could think of. I did identify what seemed to be a few significant textual patterns: answers developed in a form that reflected her progress through the text(s) in question rather than some conceptual or analytical organization; odd uses of critical terms; a tendency to not address questions. But these were symptoms, not causes. The real question was why: Why did she write answers in these ways? Exam pressure? Lack of understanding of the material? The genre of comprehensive exam writing? Or was she merely the victim of an unreliable grading system?
>
> The instructional breakthrough seemed to come after about a year when, angry with me, and probably sick of the whole business, the student wrote a rather hostile analysis of Jonson's "To

Penshurst." For the first time, her persona seemed to have the kind of authority that had been missing from all her other answers. And just a few months afterwards, she retook the comprehensives, and passed—pretty handily, I gather. Why? What had changed? That shift in persona marked a significant turning point for both of us, but what exactly did it signify? That is, what cause or causes of her unsuccessful exam writing had our interaction, and her work, affected? (41–42)

In his analysis of this student's writing problems and subsequent breakthrough, North relinquishes his search for causes because "clear though they may be in retrospect, causes are seldom much more than cloudy, changeable hypotheses." Indeed, North's purpose in telling this story is to make this very point. But the story that North tells is likely to strike a dissonant chord in many feminist readers, and the point he makes, while not in itself antithetical to feminist theories of knowledge, is premised on a model of inquiry that is inhospitable to feminist issues and methods of inquiry.

Practitioners, according to North, are interested in finding solutions to the problems they have identified, and thus, they do not search for reasons, explanations, or underlying cirmcumstances that might account for a student's literate behavior but for *causes;* they want to find the antidote that will eradicate the problem at its source and not merely treat the symptoms. Practitioner inquiry for North is thus grounded in a deterministic model of human behavior, in a behavioristic psychology that is the clinical offspring of positivist science. Writing problems are symptoms of an underlying illness; if the teacher-doctor can locate the problem at its source, he can prescribe the proper antidote or exercise that will cure the writer of her ills. The behavioristic dimensions of North's model explain his tendency to locate the problem in the writer, or more specifically, in the psychology of the writer rather than in the cultural and political circumstances of her situation: she succumbs to exam pressure, or she lacks understanding of the material, or she's unfamiliar with the genre of comprehensive exam writing. When he turns to the writer's environment to search for a probable cause of her problems, he posits an improbable cause—"an unreliable grading system." (She's failed three times, after all.) The positivist elements in North's model also explain why he relinquishes his search for the causes responsible for the student's instructional breakthrough: by the terms of his own epistemology, he must discover what is actually the case; he must separate reality from a range of appearances, symptoms, and speculations. But since practitioner inquiry, for North, always proceeds through guesswork, he has no methodological means of distinguishing reality from his own "half-formed guesses and cloudy intuitions." Thus, the "true" cause forever, and necessarily, remains elusive.

Most problematic from a feminist perspective, however, is that North's model functions, in effect, to suppress the underlying issues of gender his story inscribes. North does not consider gender as a possible source of the graduate student's difficulty, nor, in the positivist terms in which he casts his notion of causality, can he, for he would have to posit her sex as the *cause* of her difficulty and hence, as something that could be cured or that would be amenable to treatment. He could, of course, introduce gender at the point where he speculates about why the student writes answers as she does. Since he allows that the genre of comprehensive exam taking might be responsible for the student's difficulties, he could also allow that the gender of comprehensive exam writing has something to do with her difficulties. Indeed, by replacing the word *genre* with the word *gender,* he might have placed himself in a more advantageous position to begin to account for the significant textual patterns he has just identified. But (again) for North, the practitioner's desire for an immediate solution to a problem that resides solely in the writer leaves the cultural, political, and historical circumstances of the writer's situation beyond the pale of practitioner inquiry.

If North's model suppresses issues of gender, it also leaves no room for feminist approaches to practitioner research. North most clearly reveals the androcentrism of the framework in which he is working when he bypasses the student herself, her subjectivity, as a place to search for "causes." Nowhere in North's account is the woman herself allowed to speak. We simply do not know what she would say if she could tell the story for herself, how she would interpret her three failures or her eventual success. Hers is an untold story, a story we're not permitted to hear, an "other" perspective we're not allowed to share. In North's model of practitioner inquiry, the roles of teacher and student are clearly demarcated. It is the teacher-researcher who diagnoses the patient and searches for a solution ("we tried every approach I could think of"); the student is the object of inquiry, her mind, but not her subjectivity, a place to search for answers. Her subjective experiences and her writing itself never count for more than symptoms.

Interestingly, however, even as North abandons the search for causes, he leaves a door open to his readers to continue their own speculations by asking a question that his own methodological apparatus leaves him unable to answer: What does the student's turning point signify? From a feminist perspective, North's account of this student's hard-won success in taking her exams and her subsequent change in status is rich indeed in its significations. We notice first in North's narrative that it is when the student becomes angry, writing a "rather hostile" analysis of "To Penshurst," that her persona assumes a kind of authority that seemed to be missing in her earlier answers, and she goes on to pass her exams pretty handily. In other words, when she assumes an agonistic relation to a text, when she criticizes a text, she writes with what North and her exam committee recognize as authority and passes her exams. To a feminist reader the implication is obvious: the student masters the genre/gender of comprehensive exam writing. But we also notice in North's account that it is not the woman's voice that assumes a kind of authority, but a persona. Her anger, in other words, affords her a mask through which to speak. Would North have chosen to describe the student as writing behind a persona rather than speaking with authority if the student were male? Why must her hostility to a poem like "To Penshurst" (which celebrates male ownership of an estate that includes not only bountiful woods and gardens but a "fruitful" wife, "chaste withal," such that the lord of the manor may call his children "his own") be interpreted as a guise that permits her to critique and resist the text? Quite possibly, the anger with which this woman responds to a male teacher and critiques what she perceives as a sexist poem is born of her own experiences as a woman in a male-dominated culture. But if so, then this very culture ensnares her in a paradox. She must become angry to speak with the kind of critical authority required by English professors on exam committees. Her subjectivity must speak itself in traditionally defined ways, in the disputational discourse or father tongue of the academy. But when she does become angry, she is not, as a woman, allowed to own her anger, nor the authority it generates. Her authority must be perceived as speaking through a mask in order to be deemed acceptable to a male reader. We can understand the full implications of this paradox if we ask how this woman's subjectivity speaks itself (or writes itself) when it isn't speaking with (a masculinist conception of) authority. North may have provided a partial answer when he identified those "significant textual patterns" that he dismissed as symptoms. Quite possibly, she develops answers in a form that reflects "her progress through the text(s) in question rather than some conceptual or analytical organization"; she makes "odd uses of critical terms"; she has "a tendency to not address questions." Quite possibly, her writing speaks in the voice of a woman "taught early," as Adrienne Rich says, "that tones of confidence, challenge, anger, or assertiveness are strident and unfeminine" (243). Seen in this light, the shift in persona that marks a significant turning point for North and his student may indeed be a shift from voice to persona. But if so, then North may have been the unwitting agent (even as I was in my own case study) of the very process by which women's voices are rendered inaudible in the academy.

As my rereading of North and the critical reassessment of my own case study are meant to show, the aim of feminist criticism is never simply criticism for its own sake; rather, it hopes to contribute to our understanding of the gendered nature of composing, including those texts we compose under the name of "research." Feminist rereadings of the stories we have told may reveal to us the stories we have yet to tell; they may raise questions we have not thought to ask, issues (such as how women are socialized into academic discourse communities) that have remained invisible under the assumption that gender has no impact on experience. Feminist critiques may also challenge the ways in which we have traditionally constructed our stories, the processes by which we ascertain truth and impart knowledge to the larger research community. I have objected to North's search for causes and to his omission of his student's perceptions of her experiences, for example, on epistemological and procedural grounds. In doing so, I have implicitly suggested that there are fundamental differences between traditional approaches to inquiry and feminist methodology. In the next section, I hope to make these philosophical and methodological differences more explicit.

Feminist Constructions of Knowledge

If feminist critique is essentially reactive, focusing on the extant studies, theories, and text(book)s that comprise the literature of our discipline, feminist empirical research is essentially proactive: it seeks to generate new knowledge about the relationships between gender and composing that can help us counteract the androcentrism that leaves women's modes of thinking and expression suppressed and undervalued. While there are no uniquely feminist methods for gathering evidence, feminist inquiry is distinct from other types of inquiry in at least one respect:

it takes gender as its starting point. Whether the researcher is specifically interested in invention, forms of expression, ways of making meaning, or the role that audience plays in text production, he or she seeks to learn more about the ways that men's and women's different relationships to culture affect their writing processes or the specific rhetorical and linguistic features of their written texts. Examples of studies in composition that take gender issues as their starting point include Geoffrey Sirc's "Gender and 'Writing Formations' in First-Year Narratives," Donnalee Rubin's "Gender Influence: Reading Student Texts," and Cinthia Gannett's *Gender and the Journal: Diaries and Academic Discourse.* Each relies on a different set of techniques for data collection and analysis, but in each case the specific features of written discourse that form the ostensive topic of inquiry are actually subsumed under a problematic of gender.

Obviously, not all studies that locate their problematics in issues of gender can be characterized as feminist. Throughout the history of modern science, male researchers have undertaken studies of gender difference—from comparisons of male and female skull and brain size to men's and women's different methods for resolving conflict—to establish male superiority and legitimate women's exclusion from education and from positions of leadership (Fee, "Nineteenth-Century Craniology"; Gilligan).[4] Taking gender as the starting point of inquiry, then, is a necessary but not a sufficient condition of feminist methodology, for feminism has as its ideological goal the overturning of patriarchal assumptions and practices that render women's experiences invisible and undervalued. In composition studies, research on gender difference may be characterized as feminist, at least at this moment in our institutional history, if it explores relationships between gender and writing to illuminate women's distinctive modes of thinking and expression. This does not mean, as Sandra Harding points out, that feminist researchers "try to substitute one set of gender loyalties for the other—'woman-centered' for 'man-centered' hypotheses. They try instead, to arrive at hypotheses that are free of gender loyalties" (*The Science Question* 138). But since women's experiences and ways of knowing have been suppressed in the history of western culture, we first "often have to formulate a 'woman-centered' hypothesis in order even to comprehend a gender-free one" (138). In other words, we may need to focus on discourse from the perspective of women's experiences even to understand men's communicative practices as gendered rather than as representing the human.

Harding identifies three characteristics of feminist research in the social sciences that are relevant to feminist research in composition. First, it "generates its problematics from the perspective of women's experiences" and "uses these experiences as a significant indicator of the reality against which hypotheses are tested." Second, it "is designed for women." That is, "The goal of this inquiry is to provide women explanations of social phenomena that they want and need." And third, it "insists that the inquirer her/himself be placed in the same critical plane as the overt subject matter. . . . That is, the race, class, culture, and gender assumptions of the researcher her/himself must be placed within the frame of the picture that she/he paints" ("Is There a Feminist Method?" 8–9). Each of these characteristics represents a more or less radical departure from traditional assumptions and paradigms of knowledge making in the field in composition: we tend to generate our problematics from gender-neutral perspectives; we assume that we already are providing women with explanations of composing they want and need by including both men and women subjects in our various investigations and by publishing our theories and findings for a gender-inclusive audience; and those of us who conduct empirical research generally assume that we must control for our personal biases and cultural situatedness in order be objective, to paint an accurate and reliable picture of the reality we observe. Harding's characteristics, then, problematize "business as usual" in composition studies by challenging assumptions of gender neutrality, gender inclusiveness, and researcher disinterestedness. In the remainder of this chapter, I will elaborate on each of these issues in turn, though all, I believe, merit a fuller discussion than I am able to lend to them here.

In composition studies, we tend to generate our problematics from gender-neutral perspectives. We have asked what it means to compose as basic writers, nontraditional students, college freshmen, technical writers, graduate students, biologists, chemical engineers, corporate executives, and so on, and we have generally assumed that the gender of the writer was irrelevant to the problematics of composing that formed the basis of our inquiry. Thus, we have not systematically explored, as Elizabeth Flynn points out, what it means for the women writers within any of these discourse communities to compose as women ("Composing as a Woman"). In some instances, of course, the influence of gender on the writing practices of the group we are studying will be negligible. But in other cases, the assumption of gender neutrality could conceal an androcentric bias or allow men's experiences to define characteristic ways of thinking and writing for both men and women. Consider, for example, a study in which we are interested in the discourse processes by which students in an engineering class learn to become effective problem solvers. We observe the class, collect the students' writing over the course of the term, and code and analyze the data for instances of problem solving. If we do not differentiate between the male and female students in the class and do not take into account the fact that engineering is a male-dominated discipline, the mere fact that men outnumber women in the class will allow men's problem-solving and discourse practices to define the standard, the reality against which individual performances are measured. Women's cognitive styles and discourse strategies will be suppressed or marginalized, their underrepresentation in the discipline reified by our methods. Or consider, on the other hand, studies of writing and the teaching of writing where women comprise the majority of the group we are investigating. The persons we designate under the label nontraditional students, for example, are most often women, women who have raised families or who have delayed their own education to further their partners' careers. Most part-time composition faculty, too, are women—a fact we have yet to acknowledge in our professional guidelines and recommendations for the postsecondary teaching of writing.[5] Studies that concentrate on the distinctive curricular requirements of adult learners or on the inequitable labor conditions and earnings of instructors but that overlook the explicit correlation between gender and status—the fact that it is because these students and teachers are women that they have been defined as nontraditional students or have taken part-time positions—once again leave women's experiences suppressed. In the first example, generating our problematics from the perspective and experiences of the women in the engineering course could help us to learn more about the ways in which the genres and contexts of engineering discourse are gendered; instead of universal descriptions of how engineers compose in response to various writing tasks, we might uncover gender-related strategies for solving problems and hence, perhaps, empower voices we were previously unaccustomed to hearing. In the second example, enlisting the perceptions of the women and men whose experiences we are studying can tell us more about the specific educational needs of returning students and the working conditions of part-time faculty than if we assume from the outset that gender roles are irrelevant to the situation and status of these groups. Instead of the stereotypical and hierarchical modes of thinking that so often accompany outsider perspectives, our curricula and policies will be shaped and guided by those in the best position to reveal what they should be.

While generating problematics from the perspective of women's experience may, in itself, provide women with theories of composing they want and need—Harding's second characteristic—there is no guarantee that composition research designed specifically for women will reach its intended audience. Dale Spender has documented the difficulty that feminist scholars in various disciplines have had in placing research about and for women in the principal journals of their fields (*The Writing or the Sex?*), and there is evidence to suggest that similar gatekeeping practices occur in composition. In her essay, "Composing 'Composing as a Woman,' " for example, Elizabeth Flynn recounts how reviewers of her earlier essay, "Composing as a Woman," were reluctant to publish her article because her explicitly feminist and metatheoretical approach did not conform to their conceptions of research. Flynn's second piece—itself a reflective and metatheoretical essay—was published in the section of the journal normally reserved for curricular issues and pedagogical strategies, the Staffroom Interchange. Apparently, studies of writing must take everyman as their audience, to borrow the apt and ideologically revealing term that recently adorned the cover of *College English* ("Everyman's Guide to Critical Theory," March 1990) in order for those studies to be regarded as research and as worthy of professional publication. Women, of course, are tacitly assumed to be included in this generic representation of readership (everyman presumably means every man and woman) and are also, therefore, automatically assumed to be interested and concerned with issues relevant to men. But reversing this semantic configuration reveals the problem with "inclusiveness." Men cannot be subsumed under the category everywoman. And so men are not automatically assumed, at least by journal editors, to be interested in research about and for women. Indeed, the publication of Flynn's work in a regular issue of *College Composition and Communication* is something of an anomaly, for research for women is nearly always assigned to special journal issues and to essay collections devoted exclusively to feminist scholarship and pedagogy.[6] Such research is published in regular issues of our principal journals only when editors narrow their perceptions of audience exclusively to women or to feminist women and men. Research by and for men requires no such narrowing because the universal audience of composition scholarship, figured in the generic everyman, is already male. The androcentrism that pervades our conceptions of audience and the potential for sexism that attends the fact that most of our journal editors are men are feminist issues in their own right, issues, I would add, in pressing need of study.

What Harding has identified as the third characteristic of feminist research—its insistence that the inquirer her/himself be placed in the same critical plane as the overt subject matter—is likely to be especially problematic for many composition researchers because it runs counter to long-held notions about what constitutes good empirical research, perhaps even research itself. The dominant paradigm, reflected throughout works such as Lauer and Asher's *Empirical Designs* and in parts of North's *The Making of Knowledge in Composition,* dictates that the researcher must detach herself from the object of inquiry and keep personal bias and values from influencing her observations and analysis if she is to paint an objective and undistorted picture of reality. Introducing into analysis the subjective elements of the researcher's own assumptions of race, class, culture, and gender would undermine the reliability and validity of the results; in effect, the researcher would have to relinquish whatever claims to knowledge she would like to have made for her study and assign her study to the domain of opinion or speculation.

As feminist philosophers and historians of science have pointed out, however, the concept of dispassionate, disinterested inquiry has itself arisen from patriarchal ideology. Methods of analysis that presumably guarantee the objectivity of a researcher's results are actually by-products of an androcentric epistemology that has historically equated subjectivity with the feminine mind. Empirical science, in its quest for socially transcendant truths and value-neutral facts about the world, detached the knower (or the scientist) from the object of study and insulated its objects of inquiry from the contingencies of lived experience. Women's lived experiences were rendered inaccessible to inquiry, and women themselves were excluded from knowlege making. "The Enlightenment vision," Harding writes, explicitly denied that women possessed the reason and powers of dispassionate, objective observation required by scientific thinking. Women could be objects of (masculine) reason and observation but never the subjects, never the reflecting and universalizing human minds. Only men were in fact envisioned as ideal knowers, for only men (of the appropriate class, race, and culture) possessed the innate capacities for socially transcendant observation and reason. ("The Instability" 292)

Elizabeth Fee similarly notes that the objective-subjective and rational-emotional dichotomies central to the scientific enterprise are distinctively masculine, rising from man's self-definition as a being of pure rationality and man's definition of woman as the repository of emotional life and of all the nonrational elements of human experience ("Women's Nature" 11–12). The methodological underpinnings of modern science, then, have developed according to male prescriptions and proscriptions of knowledge. But since they purport to hold a nondistorting mirror up to reality, to register objectively and dispassionately reality as it is, they appear to be value-neutral and hence gender-neutral as well. Feminist scholars point to the gender bias inscribed in the history and methodology of positivist science to show that the scientific enterprise itself is ideologically interested—and to argue, therefore, that no individual project that is based on a scientific methodology can claim to be disinterested. The realities recorded and reported via so-called objectivist methodologies are always versions of a reality that is subject to revision; reality "as it is" is always someone's perception, even if a collective perception or representation. The perspective from which this reality is glimpsed, moreover, is always a situated perspective. There is no "view from nowhere," as Susan Bordo writes, no "God's eye-view" from which "one can see nature as it really is, undistorted by human perspective" (143). The researcher's own race, class, culture, and gender assumptions are not neutral positions from which he or she observes the world but lenses that determine how and what the researcher sees. In choosing to make these assumptions explicit, the feminist researcher does not decrease the reliability of her observations nor the validity of her conclusions but only the objectivism, as Harding notes, that serves to hide this kind of evidence from the public ("Is There a Feminist Method?" 9). Put another way, feminist inquiry wears its heart on its sleeve: it originates in an ideological agenda that, instead of masking, it declares up front. But all empirical research, the feminist argues, is similarly interested or ideologically motivated; the difference between feminist inquiry and the dominant, hypo-thetico-deductive model of inquiry is that the latter has produced no self-generated practice of reflection on its racial, class, and gender biases.

While the three characteristics of feminist research that Harding delineates reveal fundamental differences between a feminist approach and traditional approaches to empirical research in composition, they do not represent a wholesale rejection of empiricism by feminists but only of the positivist elements that still linger in the dominant paradigm of scientific inquiry. Feminist researchers often seek out or devise alternative empirical methodologies whose principles and procedures are consonant with feminist ideology and praxis. Many are drawn, for example, to the cluster of methods that fall under the rubrics of qualitative and naturalistic inquiry. Techniques such as open-ended interviews and case studies enable researchers to generate descriptions of composing from the point of view and in the language of the writers they are studying. Participant observation, a defining feature of ethnomethodology, allows researchers to reflect critically on their own subject position, both as researchers and as authors, in the twin sites of study—in the field and on the page. And emergent forms of teacher research are helping researchers learn more about women's and men's different experiences within the classroom contexts in which they compose, about the cultural differences among individual writers in these contexts, and about the fluid and ever-shifting nature of these contexts themselves. But whether individual researchers are appropriating or revising conventions of empirical scholarship, their work is informed by the same purpose: they are consciously seeking to create the conditions and circumstances whereby voices, stories, and discourses too long silent in the academy can be heard.

In this chapter I have sought to claim for feminist research and scholarship a central role in composition studies. I have argued that we will have to resist the desire to subsume problematics of gender under universal descriptions of how writers write and ask, instead, what difference it makes to the writing situation whether a writer is a man or a woman. To do otherwise, I have suggested, is to give our tacit assent to an ideology that has allowed men's discursive practices to define the standard against which women's writing is judged. One of the places this ideology has found expression is in the traditional methodologies—the research practices and assumptions—of our discipline. Thus, we need to inquire not only into relationships between gender and composing but into the gendered nature of our research practices, including the cultural and historical traditions that have produced them. What is finally at stake, I believe, if feminism is to become a fully realized voice within composition studies is considerably more than the special interests of a subgroup of scholars in our field. If we do not as a research community undertake to understand issues of gender difference and sexual politics, we can never hope to achieve the full understanding of composing that has been the goal of composition studies from its inception.

Notes

1. Elizabeth Flynn, in her essay "Composing as a Woman" similarly notes that "the fields of feminist studies and composition studies have not engaged each other in a serious or systematic way." My debt to Flynn's essay will be apparent throughout this chapter. I also wish to acknowledge a number of colleagues whose insights and comments on various drafts of this chapter have proven invaluable: Gesa Kirsch, Cinthia Gannett, Donna Qualley, Elizabeth Chiseri-Strater, Bonnie Sunstein, and Sherrie Gradin.

2. While I view gender as a social construction rather than a biologically determined characteristic, my references to gendered dualisms such as "male and female modes of thinking" and "men's and women's differential relationships to culture" throughout this chapter would seem to commit me to a view of homogenized difference and thus to a form of essentialism. I certainly recognize that women and men come in different races, classes, and cultures, and I believe it would be mistaken to speak collectively of "woman's experience" or "man's experience." But race, class, and culture are also always categories within gender, and our culture, as Susan Bordo writes, is in fact constructed by gender duality: "Our language, intellectual history, and social forms are 'gendered'; there is no escape from this fact and from its consequences on our lives. . . . [L]ike it or not, in our present culture, our activities *are* coded as 'male' or 'female' and will function as such within the prevailing system of gender-power relations" (152).

3. A number of works in recent years have discussed the androcentrism of academic discourse stemming from women's historical exclusion from formal education, including Aisenberg and Harrington; Bleich; Presnell; and Spender (*Man Made Language*).

4. For additional examples and analyses of gender-based distortions in the history and practices of science, see Schiebinger; Harding (*The Science Question*); and Keller.

5. See the *Statement of Principles and Standards for the Postsecondary Teaching of Writing* published by the Conference on College Composition and Communication, October 1989.

6. Composition journals that have devoted special issues to feminist theory and to studies of gender and writing include *Journal of Advanced Composition* 10.2 (1990) and *College English* 51, 52 (1990). For edited collections on feminist theory, research, and pedagogy in composition, see Caywood and Overing, and Phelps and Emig.

Works Cited

Aisenberg, Nadya, and Mona Harrington. *Women of Academe: Outsiders in the Sacred Grove*. Amherst: U of Massachusetts P, 1988.

Bleich, David. "Sexism in Academic Styles of Learning." *Journal of Advanced Composition* 10 (1990): 231–47.

Bordo, Susan. "Feminism, Postmodernism, and Gender-Scepticism."

Feminism/Postmodernism. Ed. Linda J. Nicholson. New York: Routledge, 1990. 133–56.

Caywood, Cynthia L., and Gillian R. Overing, eds. *Teaching Writing: Pedagogy, Gender, and Equity.* Albany: State U of New York P, 1987.

Fee, Elizabeth. "Nineteenth-Century Craniology: The Study of the Female Skull." *Bulletin of the History of Medicine* 53 (1980): 414–33.

———. "Women's Nature and Scientific Objectivity." *Woman's Nature: Rationalizations of Inequality.* Ed. Marian Lowe and Ruth Hubbard. New York: Pergamon, 1982. 9–27.

Flynn, Elizabeth. "Composing as a Woman." *College Composition and Communication* 39 (1988): 423–35.

———. "Composing 'Composing as a Woman': A Perspective on Research." *College Composition and Communication* 41 (1990): 83–89.

Foss, Karen A., and Sonja K. Foss. "Incorporating the Feminist Perspective in Communication Scholarship: A Research Commentary." *Doing Research on Women's Communication.* Ed. Kathryn Carter and Carole Spitzack. Norwood, NJ: Ablex, 1989. 65–91.

Gannett, Cinthia. *Gender and the Journal: Diaries and Academic Discourse.* Albany: State U of New York P, 1992.

Gilligan, Carol. *In a Different Voice: Psychological Theory and Women's Development.* Cambridge, MA: Harvard UP, 1982.

Hairston, Maxine. "Breaking Our Bonds and Reaffirming Our Connections." *College Composition and Communication* 36 (1985): 272–82.

Harding, Sandra. "The Instability of the Analytical Categories of Feminist Theory." *Sex and Scientific Inquiry.* Ed. Sandra Harding and Jean F. O' Barr. Chicago: U of Chicago P, 1987. 283–302.

———. "Is There a Feminist Method?" *Feminism and Methodology.* Ed. Sandra Harding. Bloomington: Indiana UP, 1987. 1–14.

———. *The Science Question in Feminism.* Ithaca: Cornell UP, 1986.

Keller, Evelyn Fox. *Reflections on Gender and Science.* New Haven: Yale UP, 1984.

Lauer, Janice, and William Asher. *Composition Research: Empirical Designs.* New York: Oxford UP, 1988.

North, Stephen M. *The Making of Knowledge in Composition: Portrait of an Emerging Field.* Upper Montclair, NJ: Boynton/Cook, 1987.

Phelps, Louise Wetherbee, and Janet Emig, eds. *Feminine Principles and Women's Experience in American Composition and Rhetoric.* New York: MLA, forthcoming.

Presnell, Michael. "Narrative Gender Differences." *Doing Research on Women's Communication.* Ed. Kathryn Carter and Carole Spitzack. Norwood, NJ: Ablex, 1989. 118–36.

Rich, Adrienne. "Taking Women Students Seriously." *On Lies, Secrets, and Silence.* New York: Norton, 1979. 237–45.

Rubin, Donnalee. "Gender Influence: Reading Student Texts." Diss. U of New Hampshire, 1989.

Schiebinger, Londa. "The History and Philosophy of Women in Science: A Review Essay." *Sex and Scientific Inquiry.* Ed. Sandra Harding and Jean F. O'Barr. Chicago: U of Chicago P, 1987. 7–34.

Shaughnessy, Mina. *Errors and Expectations.* New York: Oxford UP, 1979.

Sirc, Geoffrey. "Gender and 'Writing Formations' in First-Year Narratives." *Freshman English News* 18 (1989): 4–11.

Spender, Dale. *Man Made Language.* London: Routledge, 1980.

———. *The Writing or the Sex?* New York: Pergamon, 1989.

Statement of Principles and Standards for the Postsecondary Teaching of Writing. Conference on College Composition and Communication. October 1989.

Sullivan, Patricia A. "From Student to Scholar: A Contextual Study of Graduate-Student Writing in English." Diss. Ohio State U, 1988.

Writing
Theory : : Theory
Writing

SOME THINKING ABOUT WRITING theory as a foundation for research, especially about writing it, can paralyze even the most experienced composition theorists, for more than the obvious reason that theories of writing have everything to do with the act of writing itself. This stultifying thinking is legendary: "Theory" is written by the smart for the smart. "Theory" is too abstract and general to have much to do with actual writing practices that can be investigated with more concrete research methods, or with the act of teaching students to engage in and analyze these practices. A good theory must be a magnificent machine, a system applicable to explaining and predicting everything. "Theory" is written by (great, white) patriarchs, or their textual equivalents. "Theory" is, finally, simultaneously too exciting and too boring to claim as our own.

Such images too often exclude thoughtful teachers from focusing on, working through, and taking the risk of writing and publishing theoretical contributions in composition studies. We need to—and can fairly easily—demystify these images. Our historical concerns with writing as a cultural phenomenon have explained that intimidating images of theory have much to do with identifiable ways of publishing explanations, and with settings for reading them. Print and its modern industrialization in an international market toward the end of the nineteenth century gave us the comparatively late development of a textual, "neutral exposition" (Richards 40), a medium that enabled "grand theories" at their most intimidating. Reading impersonal, published voices that simultaneously addressed no one and everyone in assertive theoretical statements was quite distinct from sharing explanations in earlier, more exclusive but equally more communal exchanges. Ideas have always been imagined as reaching the most distant borders of the worlds they address, and by the seventeenth century in Europe, speculative explanations could be actually published among international but exclusive philosophical and scientific communities. But later economies of print accelerated changes in interactions between ideas and settings for receiving them. Reasoned explanations that applied formal principles to observed phenomena were no longer submerged as the natural or normal beliefs of particular local groups who unselfconsciously spoke through (if not about) them. Such explanations began to achieve status, even among nonintellectuals, *as* ideas. They also became more available to be contested in a newly visible, newly distinct, intellectual domain based on a wider circulation of texts.

Consequently, our image of the exclusivity that surrounds "big" theories has a great deal to do with nineteenth-century "high literacy," a focal point in a geneaology of ideas as texts. But the twentieth-century composition theory that I address here, as well as the possibility that its work serves and should be shared across a broader range of participants in our field, are part of another, more recent, trend in organized formal inquiry—to consider specific, local differences and the settings where they occur. Following turns toward new history in historical studies, and away from *grand recits* or master narratives in literary postmodernism and literary new historicism (which takes as its objects formerly excluded anecdotal incidents that demonstrate resistance to dominant hegemonic culture), theories are less likely to appear valid, much less true, if they are conceived of as generic explanations of globalized concepts. Archival research into historical practices in rhetoric and composition, as well as localized empirical descriptions of writers in specific, differentiated settings, demonstrate that the big picture has been painted with too broad a brush to detail the interplay of circumstance, privilege, local interests, and limited perspective that actually constitute an object of description or a researcher's claims to truth.

Paradoxically, interest in interpreting specific, local practices, and especially in focusing on their significant differences, requires a metatheoretical brand of explanation that acknowledges its own presuppositions. Accounting for any postglobalized social and/or textual practice in a way that acknowledges limits on definitions of "the" writer, "the" text, or "the" audience requires that we frame our accounts in *a* particular set of social and intellectual circumstances. Metatheory does not hide either its object or its explanation in a concern with abstract writing, or direct toward it an all-seeing, only objective, normative gaze. Focusing on difference rather than attempting to create universal accounts based on similarity invites us selfconsciously to place explanations in the circumstances that have encouraged them so that we acknowledge their limits.

From this simultaneously local and metatheoretical perspective, we might now redefine theories in a way that naturalizes their place in composition research. Theories are particular discourses that arise in specific intellectual and material circumstances, conditions that importantly constrain their content and its implications, or range of significance, at specific times. They are organized frames of intelligibility, systems that explain. But these frames of intelligibility are also variable *significations* whose sources (or signifiers) are endowed with less power than they had under earlier ideas of authorship. The content and results of theory now openly depend on actual people in a discourse community or a problem-solving group, who together define an intellectual project. As a writer of theory who takes her authority from such an interplay of texts and circumstance, I look for particular *social* circumstances that authorize ideas, allowing their production and their widespread (or perhaps only marginal) availability and recognition at particular times. Theories are interesting insofar as they are capable of rhetorical analysis. Precisely what group is saying what, about what, to whom, where, when, and for what purposes? But equally important, who is hearing—and not hearing—what, about what, from whom, where, when, and with what results? These questions are more politically oriented than those evoked by Thomas Kuhn in *The Structure of Scientific Revolutions*, but they obviously echo his work as well as that of Michel Foucault, who stresses the dimensions of power, and of pleasure, involved in discursive practice.

In composition theory, since I became aware of it in the early 1970s, we have had many powerful and pleasurable explanations of writing. Those that captured the attention of composition teachers have included valuable, directly applicable, and equally valuable but more broadly organizing explanations. "Generative rhetoric" was described by Francis Christensen (*Notes Toward a New Rhetoric*) and elaborated by Frank D'Angelo (*A Conceptual Theory of Rhetoric*), as it was by others. This theory, applied directly to teaching, explained that sentences and whole texts could be expanded or developed by the writer, as units requiring systematic, grammatically categorized additions of information. "Tagmemic invention," as described by Richard Young and his colleagues Kenneth Pike and Alton Becker at Michigan, theorized that a writer can discover relevant, interesting ideas that change both the writer's and the readers' perceptions by deploying a nine-cell grid through which an idea or concept might be explained. Young and his collaborators emphasized that ideas are not products of mysterious (vitalistic) mental processes. They are cognitively derived from thinking in systematic ways that some experienced writers internalize so thoroughly that they appear to be intuitive (*Rhetoric: Discovery and Change*).

Janet Emig, in *The Composing Process of Twelfth-Graders*, explained that many student texts are wooden because the teaching of writing relied on descriptions of the written text (the *product* of writing), not on observations of how writers write. She theorized that writing is a recursive process, not a linear transcription of ideas already in mind. Mina Shaughnessey, in *Errors and Expectations,* explained that when inexperienced adults write, they intelligently switch from their well-mastered spoken, aural code to an unfamiliar graphic code. She theorized that such writers are making sense and that their texts can be interpreted as systematically patterned representations of meaning.

I wish that each of these examples could capture the sudden "aha" that teachers of my generation felt when these and other frames of intelligibility, a range of new theories, were applied to processes and problems that had remained opaque earlier in our careers. These insights were eagerly adopted by many and have been further explored, in many more recent theories, because they offered hope that we might revise the "workbook and whip" and the "shout at foreigners" approaches in which immediate frustrations and a long history of elitist social traditions around written texts had installed us. But they also evoked less practical pleasures, assuring us that others shared our problems and that we could, in print, discuss them.

Each expression of composition theory was valuable, whether or not we ultimately applied it, because it simultaneously established and improved a community that now had its own discourse. Many now critique the structuralist oppositions underlying Walter J. Ong's categories in *Orality and Literacy,* but the value of his work, and of many others, remains significant far beyond its current propositional value. By the late 1970s, overwhelming rejection of E. D. Hirsch's argument for textual efficiency in his *Philosophy of Composition* could arise from an established perspective, a unifying boundary that divided inside from outside knowledge of writing processes and their teaching. Variously relying on language history, observation, and reasoning from principles that privilege differing epistemologies, these contributions were unified in their establishment of the act of writing as a distinct and productive object of inquiry.

But successful theories are also obvious. My readers who began to teach after each of these contributions became visible boundaries around their work may wonder why any of the foundational explanations by Young, Emig, or Shaughnessy incurred objections, or how any of them needed further verification and research. In light of what we know now, both from within and from outside a growing field of composition, it appears almost unimaginable that anyone strenuously disagreed with Young's proposition that everyone can generate new ideas, disavowed Emig's distrust of the linear, strictly followed outline, or laughed at Shaughnessy's certainty about the intelligence of inexperienced writers. Contemporary classroom teachers would not, that is, announce with an earlier Warriner's textbook that *they* thought that good writers know what *they* want to say ahead of time and say it clearly in correct, smooth sentences that fulfill a firm plan (Emig 21). And with only few exceptions, contemporary teachers certainly feel, if only peripherally, part of a field that shares and discusses its problems in refereed forums that question and sometimes reject new contributions.

But the knowledge and pleasure that these and other theories created must also be read against the issues of empowerment and signification that I raised earler. Theories of writing are significations embedded in a signifying system of writing, and their value (or meaning) is more and less apparent in particular contexts. The comprehensive accuracy of a theory of writing, as the example of Hirsch's work indicates, relies on its reception as much as it does on its assertions, and this reception in turn depends on the possibility for a significant audience to exist. Without the field of composition that now comprises this audience, composition theory could not claim institutional time for its writing or reading, could not be published (as many remember too well), could not be critiqued, could not be recognized in professional reward systems, and could not, finally, be applied. And even more recent theories that stress newer insights about the slippery, situationally significant nature of writing itself could not now be overlooked in our practices without the widely publicized configurations, the insiders' power, that this field has assumed. *Having* a theory, as we do when we make language and take actions at the intersections of our unstated assumptions in our professional, religious, or political groups, differs vastly from *saying* publically that we have one, as we do when we write and read work like Maxine Hairston's "Winds of Change," George Hillocks's "What Works in Teaching Composition," Lester Faigley's "Competing Theories of Process," Stephen North's *The Making of Knowledge in Composition,* or James Berlin's "Rhetoric and Ideology in the Writing Class."

This distinction is quite important for practices in composition teaching and research, for *having* a theory determines how we teach and interpret every kind of text, while *saying* we have a theory has a much more complex relation to actual practice. The theory we *have* determines whether frustration and blame—or interest and analysis—follow our reading of "bad" student writing; the theory we *say* we have determines many other, largely professional, interactions. For instance, literary studies in the 1950s, addressing new postwar students without a suddenly "hermetic" Latin, Greek, and biblical textual training, *had* a formalist theory of reading. But the social setting defined by these new students encouraged proponents of this formalism to *say* they simply read a text to find what students once called "deep meanings." In composition studies, we are even more ambivalent about acknowledging the theory we *have,* not because we must be, or can successfully appear to be, atheoretical, but paradoxically because we now *say* we have another.

My focus here is on the process and product theories that have made current explanations of composition teaching intelligible and that are commonly identified as sequential moves in a history of established composition theory. According to Hairston's "Winds of Change: Thomas Kuhn and the Revolution in the Teaching of Writing," the primary value of establishing the new paradigm of process in composition studies was to provide a space for systematically discovering and describing how actual writers write (85). This model, she argues, led teachers away from analyses of the product of composition, student essays, and encouraged them to intervene during the process of writing, when actual benefits could result. Hairston's case for opposing product (or current traditional) teaching to process teaching derives from the work of specific theorists mentioned earlier, especially Mina Shaughnessy. Hairston says that Shaughnessy's work on basic writers and the logic with which they approximate standard graphic representations made her the field's "essential person . . . who asked [the essential] question" (82).

Consequently, it apppeared that a new theoretical paradigm for teaching writing and organizing composition research was close at hand in 1982, when Hairston described the field, in Kuhn's terms, as technically "pre-paradigmatic." The field— which subsequent writers like Faigley, North, and Berlin describe *as* a field—had a new question, had available means to investigate this problem, and had a new practice based on answers to this question. It asked, "How do writers write?" It investigated with controlled observations and systematic textual analyses and began to practice interventionist teaching. As a "theory for teaching writing," the frame of intelligibility provided by foundations in process described positive interventions that could replace an earlier focus on the errors and infelicities of already written student texts. Variations on and elaborations of this model created a dominant model for the act of writing that we could use and continue to elaborate conceptually.

All of these benefits certainly apply in what we have *said* publically about teaching practices and in metapractical descriptions of them. The ninety model programs that comprise the contents of Neel's 1978 *Options for the Teaching of Writing,* Connolly and Vilardi's 1986 *New Directions in College Writing Programs,* and Carol Hartzog's 1986 *Composition in the Academy,* all published by the Modern Language Association, openly claim their use of this process theory for teaching. Lester Faigley and others further place process teaching in a metaperspective.

In "Competing Theories of Process," Faigley compares three categories of process theory—expressive, cognitive, and social emphases that variously describe the performance of writers. His account brings to mind such names as Murray, Bruffee, Flower and Hayes, Bartholomae, Bizzell, and Bazerman, who have written textbooks and widely recognized articles that theorize teaching. Faigley asserts that we may assume "the recognition of the study of writing as an important area of research within English" (527) and, like Stephen North in *The Making of Knowledge in Composition,* uses classifications to define schools and professional groups on which such status depends. James Berlin, in "Rhetoric and Ideology in the Writing Class," similarly classifies cognitive, expressive, and social-epistemic rhetorics that he thinks organize three distinct ideological approaches to teaching.

But in light of differences between *having* a theory and *saying* we have one, it is important to notice some flaws in the cool progress of my description. Separating two forms of composition teaching historically and oppositionally, as product both before *and* versus process, suggests that two "grand theories" have sequentially controlled the teaching of writing. Yet if a claim is made that a new theory replaces an old one, it is fair to ask how the communities representing each one interacted, whether the problem engaged by the earlier group was shifted in the latter's address to a different problem, and how extensive the change accomplished actually was. Precisely what sort of changes caused and resulted from the movement that Hairston summarized? Why did Donald Gray review the articles he had published after his editorship of *College English* ended in 1986 with the comment that "when I was told that I was living in a paradigm shift, I didn't feel the earth move" (150)?

It is obvious that the extent of a perceived shift from a "current traditional product analysis" to *teaching* based on process research must be qualified by fairly common knowledge. The traditionalism of what most teachers still actually do is verified in Richard Larson's Ford-sponsored research describing actual teaching practices across the country (Letter). And this traditional orientation toward the product, toward correcting the final text, still emerges in the topics of best-selling textbooks and in significantly better-selling handbooks and workbooks. Most have *added* process-based techniques to traditional topics and methods, thereby invalidating the claim that process is a distinct conception of what composition studies is about, or that writing has been theorized differently by all whose profession it is. The process paradigm has evidently not solved a problem that most teachers of composition perceived *as* a problem, for the teaching that Hairston claims has changed does not universally, nor even consensually, throw over its old methods with anything like the surety that makes telescopes and microscopes the normal tools of astronomers and biologists.

It is at least arguable that the normal shape of a composition course, and consequently of the theory we *have,* has remained stable even after process theories of teaching dominate in our publications. Students are not usually treated in composition classrooms as Hairston's "actual writers," with their own practices that warrant description before expansion or correction. In many courses, they read and analyze texts quite distinct from those that they read and write in actual situations. They usually are assigned generic essays that have only a metaphorical relation to the genres that constitute their other writing experiences. They still normally expect a teacher's standards, not the actual effectiveness of their writing in particular situations, to determine evaluations of this writing.

But more significantly for our purposes, when we examine actual theories of process, we find ways that the earth did not move so much or in precisely the ways that were claimed. In many descriptions of writing processes, it is still the student text that is taken as the only measure of processes, not a narration of the actual activities of its writer. Studies of student writing processes, or of changes in them outside controlled process classrooms, have not replaced studies that focus on textual features.

And in much observational process research that does highlight the activities of writers, evaluations of writing do not measure how well or poorly a student emulates the processes of the experienced and professional writers who are taken to be models. Categories of writers still follow the traditions that distinguished "good" from "bad" texts, but these categories have shifted, now, to compare "experienced" or "professional" with "unprepared" or "inexperienced" writers. This emphasis in studies of writers particularly has retained the current traditional belief that writers control, or with proper instruction can learn to control, the meaning and the results of written language. Students in most composition courses are expected to be, or to learn to be, "clear," just as current traditionalists about language claimed they could be.

In sum, neither process teaching nor process research is generally undertaken to verify a new, normalizing theory based on a revolutionary idea that set a particularly new set of problems or modes of interpretation for the field. Perhaps equally important, there is little evidence that process theory produces teaching practices, or that it contains specific formal principles, that actively compete with an earlier set of organized practices and concepts. The pointedly evaluative goals of "unity," "coherence," and "consistency" that organized a product paradigm and most of its current traditional methods have been silently retained in practice. But their articulation as defunct theories has relied on their opponents, who created them *as* theories when their own process theory was first defined.

Consequently, we can ask of composition theory what it has accomplished. If its process theory did not decisively shift teaching practices or radically redirect the field's research questions toward the settings and assumptions inherent in actual contemporary acts of writing, what great benefit has it had to the field? For our purposes, these questions might be answered by Robert Connors's article, "Composition Studies and Science," which appeared soon after Hairston's "Winds of Change." Connors recognized a special relation between Hairston's assertions and the making of theories in specific empowering circumstances. He saw in her description a particular intellectual stance. Connors focused on Hairston's argument that composition studies is a "scientific or pre-scientific" (5) field that should describe itself in the vocabulary of "paradigm" and "pre-paradigmatic" that would invoke the substance and status of science. Connors looked not at the *content* of this theory, or at its successes and failures in "problem-solving," but at its status as a discourse, encouraged and attended to by particular privileging mechanisms. Connors's critique argued that an established member of the composition teaching profession had asserted to her peers that they could change their past sense of inadequacy by comparing their new work to a *scientific* revolution. *This* change depended on stating that new interventions in writing-in-process were methods with scientific (or prescientific) validity, derived from scientifically valid research.

This message from process theory was, most certainly, heard. With none of the reservations about actual change that I have described, Hairston's peers adopted the line of her argument. They asserted that formerly *ad hoc* practices whose principles remained unarticulated, but that shared the history of literary studies' creation of "good" and "bad" texts, had become a disciplinary enterprise, with the distinct and contesting branches described by Faigley, Hillocks, North, and Berlin. Newly identified composition specialists (among whom I was one) encouraged recognition of this field, sought and received grants and book contracts, and were enabled to award new degrees in composition-rhetoric or composition studies. Their departmental colleagues heard their claims, specifically in two contexts: the "new" national literacy crisis declared after the Vietnam War, with its new definition of literacy to encompass technical skills related to the computer; and what amounted to a freeze on positions for literary scholars. With limited responsiveness, formerly disinterested colleagues recognized the field and acknowledged that its members were legitimately concerned with student writing—now that it had a theory meant to imitate scientific investigation. Writing had become a new, re-formed "problem" with a new solution close at hand. Its articulation as theory legitimated its existence, just as currently unmasked claims for literary theory empower its recent competition with philosophy for intellectual and professional recognition.

I have argued elsewhere (*Textual Carnivals*) that these results from articulating and oppposing process and product theories, insofar as they value "rigor," "hard data," and conclusions that engender more research, were symbolically gendered, specifically as male-coded "intellect." The language and mission of new articulations of a theory of composition were addressed largely to the negatively feminized situation of composition professionals, their marginalized students, and their elementary course content. A newly constructed binary opposition between product and process implied a systematic hierarchy that could claim respectable intellectual research status as against the *ad hoc,* initiative, marginalized position that composition teaching had always implied. In the style of the intimidating nineteenth-century "big" theory that still captures our imagination, effective new schools of composition theory looked for *the* pardigm that would organize a negatively domesticated space.

Process theory took as its tacit object neither the text nor the act of writing, but the *status and practices* of those who taught, which had previously been culturally and professionally blurred as simultaneously authoritarian and motherly. Its articulation drew attention to these teaching practices and improved the status of those who engaged them, but it did not, finally, define a new interpretative model of what writing is, of its purposes in contemporary settings, of how courses in contemporary acts of writing might fit these purposes, or of the social and institutional situations of students in potentially renovated courses.

Given a new status but not a new interpretative model that

foregoes evaluations of texts in favor of descriptions of them, a broad range of composition theorists rewrote diverse aspects of their formerly unorganized practice. Under this new entitlement, some created a history that was an intellectual history of rhetorical personages and their influences. These historians did not, however, address the many cultural histories of the writing situations that all students have encountered, including those who were lower class, women, or minority writers outside privileged academic settings. Cognitive theorists took as their object of study the totalized mind of the writer engaged in writing. They isolated the writer as a traditional Cartesian subject, who is assumed to control absolutely (or to be potentially able to control) a meaning sought only within written language, a "text itself." They examined negotiations between this mind and this imagined control of the supposedly fixed meanings that written language contains. Rhetorical theorists, in concert with these newly privileged schools, examined the imagined audiences for texts, taking as their object of study a similarly fixed psychology of interactions between an individual and a traditionally imagined "universal" but well-defined group whose judgments of texts can also be universalized.

While I have contributed to this work and have with many others benefited enormously from it, I am suggesting in this sketchy survey that both the theory we *have,* and much of what we now *say* we have, appear to retain an image of student writing instruction as an initiative, evaluative rite based on categories of "good" and "bad" writers and writing. In this interpretative frame, only the generic practices of a developing generic writer will earn invitations to the gatherings where ongoing conversations take place in now entirely literate but significantly diverse disciplines and extracurricular settings. In the approaches to teaching and interpretation that I have described, the written language that is the ostensible concern of composition teaching is not made intelligible as a process itself—as an action *or* as a resulting text that *approximates* meaning in uncertainly effective interactions among a temporally positioned writer, *ad hoc* readers, and specific, variable discourse situations.

Consequently, in much of the composition theory that we now display in textbooks, teaching colloquia, and program descriptions, both texts and minds are subjected to formalist interpretations. These interpretations attempt to expose imagined, essentially stable, meanings that peculiarly student texts are assumed to hide or distort. Writing itself, the object of our study, still is most frequently treated as a potentially transparent medium, a pipeline that could transmit the personal presence of a quite literally imagined authorial voice, arising from a stable, unified, coherent human subject. This voice will be heard (or not) in these views by an equally stable, unified, and purposeful audience. We do not ordinarily imagine writing, nor teach it, as though it is read by a widely scattered, often isolated readership who do not know and often will not meet its human source. Such readers inevitably rewrite and resist a text's claims on their predispositions; they are rarely persuaded by "clarity" in a text itself. But to use the vocabulary of visual representation, we have largely retained realism as our practical model for written language. Composition studies often theorizes writing as, unfortunately, the inadequacies of most entering students as against a canon of good writing and certain communication, no matter how covertly. Enduring social circumstances around institutional dispositions of writing instruction, which include retained models from nineteenth-century postsecondary curricula, often prevent alternative theories of writing from informing research or actual practice in composition courses.

I am aware that many composition theorists significantly oppose these assumptions we still have. But I am arguing primarily that the object that is theorized in composition studies remains fairly opaque because it still resides in the unarticulated but indomitable categories of "high" and "low" that first defined all academic textual studies. Writing, and its pedagogical composition, is properly assumed to be the object interpreted by descriptions of a writer's actions. Yet we have had little clarity about what such theories might predict about this globalized writing, or about the fit between its many kinds of students and their actual writing situations. We have avoided issues that constrain theorizing in other fields, especially the question of explaining a slippery phenomenon like written language as a regular result from certain conditions for its production. After the creation of a paradigm for composition studies, its theory writing has not resulted in practical challenges to the early elitist principles that modeled the form and purpose of current-traditional teaching. Nor have we genuinely questioned our evaluative assumptions and actual practices in teaching. The writing that is now a specific, locally produced, locally received, and locally evaluated medium of intellectual and social exchange often remains hidden in generic images of it as "good" or "bad" that were more appropriate in a stratified, high-literate culture whose unselfconscious claims on class entitlements valued the language and propriety of the PLU (people like us).

If I am at all correct in these observations, the discourse we call composition theory remains open, waiting for participation that examines, finds patterns in, and speculates about the causes and results of writing by another sort of "actual" writer whose cultural position, schooling, goals, and topics come up in local circumstances, not in the abstract murmur of model texts speaking only to each other, noticeably within or outside already established conventions. Any of us has available this mode of research, theorizing composition, which proceeds from assuming that practices in classrooms, the actions of writers, and the publications of our field all articulate (or resist) a prior, evaluative principle of interpretation that no longer works as a root metaphor to provide locally useful explanations. The results of this early theory are open to questions, particularly when they are revealed to reinstate the categories of "good" and "bad" that process and product have shared. This way of entering theory—questioning our observations, our opinions, and our principles in light of the complete matrix of circumstance that localize contemporary writing—would encourage a slow and recursive interplay of assertions, applications, resistances, and further assertions that describe intellectual movement more accurately than "paradigm shift" can.

One model of this interplay has already been offered by Louise Wetherbee Phelps in "Images of Student Writing: The Deep Structure of Teacher Response." Phelps suggests that writers of composition theory, always implicated in practices, have moved from particularity to self-consciousness. In her description, composition theory and its theorists have passed through (1) "a purely pragmatic phase, aimed at establishing the most effective teaching methods" (45), and (2) a transitional phase that has described processes and constructed largely psychologicistic models, using limited explanatory concepts. In her view, we might as a community be said to be now in a third phase, "a fully theoretical" time when theories are broadened to account for social activity and to include multidisciplinary perspectives, as those of social process theorists like Bartholomae, Bizzell, Bazerman, and Myers have been. Finally, Phelps says, theory writing will involve a "metatheoretical phase" in which we place studies in comprehensive cultural networks and rely on metacriticism (45).

But that metatheoretical phase, which will intersect and reform ongoing uses of the others, must base its emergence on a different sense of intellectual politics than the one we hold over from the successes of the "big" theories that it will analyze and move beyond. In this stage, whose emergence I have been encouraging and in which I hope this essay participates, it may be possible to achieve more clarity about what composition theories make intelligible. If it is how to teach students to write, we will need to critique the modeling of generic writing processes that were defined in our stage 2 research, and begin instead to describe students as *actual* "actual" writers who encounter "English" and "composition" only briefly in a complex web of public, private, vocational, and popular cultural settings. Such writers cannot, to take a primary example, always revise their writing over a long period of time. But studies of process have not included temporal pressures, despite the frequency with which all writers encounter them. Consequently, we will need to assume not only that writing is a social and socialized action, as Phelps says we have in stage 3 theorizing, but additionally consider that its purposes are never limited to the purposes *in* a text, but include the purposes *for* a text as well. We will need systematically to examine the situations in which readers read specifically identifiable kinds of writing, including our own readings of student texts, so that readers' expectations, requirements, and cultural or idiosyncratic prejudices become visible to student writers. We will need to account for evaluations of writing not in terms of its meaning or correctness, nor by gauging its expressiveness, but by investigating the actual results that a specific piece of writing—however well or ill formed it may be—has when both intended and accidental readers read it.

By defining the situations of writers and their texts in this way, I am obviously returning to my claim that contemporary courses in writing should be theorized as courses in contemporary writing. This contemporary object of study is no longer usefully described or taught as a container for thought. In its current configurations, writing is a slippery, overdetermined signification. Its "authorship" results from resistances among competing and already articulated ideas, a writer's specific access and reaction to them, a specific motive and occasion for writing, and the constraints of language itself as a writer encounters them. Like government documents and some academic publications, a text may be written *to have been written,* not to record, develop, or express thought, and not to be closely, or even casually, read. This and much other writing is not best discussed as though its meaning were entirely contained in its writer's or its idealized reader's mind, nor as if its significance is revealed in its relation to traditional conventions of formal discourse.

This "text we are already in," a complex, multimedia, culturally diverse setting that we and our students share, requires that we limit our claims to produce generic writers and theories that describe them. If theory, in a new mode as metatheory, is to be more than a professional boundary and privileging mechanism, it cannot exempt itself from valuable analyses of the assignment-making, student texts, and cultural subtexts for teaching composition that distinguish our field by focusing it on *learning* to write. To theorize teaching in a particular situation, we may need to decide whether it is formal academic, or personally expressive, nonacademic writing that composition actually addresses in any particular course. The nature of the student in this course in composition may additionally need new interpretative attention, for the imagined "you" addressed in most textbooks is now frequently nonnative, postadolescent, employed, sexually active, gendered, economically positioned, and a fully political subject of many cultural codes that do not privilege absolute standards for writing. In vital stage 4 composition theory, our metacritical stance might recognize that whatever philosophical alliances we claim, we will as both writers and readers inevitably encounter postmodern fragmentations of discourse. Our students cannot be assimilated into global requirements in the academy, or into a universalized role as the traditional citizen after they leave it, without violently distorting their actual writing and reading experiences. Consequently, composition theory may address much variable knowledge and many variable pleasures in it, the elements of interactive textual cultures.

We have a great deal of evidence that such multiplication is already at hand. Many of us who were once composition theorists have renamed ourselves in particular and specific ways that allow us to question, and to change, our formerly evaluative assumptions about the nature of composition studies. We have directly and indirectly identified with subfields in textual studies that redefine our political, not simply our intellectual, relations to other groups in the academy. Some have joined new historians to become archivists of a wide chronology of written texts and of the rhetorical theories that described them. Some have joined social-scientific researchers in, for example, reevaluating theories of reading and cognition. Some have investigated the political and nonacademic conditions that create public definitions of and instructional programs in literacy. Some study distinct textual communities through the lens offered by text linguistics, to determine the liminal social boundaries around specific kinds of successful prose. Others have applied new literary theories to the text of student writing, which these theories make less underprivileged than it was in an era of literariness in English studies.

This diversity no longer aims to solve the "problem" that first named student writing and later articulated its theories, but instead takes seriously the multiple and overlapping historical situations, purposes, readerships, forms, registers, and results of all writing. I do not describe these new approaches to emphasize that composition is a multidisciplinary or interdisciplinary discipline, borrowing at will from other methods and research tools in a unity around the traditionally globalized (good) writer or *the* course in composition. On the contrary, participation in a metatheoretical and later phase will involve imagining our own community of texts as local and singular in its focus on the significance of written texts and their generation.

The current entrenchment of composition as a field beginning a new phase thus allows us to export knowledge—the data and rigor that we once imported to break boundaries that isolated a culturally initiative and purposefully corrective and discriminatory teaching practice. The unstated evaluative principles of interpretation that this practice *had,* but which could go without saying, precisely fit its cultural mission, to monitor the vernacular writing of the unentitled. In that earlier cultural situation, composition theory necessarily insisted on and described an abstract "good writing" that became its model for later, process-oriented considerations of generically good writers. But now, in a new text of simultaneously local and metacritical impulses, we are, or are positioned to become, a necessary gloss on new historical and descriptive research, cultural studies, American studies, and newly politicized literary theory. We study writers and writing that remain unprivileged, so we are eminently qualified interpreters of a broad but previously unexamined store of information and insights about diverse written texts. If we can together self-consciously acknowledge the cultural situations of our earliest students and their writing—our roots in marginalized texts—this marginalization and its theoretical and principled sources may empower our purchase on hitherto overlooked writing, writers, and writing situations. Our history in anti- and anteprivilege, not the elitist rhetorical traditions that we have *said* we had, can be reversed to open composition studies to parity with more than its local neighbors. Among them, our research, new interpretative principles that comprise a theory for conducting it, and the specific information we have about extracanonical texts all have their own unqualified authority.

Works Cited

Berlin, James. "Rhetoric and Ideology in the Writing Class." *College English* 50 (1988): 477–94.

Christensen, Francis. *Notes Toward a New Rhetoric: Six Essays for Teachers*. New York: Harper, 1967.

Connolly, Paul, and Teresa Vilardi. *New Methods in College Writing Programs: Theories in Practice*. New York: MLA, 1986.

Connors, Robert. "Composition Studies and Science." *College English* 45 (1983): 1–20.

D'Angelo, Frank. *A Conceptual Theory of Rhetoric*. Cambridge, MA: Winthrop, 1975.

Emig, Janet. *The Composing Processes of Twelfth-Graders*. NCTE Research Report No. 13. Urbana, IL: NCTE, 1971.

Faigley, Lester. "Competing Theories of Process: A Critique and a Proposal." *College English* 48 (1986): 527–42.

Gray, Donald. "New Ideas About English and Departments of English." *English Education* 18 (1986): 147–52.

Hairston, Maxine. "The Winds of Change: Thomas Kuhn and the Revolution in the Teaching of Writing." *College Composition and Communication* 33 (1982): 76–88.

Hartzog, Carol. *Composition and the Academy: A Study of Writing Program Administration.* New York: MLA, 1987.

Hillocks, George."What Works in Teaching Composition: A Meta-Analysis of Experimental Treatment Studies." *American Journal of Education* 93 (1984): 133–170.

Hirsch, E. D. *The Philosophy of Composition.* Chicago: U of Chicago P, 1977.

Larson, Richard. Letter to the author. 23 July, 1987.

Miller, Susan. *Textual Carnivals: The Politics of Composition.* Carbondale: Southern Illinois UP, 1991.

Neel, Jasper, ed. *Options for the Teaching of English: Freshman Composition.* New York: MLA, 1978.

North, Stephen. *The Making of Knowledge in Composition: Portrait of an Emerging Field.* Upper Montclair, NJ: Boynton/Cook, 1987.

Ong, Walter J. *Orality and Literacy: The Technologizing of the Word.* London: Methuen, 1982.

Phelps, Louise Wetherbee. "Images of Student Writing: The Deep Structure of Teacher Response." Ed. Chris M. Anson. *Writing and Response: Theory, Practice, and Research.* Urbana, IL: NCTE, 1989. 37–67.

Shaughnessy, Mina. *Errors and Expectations: A Guide for the Teacher of Basic Writing.* New York: Oxford UP, 1977.

Richards, I. A. *The Philosophy of Rhetoric.* London: Oxford UP, 1936.

Young, Richard, Alton Becker, and Kenneth Pike. *Rhetoric: Discovery and Change.* New York: Harcourt, 1970.

Context-Sensitive Text Analysis

AFTER MORE THAN A decade of relative neglect, the linguistic analysis of written texts should become once again a major component of composition research. This renewed interest will come about, I believe, as a result of the increasing emphasis now being given to the role of contextual factors in composition. Instead of focusing exclusively on the individual writer and his or her plans, strategies, or voice, more and more researchers are drawing attention to the social dimension of writing. They are seeing the writer not as an autonomous agent but as a member of one or more discourse communities, each having its own values, norms, and ways of knowing and communicating. Since discourse communities are defined primarily by texts, those texts become a major part of the context within which any act of writing takes place. In producing texts of their own, writers typically respond to questions or issues raised in other texts; and, in so doing, they borrow ideas, language, genre conventions, and other aspects of prior texts. It is especially this recognition of the *intertextuality* of writing (and reading), I believe, that is stimulating new interest in text analysis.

The new style of text analysis that we see emerging is more rhetorical than the text analysis of old. In the past, the teaching of composition relied heavily on generic, decontextualized notions of textual well-formedness. Text linguists working in this tradition did research on the paragraph (Christensen; Becker; Rodgers), the essay (Grady; D'Angelo), discourse blocs (Pitkin), sentence combining (O'Hare), and other aspects of written language thought to be essential to "good writing." This tradition did not entirely die out, even as the field shifted from a product orientation to a process one. In the late 1970s and early 1980s, for example, work done on such topics as cohesion and coherence (e.g., Winterowd; Halliday and Hasan; Witte and Faigley), topical structure (Witte), discourse structure (Colomb and Williams; Coe), structural plans (Meyer), and given-new ordering (Vande Kopple) paid little attention to contextual variables. In all of these studies, the focus was not on the rhetorical effectiveness of a particular set of linguistic features in a particular situation but rather on what makes a text readable.

What we see emerging today, however, is a broader conception of text analysis that includes not only the cognitive and expressive aspects so closely associated with the process movement but sociological and cultural dimensions as well. The process movement has served the valuable purpose of shifting attention away from generic models and finished products, emphasizing instead the inventional aspects of writing and the processes by which individuals produce texts. But individuals do not write in a vacuum. They belong to discourse communities, they have socially influenced purposes and goals, they borrow language and ideas from other people—in short, they live and perform in some multivariegated, sociocultural *context*. The processes by which competent writers produce successful pieces of writing are not decontextualized cognitive operations or expressive acts carried out by isolated individuals; rather, they are more broadly based processes embedded within and influenced by community affiliations. Sociolinguistic research has shown that communities are created and maintained largely by their language-using practices. Studying particular texts in this light can tell us much about the communities and individuals involved and how the tensions and relations between them affect the composing process. Some good examples can be found in Fowler; Brown and Herndl; Bernhardt; Faigley; Berkenkotter, Huckin, and Ackerman; Kress; and Fairclough.

The purpose of this chapter is threefold: (1) to examine the epistemological assumptions a researcher makes when choosing to do context-sensitive text analysis, (2) to outline some of the methodological characteristics that result from these assumptions, and (3) to illustrate and discuss these points in a specific case.

Epistemological Assumptions

Researchers who engage in context-sensitive text analysis generally subscribe to a number of basic assumptions, as follows:

Texts exist. They are not "fictions," they do not exist only in the mind of the reader. Although texts are usually open to multiple interpretations, the number of plausible interpretations is constrained by various linguistic conventions that are manifested in the text. The meanings of these conventions are tacitly agreed upon by members of a discourse community (cf. de Saussure's "l'arbitraire du signe"). Even Stanley Fish, David Bleich, and other reader-response theorists seem to agree that interpretation cannot take place except through interpretive communities. They fail to recognize, however, that such communities are formed and maintained around a body of tangible, linguistically constituted texts, and that these texts contain observable patterns of language usage that come to mean certain things to the members of a given community. Text analysts make the epistemological assumption that analyzing these patterns in certain ways (see below) can give us insight into the meaning-making practices of the community and its individual members.

Texts are the product of an attempt by a writer to communicate meaning to one or more readers. This is not to say that we can know for certain what that meaning is, or that readers do not themselves construct meaning from a text, or that the reader's intepretation may not differ from the writer's intended meaning. The assumption simply recognizes that writers have something to say and that they invest thought and effort in the construction of text in order to share that something with their readers. From this it follows that writers try to use language in ways that will be recognized and understood (i.e., in conventional ways, including so-called imaginative usages that rely on convention, only less obviously), and that, if writers are competent, many if not most of their intended readers will be able to glean their intended meaning. Text analysts assume that by paying attention to these linguistic conventions, with appropriate help from insiders, they can gain knowledge about various aspects of the writing-reading process.

Meaning includes not only propositional content but metalinguistic and interpersonal content as well. This echoes Halliday's tripartite distinction of ideational meaning, textual meaning, and interpersonal meaning, and it underscores the belief (1) that texts are meaningful only insofar as they are interpreted by writers and readers, (2) that information does not exist in any pure form but is subject to interpretation, and (3) that interpretation is based on values, goals, purposes, and other variables that are community-based. In other words, propositional information in a text is usually accompanied by metalinguistic and interpersonal information that helps to guide interpretation. Epistemologically, this means that the text analyst should avoid focusing exclusively on propositional content, as was done, for example, in a number of psycholinguistic and text-linguistic studies in the 1960s and 1970s.

Writers try to use language in cognitively efficient ways. All writers labor under short-term memory limitations. Therefore, they need to use language as efficiently as possible, maximizing expressiveness while minimizing cognitive effort. The major way of doing this is by relying heavily on linguistic conventions, which encode a relatively rich body of community knowledge yet are easy for both writer and reader to access. All language users have extensive experience with this strategy, using it in daily speech all their lives, so they can be expected to know the basic principle. Epistemologically, this is one more reason to expect that writers' and readers' efforts at communication will be governed largely by linguistic patterns and conventions and that errors and other infelicities often have good reasons behind them. Mina Shaughnessy's great contribution in *Errors and Expectations* was to demonstrate how even the errors made by basic writers could be seen as intelligent, system-governed attempts to express meaning.

There are no two ways of saying exactly the same thing; thus, even minor details of language usage can be significant in interpreting the meaning of a text. This is an extension of the efficiency principle just described. Whenever a language offers what appears to be two different words for the same thing (e.g., *plume* and *feather* in early Middle English), the users of that language usually find it convenient to discriminate among those words and use them to refer to different things (or to the same thing in different ways). This increases the speakers' expressive power. Over time, the different usages become conventionalized, making it easier for succeeding generations of speakers to learn and use the words. Thus, both expressiveness and cognitive accessibility are served. In short, the historical development of a language mirrors the highly rational behavior of its individual users, and it would be inefficient for things to be otherwise. With regard to text analysis, this means that if a writer uses a certain word in favor of another nearly synonymous word, there is probably a reason for it. If a pattern of language usage appears in a writer's text, there is probably a reason for that. This is not to say that writers always choose the right words or always express themselves to best effect, only that they always *try* to.

Writers belong to multiple discourse communities, and the texts they write often reflect their divided loyalties. Every language user belongs not just to one but to many discourse communities, including familial, occupational, social, religious, avocational, and others. In LePage's terms, every individual is located in a unique "multidimensional linguistic space." If, as Hudson claims, every individual uses language in a way that reflects his or her allegiance to different discourse communities, then we can see how a close analysis of individual texts can provide possible explanations of nonstandard usage, errors, voice, and other stylistic features. Membership in multiple discourse communities may even help account for inventional aspects of writing. Kress argues that texts arise out of discoursal differences (i.e., that people create texts in order to resolve tensions between competing discourses).

Methodological Characteristics of Context-Sensitive Text Analysis

Given the epistemological assumptions just discussed, certain methodological characteristics naturally emerge. First of all, context-sensitive text analysis is *problem-driven,* not theory-driven. Various kinds of theories, including political, sociological, and other, may guide the analysis or different parts of it, but the purpose of the analysis is to solve some problem in the teaching of composition, not to help build someone's theory of language. Therefore, analysis does not proceed deductively and is not bound by the rules and algorithms of any one particular theory. Instead, it is free to use various methods and apply various ideas as the situation demands. In short, it is naturally *eclectic* and *interdisciplinary.*

Second, context-sensitive text analysis tries to account for as much of the *context of situation* as possible (Malinowski), without becoming overly speculative. It assumes that people's reasons for writing things in certain ways are influenced by a broad spectrum of contextual factors, including social, cultural, and other factors that are not readily formalizable.

Third, it relies openly on *plausible interpretation* rather than on any kind of proof. Given its ambitious scope, context-sensitive text analysis cannot possibly be a highly formalized and testable scientific endeavor. It cannot control for all possible variables and it cannot insist on any one interpretation of findings. It can only try to assemble enough evidence to make a strong case for a certain point of view.

Finally, context-sensitive text analysis combines *multiple forms of analysis*, both qualitative and quantitative. This feature recognizes the fact that by trying to embrace as much of the context as possible in one's analysis, a certain amount of rigor must be sacrificed. Methodological triangulation (Denzin), including empirical data-gathering, can produce converging results that support the plausibility of one's argument.

Procedural Steps

Context-sensitive text analysis typically proceeds through at least six general stages, as discussed below. These stages are depicted in the final write-up as being sequentially ordered, but during the investigation they are actually carried out in a more recursive fashion. This is because the procedure is not a discovery procedure per se but a process of constructing an interpretation that will make sense to the composition community, be interesting, and bear up under their scrutiny. Interpretation takes place not just at the end of the process but throughout.

1. *Selection of an initial corpus.* For inventional purposes, one usually starts with an informally selected set of texts. It is desirable, though not necessary, that these texts be of some intrinsic interest to one's intended audience. For example, I am currently doing a text-based study of *ad hoc* discourse communities, a topic of general interest, I believe, to composition specialists. Although I could have used texts from various noncomposition communities, I decided to use texts that would be more immediately interesting to composition specialists (viz., CCCC's proposals).

More importantly, though, the investigator usually has a hunch that there is something about these texts, some linguistic pattern, that will be of interest to his audience. This step anticipates steps 2, 3, and 6, and requires considerable knowledge of the field.

2. *Identification of salient patterns.* Looking through these texts, one may notice an unusual pattern of language use, a sharp deviation from some putative norm. I find it best at this stage to

scan the texts holistically, looking for general patterns rather than detailed ones. This is because I know that in the end I will want to construct an argument that will appeal to compositionists in general, not just to those trained in linguistics. The perception of patterns in a text will vary from one person to another, of course, depending on training and experience. For that reason, it's a good idea to have colleagues from different fields or subfields also peruse the texts.

3. *A determination of "interestingness."* Is there anything in this pattern that might be of interest to composition teachers or researchers? Answering this question obviously requires considerable current knowledge of the field and a sense of where it is heading. Simply gathering and analyzing data is of no value if it doesn't support a point that people in composition find interesting. In my experience, that usually means something that is perceived as both *useful* to theory building or pedagogy and *original*. (But not *too* original: it should accord with one or more of the conventional story plots of the field [cf. Newkirk's chapter in this volume].)

4. *Selection of a study corpus.* Sometimes, what appears to be a striking pattern of language use turns out to be an artifact of selective attention on the part of the investigator. That is, in dealing with the initial corpus, one may inadvertently concentrate on only a subset of the texts, arbitrarily selected. If one plans to make any claims of generality at the end of the study (thereby increasing the interest of the study), it is important at this point to use a principled procedure to create a study corpus. For example, in the CCCC's project just mentioned, I have created a stratified random sample of 350 proposals by randomly selecting one proposal from each of the four grading categories for each of the twenty-five or so program areas for each of the past three years.

5. *Verification of the pattern.* Now that there is a well-defined study corpus, one can do some empirical data gathering and, if appropriate, some statistical measurements on the data to see if the pattern perceived in step 2 still exists under these more con-

trolled circumstances. Not all readers in composition studies today are receptive to empirical evidence, but many are. The key to this step is the proper selection of text features that are both indicative of the pattern and reliably quantifiable. How do you select text features that are indicative of the pattern? Generally you go back over the initial corpus and try to identify those features that you think gave rise to the holistic impression you got in step 2. For example, if you perceived a pattern of textual impersonality, you might look for linguistic features known to convey an impersonal tone of voice (i.e., agentless passive constructions, nominalizations, stative verbs). I always try to use features that either have face validity for composition specialists or are widely supported in the research literature (a useful partial checklist, given in Fowler, includes lexical processes, transitivity, syntax, modality, speech acts, implicature, and personal reference). Sometimes you have to create a baseline corpus in order to have something against which to compare the target corpus. For example, if you think freshman composition students begin too many sentences with the word *there,* you might want to examine not only freshman essays but other, more advanced essays as well, so as to be able to make some kind of comparison (cf. Huckin and Pesante).

6. *Functional-rhetorical analysis.* Why does this pattern exist? By now the investigator has probably already formed an opinion, but here is where a full answer must be constructed. Constructing a plausible, if tentative, explanation requires considerable wide-ranging knowledge. Using the epistemological assumptions given at the beginning of this chapter, the investigator must look at the data from different perspectives and build the most faithful interpretation she can, revising her earlier hypothesis if necessary. To this end, one should draw on whatever knowledge one has of various relevant fields (i.e., sociolinguistics, psycholinguistics, textlinguistics, rhetoric, composition studies, cultural studies). Working with colleagues from these fields is particularly helpful

at this point, as it not only provides important knowledge and ideas but helps guard against wrongheaded interpretations.

An Example

The assumptions, characteristics, and procedural steps just described can perhaps best be understood by seeing how they have been operationalized in an actual study. I've selected a study I worked on myself (Berkenkotter, Huckin, and Ackerman), not because I think it's better than any of the other studies mentioned above but simply because I happen to know it better.

The case to be discussed here is that of a graduate student ("Nate") making his way through the first year of a Ph.D. rhetoric program. The project began quite innocently: although my two collaborators (Carol Berkenkotter and John Ackerman) and I thought we might notice some interesting things about Nate's socialization into a new discourse community (this was 1986 and the social-epistemic view of writing was beginning to command considerable attention among composition researchers), we did not start with any particular preconceptions or hypotheses; rather, we decided to simply track Nate's progress and see what happened (i.e., work inductively). Accordingly, we collected Nate's writings, interviewed him, followed him around, took notes, and did other activities of a quasi-ethnographic nature for a period of about ten months.

The project became interesting midway through when we noticed clear changes in Nate's style of writing: it seemed to be becoming more complex and abstract on all levels (word, sentence, text). This was the "triggering observation" that caused us to entertain several possible working hypotheses. One hypothesis was that Nate was simply displaying the effects of stress—the stress of being in a new environment with all sorts of uncomfortable demands placed on him. This seemed possible, but the changes we were seeing in his writing were not negative ones indicating some kind of dysfunction. Rather, they seemed to form a pattern of increasing stylistic complexity. Another possibility was that Nate was simply undergoing developmental changes as part of normal maturation. That seemed unlikely, though, since Nate was in his mid-thirties and was already a demonstrably competent writer at the beginning of the year. A third, more likely possibility was that Nate was trying to learn a new way of writing, one that would be more acceptable to his new community of peers and mentors. Since this view had considerable face validity and no strong counterevidence, we provisionally adopted it as our working hypothesis.

Was this hypothesis of interest to composition teachers? We thought so, because writing courses typically try to teach students how to write in new ways for new audiences, and indeed, the writing class itself can be seen as a new discourse community. There was considerable discussion in the composition literature about this aspect of writing pedagogy (e.g., Bizzell; Bruffee; Bartholomae), but no actual case studies. By tracking the progress of a student entering a new discourse community, we thought we could contribute to the literature in a way that had not been done before.

Were we seeing a real pattern in Nate's writing or just an illusory one? To find this out, we had to establish a study corpus and do some quantitative measurement of key textual features. Nate had written twelve academic papers (about 31,500 words) during his first year, so we used these papers as our initial corpus (for detailed analysis, we used only the first fifty T-units of each of these papers). Later, to control for the audience variable, we concentrated on four of these papers, plus an informal memo, all of which had been written for the same professor. Selecting the right features is crucial to success in research of this type. The features chosen should be reliably identifiable and quantifiable, and of course they should test one's impressionistic judgments about the text(s) at hand. In Nate's case, we had noticed changes in diction, sentence structure, and textual coherence and cohesion, so we needed to select and measure linguistic features on all three of these levels.

On the word level, what we had noticed most of all was that when he tried to write formal papers, Nate sometimes used expressions like *horribly, mindframe,* and *cheesy dilemma* that were distinctly uncharacteristic of the diction used by established scholars. It seemed to us that this tendency was more pronounced in his early writings than in his later ones. Trying to find out if our impressions were accurate was not an easy matter. We could not simply go through his texts and identify off-register terms ourselves; we had a vested interest in finding such terms and thus would not be considered impartial judges. In theory, one could imagine using a computer to do the job. A computer could sort through a large number of recently written scholarly texts in composition, build a frequency list of words and expressions found therein, and then analyze individual texts (such as Nate's) against that list. But that has not been done, and it would require a massive effort even more daunting than that of Francis and Kucera, who used a different sort of corpus in the 1960s. Also, we had no way of knowing what such a count would mean, since we did not have any comparative data on other writers' use of off-register words.

To solve the problem, we started with the ethnomethodological assumption that the best judges of off-register diction would be disinterested members of the particular discourse community that uses that register. Accordingly, we asked three mainstream scholars in composition research to go through five of Nate's texts (written over a period of ten months) and independently identify all off-register words and phrases. For purposes of comparison, we also had them do the same for ten published texts written by other well-known scholars in the field, texts that we knew Nate was reading and admiring. In all cases, we used only the first one thousand words of each text. The raters did not always agree on their identification of particular off-register expressions, but the overall results of their evaluations showed that

Nate's percentage of off-register expressions was much higher than that of the ten established scholars. The results also showed that Nate's use of off-register expressions decreased steadily and markedly over a period of ten months, from 3.7 to 1.1 percent (the ten established scholars scored an average .4 percent). Thus, there is empirical evidence that in the space of ten months Nate gained considerable control over the vocabulary of his new discourse community.

On the sentence level, there were two text features in Nate's writing that showed dramatic variation over time. One was the length and complexity of his sentences. The relatively short, simple sentences of his early writings seemed to become long, complex ones later on. It was easy to count up words and sentences, and we knew that sentence length usually correlates with complexity. So, we decided to use average number of words per sentence as our indicator of both sentence length and sentence complexity. Nate's five writings showed the following figures for average sentence length: 18.3, 15.1, 19.1, 26.7, and 34.3. If we exclude writing number 2, the only informal piece in the set, we find that there was a steady increase in sentence length over a period of ten months. By comparison, the average sentence length for the ten scholars' writing was 26.3 (range: 21.7–29.4). Thus, if we hypothesize that Nate was trying in some fashion to emulate these scholars' writing, it would appear that he succeeded in approximating the length and complexity of their sentences by the end of his first year in the program (cf. text number 4) but that he overshot the target with text number 5.

The other noticeable sentence-level feature was the use of the word *I*. In his early writings, Nate began about half his sentences with this subject pronoun. In his last two papers, which had much longer and more complex sentences, he used only one *I* in each. The ten scholars' writings averaged only 2.7 *I*'s per thousand words, and four had none at all.

At the full-text level, it seemed to us that Nate's early writing lacked some coherence and cohesion. Much has been written about coherence and cohesion in the composition literature, so a number of measures were available to us. For example, we could have analyzed the topical structure of Nate's texts (Witte), the given-new patterning (Vande Kopple), the lexical cohesion (Stotsky), the discourse structure (Meyer), and the text structure (Nold and Davis; Coe). But none of these methods were well suited to the case at hand. For example, topical structure analysis depends on the identification of individual sentence topics. In much expository writing this is not a problem, since the grammatical subject of a sentence is often also the topic of that sentence. But in Nate's writing, as already pointed out, the grammatical subject of many of his sentences was the pronoun *I*, which hardly seemed to be what the sentence was about. In sentences like these, and in many others, it was difficult to ascertain the true sentence topic.

In a similar vein, although the principle of putting given information before new information may be valid in general, we often found it difficult to identify exactly what constituted new or given information in Nate's texts. His heavy use of *I* in sentence subject position created what was technically a given-before-new pattern, but it was not an effective use of the pattern in that it did not "push the communication forward" (Firbas). Also, we encountered many cases where the information status of a particular noun phrase was simply unclear between a given or new interpretation. We thought of invoking Ellen Prince's notion of "inferable" entities (Prince; cf. Jordan's "associated nominals") for these unclear cases, but decided that we had no principled way of making the proper identifications and that in fact interpretation could vary from one reader to the next. In general, trying to identify lexical cohesion proved problematic. Lexical cohesion is often created not through repetition, synonymy, or set-subset relations but through intertextual lexical collocation (words that often co-occur). As Sandra Stotsky has noted, intertextual lexical collocation derives not from the linguistic system but from the reader's prior textual experiences; hence, it will vary from reader to reader. Trying to identify intertextual lexical collocations in

Nate's texts, like trying to identify given and new information, would have been highly subjective, unreliable, and laborious.

Therefore, to test our impression about the lack of cohesion in some of Nate's writing, we decided to focus on three other sets of features that could be measured more reliably: connectives, discourse demonstratives, and ratio of definite articles to indefinite articles. (Definite articles typically mark given information while indefinite articles mark new information; hence, according to Johansson, a high article ratio indicates thematic continuity.) Although we harbored some uncertainty about the validity of these different measures (all had been used elsewhere as measures of cohesion, but none had really been thoroughly tested), we thought that if we used multiple measures and had converging results, we would be on safe ground. As it turns out, our results did all point to the same conclusion: Nate's writing was less cohesive than that of the ten well-known scholars. He used significantly fewer connectives and fewer discourse demonstratives and had a significantly lower article ratio than they did.

Somewhat troubling, however, was the fact that the findings from these three measures gave no evidence of improvement over time. Our earlier holistic judgments had given us the impression that Nate's writing was getting more cohesive, but our quantitative results suggested otherwise: there was no change in his use of connectives or articles, and his use of demonstratives had actually declined. Thus, we were faced with the choice of either trusting our holistic impressions or trusting the linguistic measures we were using. Since the results of the three measures essentially agreed with each other, we decided to trust them rather than our intuitions. Accordingly, we claimed that our subject "did not appear to have made much improvement in coherence and cohesion."

This may have been a mistake. In a recent article, Richard Haswell points out that the use of explicit ties to measure cohesion has never been shown to be consistently valid. Indeed, he argues quite persuasively that competent writers are often able to create cohesion and coherence *without* using many demonstratives, connectives, or other explicit ties, relying instead on the reader's ability to detect familiar discourse patterns, or "unstated structures of expectation" (Haswell). Haswell's argument is persuasive not only because it is based on a body of empirical data but because it makes sense in terms of the efficiency principle mentioned above. That is, why should competent writers clog their prose with connectives, demonstratives, and other transitional devices if these devices aren't needed? If Haswell is right, we may have erred by focusing on cohesive devices that are not used consistently by competent writers and thus are not entirely valid indicators of cohesion. There are several lessons in this. First, some aspects of textuality, such as cohesion and coherence, are very difficult to assess analytically (i.e., using linguistic features), at least for now. In such cases, holistic judgments using several independent raters may be more valid. Second, converging measures may help inspire confidence in one's findings, but they do not guarantee validity. Third, one should not use *any* linguistic measure uncritically (i.e., without testing it against one's own intuition). Unlike the register index, which did strike us as intuitively right, we had harbored some doubts about using connectives, demonstratives, and definite articles as measures of cohesion; we should have acted on these doubts (just as Haswell did). Finally, one should never consider a textual analysis to be fixed and conclusive. There is always room for reinterpretation, especially as we learn more about the strengths and weaknesses of the tools we use.

Despite these problems with measuring cohesion and coherence, however, we still had gathered considerable data from various levels of analysis supporting our impression that there was a real pattern to the changes in Nate's writing over time. Therefore, we now had to try to explain this pattern. Our working hypothesis, it may be recalled, was that Nate was trying to learn a new way of writing, one that would be more acceptable to his new community of peers and mentors. Was this a valid hypothesis? At first we concluded that it was. But there was more to the story. In trying to sort out what we had learned from this study, we found it essential to not only review the textual evidence we had collected but also (1) to consult the literature from sociolinguistics, composition studies, psychology, and other possibly relevant fields and (2) to consult with Nate himself. These efforts enriched our interpretation of our findings and saved us from committing a serious interpretative error.

We knew from earlier discussions with Nate that he had come to the Ph.D. program (strongly empirical in orientation) from a very different background (expressive writing). Accordingly, when we first noticed the changes in his writing, we had tentatively concluded that he was making a transition from one community to the other, in effect rejecting the one for the other. But when we talked with Nate about this, he emphatically denied having rejected his earlier community or his earlier style of writing. Indeed, he claimed that he deliberately *used* expressive writing for compensatory purposes (e.g., for invention and problem solving) while going through his first year in the doctoral program. This caused us to revise our perception of what was going on in his writing.

Armed with this insider information, we were able to see that the changes in Nate's writing style did not signal a rejection of his earlier community but simply an adaptation to another one. It was like learning a second language: he was not rejecting his native language, just adding to it. Nor had he lost his voice. Consistent with the epistemological assumption about multiple discourse communities discussed earlier, Nate was using different voices and various blends of voices for different situations and purposes. This gave us an enriched view of Nate's accomplishment and a better understanding of what it means to enter a new discourse community.

Closing Comments

One example, however extended, does not adequately illustrate the various aspects of doing context-sensitive text analysis.

It does, however, bring out at least the following points. First, in order to identify an interesting and worthwhile issue, select appropriate text features, and provide plausible accounts of the data, one should have some knowledge of as many relevant disciplines as possible, including sociolinguistics, psycholinguistics, rhetoric, reading research, composition studies, linguistic theory, discourse analysis, pragmatics, cognitive psychology, and literary theory. Since it is virtually impossible for any one person to know so many fields, one should try to collaborate with other investigators from different areas. Second, to compensate for the relative lack of rigor inherent in context-sensitive studies and for the inadequacy of any one particular method, one should seek to use multiple methods of analysis. (Point 1 above should facilitate this effort by making diverse methods available.) Third, the value of ethnomethodological work (Garfinkel) should not be overlooked, in particular the use of specialist consultants from within the community being investigated. In the case discussed here, Nate's input was critical to the success of the project. Finally, since plausibility rather than proof is the standard by which a context-sensitive text analysis will be judged, no analysis should be considered definitive. The investigator should always be on the alert for any mismatch between data and interpretation and should always be willing to revise his or her interpretation accordingly.

I close with this quote from John R. Firth, the most influential forerunner of contemporary text analysis:

> We may assume that any social person speaking in his own personality will behave systematically, since experienced language is universally systemic. Therefore, we may study his speech and ask the question, "What is systemic?" We must not expect to find one closed system. But we may apply systematic categories to the statement of the facts. We must separate from the mush of general goings-on those features of repeated events which appear to be parts of a patterned process, and handle them systematically by stating them by the spectrum of linguistic techniques. (187)

Works Cited

Bartholomae, David. "Inventing the University." *When a Writer Can't Write*. Ed. Mike Rose. New York: Guilford, 1985. 134–65.

Becker, Alton. "A Tagmemic Approach to Paragraph Analysis." *College Composition and Communication* 16 (1965): 237–42.

Berkenkotter, Carol, Thomas Huckin, and John Ackerman. "Conventions, Conversations, and the Writer: Case Study of a Student in a Rhetoric Ph.D. Program." *Research in the Teaching of English* 22 (1988): 9–43.

Bernhardt, Stephen. "Applying a Functional Model of Language in the Writing Classroom." *Functional Approaches to Writing: Research Perspectives*. Ed. Barbara Couture. Norwood, NJ: Ablex, 1986. 186–98.

Bizzell, Patricia. "Cognition, Convention, and Certainty: What We Need to Know about Writing." *PRE/TEXT* 3 (1982): 213–43.

Brown, Robert, and Carl Herndl. "An Ethnographic Study of Corporate Writing: Job Status as Reflected in Written Text." *Functional Approaches to Writing: Research Perspectives*. Ed. Barbara Couture. Norwood, NJ: Ablex, 1986. 11–28.

Bruffee, Kenneth. "Collaborative Learning and 'The Conversation of Mankind.' " *College English* 46 (1984): 635–52.

Christensen, Francis. "A Generative Rhetoric of the Paragraph." *College Composition and Communication*. 16 (1965): 144–56.

Coe, Richard M. *Toward a Grammar of Passages*. Carbondale: Southern Illinois UP, 1988.

Colomb, Greg, and Joseph Williams. "Perceiving Structure in Professional Prose: A Multiply Determined Experience." *Writing in Nonacademic Settings*. Ed. Lee Odell and Dixie Goswami. New York: Guilford, 1985. 87–125.

D'Angelo, Frank. "A Generative Rhetoric of the Essay." *College Composition and Communication* 25 (1974): 388–96.

Denzin, Norman K. *The Research Act*. Chicago: Aldine, 1970.

Faigley, Lester. "The Problem of Topic in Texts." *The Territory of Language: Linguistics, Stylistics, and the Teaching of Composition*. Ed. Donald McQuade. Carbondale: Southern Illinois UP, 1986. 123–41.

Fairclough, Norman. *Language and Power*. London: Longman, 1989.

Firbas, Jan. "Non-Thematic Subjects in Contemporary English." *Travaux Linguistiques de Prague* 2 (1966): 239–56.

Firth, John R. *Papers in Linguistics, 1934–1951*. London: Oxford UP, 1957.

Fowler, Roger. "Power." *Handbook of Discourse Analysis. 4 vols*. London: Academic, 1985. 4: 61–82.

Francis, W. Nelson, and Henry Kucera. *Frequency Analysis of English Usage: Lexicon and Grammar*. Boston: Houghton, 1982.

Garfinkel, Harold. *Studies in Ethnomethodology*. Englewood Cliffs, NJ: Prentice, 1967.

Grady, Michael. "A Conceptual Rhetoric of the Composition." *College Composition and Communication* 22 (1971): 348–54.

Halliday, Michael A. K., and Ruqaiya Hasan. *Cohesion in English*. London: Longman, 1975.

Haswell, Richard. "Textual Research and Coherence: Findings, Intuition, Application." *College English* 51 (1989): 305–19.

Huckin, Thomas, and Linda Hutz Pesante. "Existential *there*." *Written Communication* 5 (1988): 368–91.

Hudson, Richard A. *Sociolinguistics*. Cambridge: Cambridge UP, 1980.

Johannson, Stig. "Word Frequency and Text Type: Some Observations Based on the LOB Corpus of British English Texts." *Computers and the Humanities* 19 (1985): 23–36.

Jordan, Michael. "Some Associated Nominals in Technical Writing." *Journal of Technical Writing and Communication* 11 (1981): 251–64.

Kress, Gunther. *Linguistic Processes in Sociocultural Practice*. Oxford: Oxford U P, 1989.

Kucera, Henry, and W. Nelson Francis. *Computational Analysis of Present-Day American English*. Providence, R.I.: Brown UP, 1967.

LePage, Robert B., et al., "Further Report on the Sociolinguistic Survey of Multilingual Communities: Survey of Cayo District, British Honduras." *Language in Society* 3 (1977): 1–32.

Malinowski, Bronislaw. "The Problem of Meaning in Primitive Languages." Supplement 1. Ed. C. K. Ogden and I. A. Richards. *The Meaning of Meaning*. New York: Harcourt, 1923. 451–510.

Meyer, Bonnie J. F. *The Organization of Prose and Its Effects on Memory*. Amsterdam: North Holland, 1975.

———. "Reading Research and the Composition Teacher: The Importance of Plans." *College Composition and Communication* 33 (1982): 37–50.

Nold, Ellen, and Brent Davis. "The Discourse Matrix." *College Composition and Communication* 31 (1980): 141–52.

O'Hare, Frank. *Sentence Combining: Improving Student Writing without Formal Grammar Instruction.* NCTE Research Report No. 15. Urbana, IL: NCTE, 1965.

Pitkin, Willis. "Discourse Blocs." *College Composition and Communication* 20 (1969): 138–48.

Prince, Ellen. "Toward a Taxonomy of Given-New Information." *Radical Pragmatics.* Ed. Peter Cole. New York: Academic, 1981.

Rodgers, Paul. "A Discourse-Centered Rhetoric of the Paragraph." *College Composition and Communication* 17 (1966): 2–11.

Shaughnessy, Mina P. *Errors and Expectations: A Guide for the Teacher of Basic Writing.* New York: Oxford UP, 1977.

Stotsky, Sandra. "Types of Lexical Cohesion in Expository Writing: Implications for Developing the Vocabulary of Academic Discourse." *College Composition and Communication* 34 (1983): 430–46.

Vande Kopple, William. "Given and New Information and Some Aspects of the Structures, Semantics, and Pragmatics of Written Texts." *Studying Writing: Linguistic Approaches.* Ed. Charles Cooper and Sidney Greenbaum. Beverly Hills: Sage, 1986. 72–111.

Winterowd, Ross. "The Grammar of Coherence." *College English* 31 (1970): 828–35.

Witte, Stephen. "Topical Structure and Revision." *College Composition and Communication* 34 (1983): 313–41.

Witte, Stephen, and Lester Faigley. "Coherence, Cohesion, and Writing Quality." *College Composition and Communication* 32 (1981): 189–204.

Analyzing Talk about Writing

TALK SURROUNDS WRITING, ENVELOPES IT. We talk our way into writing, and we talk our way out of it. And in between, very often, we let talk diffuse into acts of inscription: it breaks the silence between thinking and writing. Given the immediacy of talk to writing, then, we need to consider talk *about* writing a domain of special inquiry in composition studies. To do so, we must develop methodologies for explaining why, as Roland Barthes puts it, "writing begins at the point where speech becomes *impossible*" (190). This chapter offers an exploration and critique of such methodologies.

The agenda for this exploration is straightforward: I define talk about writing and examine how composition researchers have analyzed it. In doing so, I attend closely to the methodological cues these researchers take from work in other disciplines. The agenda for critique, however, complicates my exploration. I maintain that to analyze talk about writing adequately, we must understand what we are (and are not) studying, and from this, what we can (and cannot) hope to learn. More importantly, I contend that we must assess how the knowledge produced by analyzing talk about writing fits into the mosaic of knowing we call composition studies.

To begin, then, I wish to propose a working definition of talk about writing: conversation in which speakers attend to text or the processes of creating text. Many forms of talk about writing fit this definition, among them concurrent verbal reports of composing processes (Swarts, Flower, and Hayes), retrospective accounts of composing (Sternglass), discourse-based interviews

(Odell, Goswami, and Herrington), and published interviews with literary figures (Tomlinson). This chapter examines yet another kind of talk about writing that fits our working definition: the talk that occurs whenever and wherever writers of any stripe come together to discuss their work. A high school classroom, a college instructor's office, a place of business, a dining room table—all are sites of talk about writing. All imply contexts that shape written products.

Now let me complicate this definition. While talk about writing occurs in many venues and for many purposes, our representations of that talk in research reports cannot begin to capture the texture of what people say when they discuss a piece of writing in progress. Such representations are necessarily narrow and selective because they must mold to the narrative form and serve the arguments readers expect to find in published reports of research. Consequently, the value of these representations is primarily rhetorical. Effective representations of talk about writing make for persuasive arguments about the nature of discourse.

What do these persuasive arguments look like, and what distinguishes them from unpersuasive ones? In the next few sections I will attempt to answer this question.

Analyzing Talk about Writing

A survey of cross-disciplinary work on discourse analysis suggests several frames within which we might view talk about writing. Accompanying each methodological frame, of course, are assumptions about language and the world that shape what we can and cannot learn by using it. I begin here by discussing a family of analytical methods that falls under the heading "conversation analysis." I then go on to describe two other approaches—pragmatic and functional—that differ in how and where they locate meaning in conversational discourse.

Conversation analysis. Practitioners of conversation analysis attempt to make sense of talk from the perspective of its participants. Practitioners generally accept the basic tenet that people use conversation to negotiate the tacit rules that govern their actions in social settings. As John Heritage and J. Maxwell Atkinson put it,

> In examining talk the analyst is immediately confronted with an organization which is implemented on a turn-by-turn basis, and through which a context of publicly displayed and continuously updated intersubjective understandings is systematically sustained. It is through this turn-by-turn character of talk that the participants display their understandings of the state of the talk for one another, and because these understandings are publicly produced, they are available for analytic treatment. (11)

Just how available these "intersubjective understandings" are to analysts is a matter of some debate among those who engage in conversation analysis. According to Aaron Cicourel, this debate centers in part on how to interpret speakers' references to events outside their conversation, events that cannot be explained without expansion of meaning suggested by the surface features of conversational discourse (111). Cicourel warns that all attempts at expansion, inevitable as they are, necessarily introduce analysts' presuppositions about the world into the interpretive frame.

Given the distortion inherent to expansion, some conversation analysts proscribe any expansion at all, restricting interpretation to what appears explicitly in the transcription of talk. Other analysts consider carefully selected aspects of conversational context, but only those very clearly referenced in the transcript. In either case, though, analysts must announce to their audiences their own positions vis-à-vis the situations they interpret; they must acknowledge their roles *within* the social contexts they describe (Cicourel). For researchers studying talk about writing, this means revealing their familiarity with many aspects of the conversational context: knowledge of the participants and their reasons for talking about writing, the purposes of the writing they are talking about, and so on. Such disclosures assist us as readers in two ways. First, they help us judge the validity of researchers' expansions of conversational meaning. And, perhaps more importantly, they remind us of researchers' ideological interest in their work: researchers' knowledge and experience are always integral parts of the domains they claim to analyze.

A recent study of talk about writing conveys the salient characteristics of conversation analysis. In this study, Sarah Warshauer Freedman and Anne Marie Katz inquire into the nature of writing conference conversations that "become part of the writing process itself" (59). They observe that talk during a writing conference blends elements familiar from two contexts: everyday one-on-one conversation and teacher-student conversation in classrooms.

According to Sacks, Schegloff, and Jefferson, whom Freedman and Katz cite, the everyday conversation of American adults follows a fairly small set of tacit rules that suggest preferred patterns of turn-taking. These patterns have as basic units co-occurring "adjacency pairs" that specify a preferred response to an initiating query or statement. (For example, the preferred response to a "greeting" is a "greeting": I say, "Hello," and you respond, "Hi.") Speakers orient themselves to these rules, but are not strictly bound by them. However, speakers know that their conversational partners may call them to account for utterances that depart from the preferred and expected. (If, in the previous example, you had replied, "My rent is due today," I might prompt you to explain why you offered a "dispreferred" response.) A variety of adjacency pairs may occur in everyday conversation: invitation-acceptance/refusal, assessment-agreement/disagreement, self-deprecation-disagreement/agreement, to name just a few.

Compared to everyday talk, conversation in American classrooms follows a somewhat more restricted set of tacit rules, according to Freedman and Katz. They cite Hugh Mehan's ethnographic study of schooling in which he argues that regular classroom utterances co-occur in a predictable triplet: the teacher *initiates*, the student *responds*, and the teacher *evaluates*. Here, too, Sacks, Schegloff, and Jefferson's notion of accountability remains in force. Student and teacher orient themselves to the preferred sequence—initiate, respond, evaluate—and deviations from it usually require an explanation.

Freedman and Katz analyze several stretches of teacher-student conversation in an effort to demonstrate the hybrid nature of writing conference conversation. In its basic structure of turn-order, conference conversation tends to follow Mehan's tripartite formula. But in terms of turn-allocation, conference conversation appears quite unlike the classroom discourse Mehan observed. Freedman and Katz found that the typical *responses* students offered to teacher *initiations* were much lengthier than those Mehan's younger students supplied. In this respect, conference talk can resemble everyday conversation: one speaker (the student) may take an extended turn so long as the other speaker (the instructor) remains silent or interjects supportive cues (e.g., okay, uh huh). Such cues signal that the length of a turn is still appropriate. This sort of writing conference talk is conducive to learning, Freedman and Katz conclude, because within a predictable structure resembling classroom interaction, students can raise topics and elaborate upon them just as they might in less restricted conversations outside the classroom (78). Consequently, students have a rare opportunity in writing conferences to solve problems and rehearse arguments that translate into invention or revision of the texts about which they speak.

Freedman and Katz's application of conversation analysis raises two interesting problems of methodology—problems that are interpretive and ultimately rhetorical.

The first problem has to do with the assumption that speakers contribute to conversational exchange in normal ways—that is, unless they intend to make a special point by departing from the norm. Who defines what is normal in everyday conversation? Sacks, Schegloff, and Jefferson would argue that the speakers themselves do; such a definition is fundamental to the speakers' mutual construction of an intersubjective space for their conversation. So, then, who defines what is normal in classroom conversation? As Mehan shows and others argue, the authority to negotiate and ratify what is normal in classroom conversation—and conference conversation—belongs mostly to the teacher. Indeed, much of the overt authority students assert in one-to-one negotiations with teachers is granted them by their teachers. But students can also exercise covert forms of authority. Students can direct the course of a conversation by questioning, resisting, or ignoring a teacher's assertion of authority. We should construe this covert action as normal behavior, too.[1]

Because Freedman and Katz seem to define normal interaction fairly broadly, they largely avoid skewing their interpretation in favor of the teacher. They also avoid such skewing by following, to some extent, Cicourel's advice: disclose your interests in the research scene; interpret what you see, as much as possible, within the institutional constraints governing the conversation. In this way, the interactional norms are rooted more in the conversation and less in the analyst's speculations about conversational context. To further ground their analysis in the conversational text, Freedman and Katz might have solicited interpretations from the involved student and teacher. These participants' contributions to analysis could well have illuminated or challenged the researchers' own careful interpretations.

The second problem raised by Freedman and Katz has to do with their attention to the structural elements of talk about writing. Irene B. Wong suggests that we cannot rely "only on structural analysis for understanding the nature of conference talk"—and presumably other forms of talk about writing (450). She stresses that in addition to turn-order and turn-allocation, we also need to attend to the "exchange of information" and the context in which speakers "determine the agenda of the discussion" (450). Wong accomplishes this by analyzing the "negotiability" of the content of each topic raised in conversation. She claims that distinguishing between topics with high and low negotiability helps us identify differences in speakers' knowledge about the topics. For example, in her study Wong found that technical writing teachers allowed a great deal of negotiation on topics in student texts the teachers knew little about. The teachers permitted much less negotiation of content issues that fell within their domain of expertise. Actually, Freedman and Katz do not ignore the content of the conversations they analyze. Rather, they simply—and correctly—refrain from marking content and form as separable categories, and they incorporate Wong's category of negotiability into their treatment of topic shifts within students' responses to teachers' initiating utterances (Freedman and Katz 72–77).

Wong's criticism of Freedman and Katz does raise an interesting point about the rhetoric of reporting results of conversation analysis. A rich presentation of the "data"—a detailed transcription of the talk being analyzed—is essential. Freedman and Katz provide three short excerpts from a writing conference conversation. The excerpts are punctuated so as to hint at the "messiness" of everyday conversation: pauses, overlaps, interruptions, rising and falling intonation, and the like. It is out of these messy details that speakers construct interpretations of their unfolding dialogue, and so must analysts. To bracket such details as *meaning-less* "form" in an attempt to look at pure, *meaning-ful* "content" imposes an operation on the conversation that is alien to its participants, and that therefore lacks validity for the conversation analyst.[2] Still, it is impossible to render an accurate transcription of a conversational exchange, and analyst and audience alike must always acknowledge this inherent shortcoming of the approach.

Other ways of analyzing conversation. I want now to turn to other modes of analyzing talk about writing, modes that make different assumptions about language and intersubjective states of consciousness. They, too, have rich explanatory power within the worlds of discourse they posit. I will consider two modes in this section: a pragmatic mode and a functional mode. Pragmatic analysis differs from conversation analysis in several ways. The most marked difference is that the *descriptive* rules conversation analysts recognize in the pragmatic view become *prescriptive* rules that specify what normal conversation ought to be. Functional analysis differs from conversation analysis in its assumption that speakers employ a nonnegotiable "fixed code": that is, the words exchanged in conversation are held to be either inherently unambiguous or rendered so by the context in which they occur.

Pragmatic theories of discourse focus on the interpretation of utterances (Taylor and Cameron 81; Ducrot and Todorov 81, 338). To guide these interpretations, analysts observe, among other things, "conversational principles" that specify how inferences can be made from utterances situated in context. The best known of these principles are embodied in H. P. Grice's "cooperative principle" and its four associated "maxims." Grice's principle and maxims, according to Stephen Levinson, "specify what participants have to do in order to converse in a maximally efficient, rational, cooperative way: they should speak sincerely, relevantly and clearly, while providing sufficient information" (102). Utterances that initially appear to violate a maxim challenge the analyst to construct an inference explaining how the utterance, in fact, complies with the cooperative principle. Thus, if we were to overhear the following exchange between writing teacher and student, we might initially think that the student was answering in an irrelevant way:

TEACHER: Where's the reference for this quotation?

STUDENT: I lent the book to someone else in the class.

Given the pedagogical context, however, it is fairly easy to imagine that we (and the teacher) are meant to infer that, because the student lent her book to another student, she was unable to document the source of the quotation. The student's answer, in short, is relevant, and perhaps as much to the point as the seemingly direct response, "The reference is at the bottom of page four." It should be noted, too, that conversational maxims can be strategically violated, which is to say that meaning can be intended and interpreted even if speakers disregard the cooperative principle.

Insofar as pragmatic principles offer a way to describe utterances—and not prescriptions for forming them—they are akin to the descriptive bent of conversation analysis. The difference between the two analytical modes, however, becomes clear when we compare their scopes. According to Michael Toolan, the distinction "lies in that Grice had the audacity to propose universal rational and moral grounds, in his maxims for cooperative talk, while the conversation analysts are far more circumspect, and sensitive to local ethnological norms of talk, in their formulations" (262). Still, with care and qualification, Grice's principle and principles like it (for example, principles of conversational "politeness") can serve well the analysis of talk about writing. Marilyn Cooper made a move in that direction by adapting Gricean pragmatics for use in interpreting the development of student texts. It is clear that her program could be further refined to apply to talk about writing, so long as conversational principles are formulated, Toolan would suggest, as regulative and descriptive, rather than constitutive and prescriptive (262).

But it is certainly possible to view conversational principles as both constitutive and prescriptive. This form of discourse analysis discounts intersubjective states as important to understanding the nature of conversation. Instead, this approach assumes that conversations appear orderly and coherent because speakers are predisposed to agree on the rules that govern what units can be combined to make well-formed utterances. Taylor and Cameron explain that "conversationalists recognize the 'distinguishing marks' which identify an utterance as a token of a particular type of unit and because they know in advance what the rules of conversation will allow as possible combinations of such units. Thus, their 'conversational competence' guides them in identifying and combining types of conversational acts" (123). In other words, two people generate a conversation much as they might individually produce correct English sentences according to the prescriptive rules of certain generative grammars. The world view implied by this theory entails two important assumptions about the nature of language and communication. The first assumption has to do with the stability of language. Conversation works only if "all speakers in a community share the same 'fixed code', unproblematically associating particular graphic/phonic forms with particular meanings" (Toolan 255). The second assumption has to do with how these fixed meanings are exchanged in conversation. This process of exchange enables interlocutors to have the same thoughts; it allows speakers to strike simultaneously the same mental chord in their listeners' minds and their own (Taylor and Cameron 161). Both of these assumptions presume an idealized form of intersubjectivity, one that tends to universalize the notion that "good" conversations are predestined to conclude in agreement. This approach downplays the role negotiation plays in mediating ambiguity inherent in the language people use to represent experience.

This mode of discourse analysis has had measured influence on composition research. An example of such influence can be found in Anne Ruggles Gere and Robert D. Abbott's study of talk occurring in high school English writing groups. Gere and Abbott analyze teacherless writing group talk in part according to a "functional taxonomy" of utterances proposed by J. McH. Sinclair and R. M. Coulthard. Sinclair and Coulthard developed their taxonomy to classify the forms of classroom talk they found in British schools. As its name suggests, the taxonomy distinguishes utterances by function. An utterance might, for instance, *elicit* a verbal response (e.g., What day is it?). It might *direct* someone to act nonverbally (e.g., Take out the trash). Or it might *inform* someone of something (e.g., The room is blue). Utterances shift function according to context, so that while in one case the question, What day is it? might elicit the response, Tuesday, in another situation, the query might direct someone to, say, take out the trash. Here, context fixes the meaning of an utterance, enabling meaning to be transmitted unambiguously from speaker to listener. Meaning is not openly negotiated; it inheres in words and is merely elaborated in context.

Gere and Abbott use the functional taxonomy to quantify their assertion that, in writing groups, students make use of language functions they do not have access to in the typical classroom setting. Specifically, they found that students use directive language in ways they almost never do when a teacher is involved in group talk. This insight might well elude the conversation analyst whose focus is on a small segment of oral discourse and whose intent is to document the interaction that segment reveals. We can see, then, that a functional approach to analyzing talk about writing complements other methods of conversation analysis. It can point to problems in talk about writing that can be subsequently addressed in finer-grained, interactional analyses.

Reading Analyses of Talk about Writing

Published research on talk about writing initially appeared in response to two phenomena in composition pedagogy: writing conferences and writing groups. While teacher-scholars promoted their successes with one-to-one and small-group writing instruction (e.g., M. Harris; Murray; Carnicelli; Elbow; Hawkins, to list but a few), researchers looked for ways to validate these approaches empirically. Experimental studies utilizing pretest and posttest designs proved inadequate to the task; such studies could not account for the complex interaction of oral and written discourse that occurs in writing conferences and writing groups (for such a critique, see Freedman and Nold on Budz and Grabar). Researchers subsequently broke fresh methodological ground by appropriating analytical techniques such as discourse and conversation analysis from the burgeoning fields of sociolinguistics and ethnomethodology. Applying these techniques, which I detail in a later section, researchers have undertaken to answer questions about what happens when people in pedagogical settings talk about writing.

Studies of teacher-student and tutor-student conversation include those by Fitzgerald and Stamm; Matsuhashi, Gillam, Conley, and Moss; Newkirk; Wong; Walker and Elias; Freedman and Katz; Freedman and Sperling; and Jacobs and Karliner. Investigations of talk about writing in groups have been reported by Shuy and Robinson; Gere ("Talking"); Brooke, O'Connor, and Mirtz; Nystrand and Brandt; Gere (*Writing*); Nystrand; Gere and Abbott; and Gere and Stevens.

It would be a mistake to infer from this brief overview that composition researchers arrived inevitably, and in numbers, at the conclusion that analyzing talk about writing might reveal something interesting about writing. Certainly such analysis does not provide the only source of evidence valid in an argument about what happens in classrooms, conferences, and groups. It does, however, provide evidence with intuitive appeal—the unselfconscious commentary of writers at work.

But intuitive appeal does not establish the authority of evidence. That authority derives from a deep understanding of the method that yields the evidence. For example, methods for analyzing talk about writing come from various disciplinary sources that hold conflicting assumptions about the nature of language and the location of its meaning. Should these conflicts matter to us? How should we account for them in our own work? And, too, we have yet to clearly describe what we hope to find by looking at talk about writing, or even why it is we should bother to look. How, then, should our research interests and goals be articulated with respect to talk about writing? Addressing these problems will help us explain the rhetorical power of talk as evidence in arguments about writing.

Theoretical Perspectives on Talk about Writing

By definition, talk about writing assumes *writing* as its primary object. But what is writing? Its territory is expansive; its horizons difficult, if not impossible, to survey. The same holds for talk. On our way to understanding talk about writing, then, we must attempt some clarity in relating two fuzzy concepts, talk and writing. We can do this by contrasting some contemporary and traditional ideas about discourse and human consciousness. And, ultimately, by situating discourse as constitutive of consciousness, we will arrive at a theoretical sense of how talk about writing contributes to the social construction of written discourse.

Since antiquity, writing has been considered one component of discourse—the other being speech. And writing and speech have long been viewed as different, often oppositional modes of thought and experience. From a neo-Platonic perspective, speech is identified positively with what is real, natural, and good, while writing is identified negatively as abstract, artificial, and bad. But this evaluative scale can be (and has been) easily inverted. Western metaphysics prizes writing as the medium of rational, reflective thought, while it consigns speech to the realm of the transient, the insubstantial, the irrational.

Against this metaphysical backdrop, one project of poststructuralist critical theory has been to question the primacy of writing over speaking in Western culture, and to interrogate the consequent privileging of literacy over orality as indices of social and economic power. The paradigmatic inquiry here is Derrida's deconstruction of writing: his claim that writing is, as Louise Wetherbee Phelps puts it, "shifting, indeterminate, endlessly mediated" (63). Writing thus contrasts with the stable, unmediated, totalizing presence that speech represents; speech claims a foundational presence in the world that writing can never obtain. In recasting the relationship between speech and writing, Phelps reads Derrida as positing the two acts "as interpenetrating, similar as well as different, mutually qualifying, and interdependent" (64).

Speech and writing are thus in dialogue with one another. Propositions formed in speech inform writing; propositions formed in writing inform speech. But something is missing from this dialogic sense of speech and writing, and that something is the subject—the speaking, writing, listening, reading subject, a casualty (perhaps) of the poststructuralist perspective. We need to restore subjects—people—as the speakers and writers whose activity yields writing and talk about writing. But we must be careful how we figure such subjects. Susan Miller argues that while we need not "proclaim the absolute 'death' of an oratorically modeled Cartesian subject," we do need to conceive of writers as subjects who do more than inscribe what they might otherwise speak (14). Miller proposes a "rhetorical view" of writers whose writing "treats the mixed and unstable confluence of anterior intentions and purposes and posterior 'readings,' 'meanings,' or outcomes *as though* they could be fixed. It is a living fiction of, not an achievement of, stability" (19). This view of the writing subject demands that we attend not only to inscription, or to the moment of inscription, but also to the panorama of human activities that condition intention and interpretation. Talk about writing is one occasion of this conditioning, and so it must be considered part of that which constitutes Miller's rhetorical writing subject.

Taking stock of both Phelps's and Miller's arguments, we can see that writers in oral dialogue pose numerous possibilities for analysis that extend beyond the commonplace. For example, such dialogues are simultaneously *intertextual* and *intersubjective*. That is, talk about writing blurs the borders that have traditionally bounded individual texts and individuals' consciousness. A brief explanation of intertextuality and intersubjectivity will suggest what we might be looking for when we analyze talk about writing.

Intertextuality works against notions of textual autonomy and unity. It suggests, instead, that all texts are related through the references they make to one another, whether subtle or obvious. There are at least two types of intertextuality of interest to composition scholars: iterability and presupposition. According to James Porter, "Iterability refers to the 'repeatability' of certain textual fragments, to citation in its broadest sense to include not only explicit allusions, references, and quotations within a discourse, but also unannounced sources and influences, clichés, phrases in the air, and traditions. . . . Presupposition refers to assumptions a text makes about its referent, its readers, and its context—to portions of the text which are read, but which are not explicitly 'there' " (35). Talk and writing thus fuse along at least two fronts. A text, as it evolves, may repeat or appropriate what has been said about it; a text may also refer to assumptions that presuppose talk about it. These transactions leave "traces" that we can document and analyze, and so we have a tangible object of analysis that can enter into our arguments on talk about writing.

Texts do not exist, however, in the absence of people to make them—and neither does intertextuality. To understand the intertextual nature of talk and writing, we must also understand the human agency that makes intertextuality possible. Human subjectivity and agency (roughly, people and how they do things) can be viewed from a social perspective, but we need a concept that explains how individuals share a social space and draw from it common resources that enable them to communicate. That concept is intersubjectivity, and as mentioned before, it is the touchstone for several approaches to analyzing talk, and talk about writing in particular.

Theories of intersubjectivity owe much to the work of Edmund Husserl, G. H. Mead, and L. S. Vygotsky. David Bleich appropriates these theories for composition studies in arguing that "to speak or use language in a certain way means not that there is meaning 'behind' the words, but that the presentation of the words themselves is the nucleus of social behavior. . . . Contributing one's words to a conversation is an interpersonal act that *counts*. No matter how rapidly one's conversation is forgotten, it still marks a key moment of a social achievement, the establishment of an intersubjectivity, the reidentification of a human relationship" (66). In this perspective, the social structures that shape human relationships are held to be prior to the construction of individual minds, a challenge to Cartesian dualism that posits the self as prior to (and wholly differentiated from) any collective sensibility. One problem with this line of thinking—a problem Bleich acknowledges and Derrida identifies in his "deconstruction" of Husserl's *oeuvre*—is the tendency to end up arguing for a "transcendental" or "universal" intersubjectivity. Vygotsky provides a corrective to this excess in his claim that intersubjective states are temporary, their existence contingent upon negotiating, utterance by utterance, the contours of the social world they together inhabit (Wertsch 161). This key term, negotiation, grounds intersubjectivity in a discernible realm. The action of negotiating gives us tangible evidence of intersubjectivity, evidence of the social worlds that people in conversation construct around themselves.

In talk about writing—in any talk, for that matter—negotiating to create a social world entails a whole spectrum of human problems. To understand why, consider how the idea of an intersubjective social world resembles the notion of community. Both are the fluid and transient products of ongoing dialogue. Such "discourse communities" must be seen as accommodating "both consensus and conflict" (J. Harris 20). Insofar as communities produce consensus, they sponsor the negotiation of conventions: conventions that suggest preferred ways of speaking and writing, conventions that allow speakers and writers to speak and write with recognized authority. But insofar as communities also contain conflict, the outcome of negotiation can be the subversion of convention, a move that challenges conventional authority. Since talk involves both consensus and conflict, to document this is to document negotiation of both the consensus and the conflict that constitute communities. These negotiations determine nothing less than who is allowed to say what to whom, when, how, and why—the social construction of texts.

Theoretically, then, analyzing talk about writing gives us a way of studying how texts are socially constructed. As a method, it offers a frame in which to arrange and interpret observations about the writing experience. But methodological frames limit just as much as they clarify. They define not windows onto reality, but canvases upon which we claim to depict the real. We color these canvases—we represent the real—according to modes of analysis that emerge from our varied ways of understanding language and consciousness.

Prospects for Studying Talk about Writing

In plotting the epistemological terrain of conversation analysis, I have been emphasizing two concepts: intersubjectivity and intertextuality. As my discussion of theory and methodology suggests, many modes of conversation analysis are premised on some notion of intersubjectivity. But in most analyses of talk about writing, the companion notion of intertextuality tends to receive less attention than intersubjectivity. While many studies focus on what people say about writing, few as yet attempt to demonstrate the influence of talk *on* a particular piece of writing, and vice versa.

Several recent studies do investigate this area. Among them are Jill Fitzgerald and Carol Stamm's study of writing conferences involving first grade teachers and students. The researchers draw connections between the types of comments students and teachers make about writing, what students know about revision, and what they actually do when they revise. Fitzgerald and Stamm found, against their expectations, that talk about writing most influenced students who knew least about possible revision strategies and whose writing indicated they were least accomplished at revision. From a methodological perspective, these are compelling conclusions, compelling because they show the potential for the method to yield unexpected findings. Such findings answer critics who suggest that conversation analysis reports only common sense observations of human interaction. Fitzgerald and Stamm's study also broadens the range of pedagogical settings in which conversation analysis has been applied; most studies to date have focused on writers in high school and college.

Of course, nothing in the methodologies I have examined restricts their application to pedagogical settings. Yet few studies explore the nature of talk about writing outside schools and colleges. One recent study that does venture beyond the academy is Roger Shuy and David Robinson's analysis of a conversation in which a small group discusses drafting a business letter. (The conversation was tape-recorded as evidence in an FBI sting operation.) This study provokes us to think about how we collect talk about writing for analysis. Shuy and Robinson claim a special authenticity for their "naturally occurring conversation" because it was recorded surreptitiously; only one participant in the conversation, a government agent, consented to the surveillance that produced the recording. Indeed, most studies make the argument that audio- or videotaping did not significantly alter what participants had to say. Some studies explain how tape-recording was accomplished in the absence of researchers (e.g., Walker and Elias 268). Others point to unguarded remarks that participants would have probably withheld had they remembered the conversation was being tape recorded (e.g., Gere and Stevens 90–91).

The question of researchers being present at the scene of inquiry opens out onto larger and related problems of discovery and justification (Harding 183). What are we discovering—revealing and learning—when we analyze talk about writing? And how do we justify these discoveries? I attempted to answer the first question earlier in this chapter in my discussion of the assumptions underpinning various modes of analyzing conversation. I now want to come at the question from another angle.

What we discover largely depends on what we choose to look at and what we choose to ignore. Researchers have studied primarily college and high school students. To a lesser extent, the conversation of younger writers has been the subject of inquiry.[3] But a vast constellation of writers and writing practices surrounds this small academic realm. Talk about writing in the workplace, for example, remains largely unexamined. We cannot say, then, that we have discovered very much about the majority of writers and their talk about writing. Nor, within the most-studied groups, do we know much yet about how gender, ethnicity, and class influence talk about writing. Presumably they do in rather profound ways.[4]

It will not be enough simply to apply the methods we now have to understand how heretofore marginalized subjects talk about writing. The methods themselves, because they grow out of the experiences of researchers who identify with the dominant culture, must be changed. Such changes, at base, entail revising how we justify the analysis of talk about writing.

At present, such justification seems bound to the assumption that analyzing talk about writing represents, within the domains individual studies stake out, what *really* happens when people write. Consequently, more and more studies of talk about writing contribute to an increasingly comprehensive depiction of the phenomenon. Stephen North argues that this attitude toward knowledge situates analysis of talk about writing within what he calls the "clinician" mode of inquiry (198). I would argue, though, that there are better ways to justify what we learn from examining talk about writing. For instance, borrowing an aspect of North's "ethnographer" inquiry, we might take pains to acknowledge how research on talk about writing creates "fictions" that relate the researcher's experience of the phenomenon under study.[5]

As part of a fiction, then, the intersubjectivity and intertextuality of talk about writing become not only empirical facts, but also features of a narrative discourse. As such, they relate in important ways to other features of the discourse: the narrator and the narrated, the researcher and her subjects. In the fictional discourse of the research report, subjects need not be placed in a passive role with respect to the researcher's active stance.

Rewriting the role of research subjects does not alter the status of the research report; it remains a fiction. But it does change how that fiction gets played out. As Donna Haraway insists, researchers must respect the agency of their subjects, and not cast them as purely "resources" from which to appropriate knowledge for reproduction in the sterile field of scholarly text (594). Only when we reorient our thinking in this way, Haraway argues, can we begin to conduct research that conveys "situated knowledges": the result of "partial sight and limited voice—not partiality for its own sake but, rather, for the sake of the connections and unexpected openings situated knowledges make possible" (590). Studying talk about writing allows for the discovery of unexpected openings among people, ideas, and discourse. And it allows us to see how these openings permit both the consensus and conflict that, rhetorically, make and break the bonds of community.

Talk about writing tells us much about the community that makes that talk—the people who talk that talk. Our reporting of that talk in a sense continues the conversation. It is a conversation to which we have the privilege of contributing, and over which we all too often exercise privileging and exclusive control.

Notes

Friends and colleagues who influenced the shape of this chapter include Evan Adelson, Christine Cetrulo, Janet Eldred, Kate Gardner, Keith Grant-Davie, Barbara Kennedy, Gesa Kirsch, Barry Saferstein, Patricia Sullivan, and especially Barbara Tomlinson. I am grateful for their thoughtful counsel.

1. In a study of writing conference conversation (Mortensen), I document how students covertly assert oppositional authority. I argue that such oppositional authority is a feature of most any speech situation in which one speaker controls the other speaker's access to institutional authority.

2. See Keith Grant-Davie's chapter in this volume for a discussion of what constitutes *data* for composition researchers.

3. See Celia Genishi and Anne Haas Dyson's *Language Assessment in the Early Years*, especially chap. 7, "Six- to Eight-Year-Olds: Interacting Through Text and Talk" (189–242). Indeed, much of Dyson's recent

work attends to children's talk about writing (e.g., Dyson). On talk and emergent literacy, see also Galda and Pellegrini.

4. A few studies do attempt to situate talk about writing in relation to class, gender, and ethnicity. Sarah Warshauer Freedman and Melanie Sperling consider how ethnicity figures into a writing conference dialogue in which the student expresses dismay that her teacher discriminates against her because she is Asian American. Freedman and Sperling show that, in fact, the teacher does treat the student differently, and problematically. Gere, in a historical survey, suggests how gender might influence the shape and purpose of writing groups (*Writing*).

5. See Beverly Moss's chapter in this volume for a fuller discussion of discourse analysis from an ethnographic perspective.

Works Cited

Barthes, Roland. "Writers, Intellectuals, Teachers." *Image-Music-Text*. Trans. Stephen Heath. New York: Hill, 1977. 190–215.

Bleich, David. *The Double Perspective: Language, Literacy, and Social Relations*. New York: Oxford UP, 1988.

Brooke, Robert, Tom O'Connor, and Ruth Mirtz. "Leadership Negotiation in College Writing Groups." *Writing on the Edge* 1.1 (1989): 66–85.

Budz, Judith, and Terry Grabar. "Tutorial versus Classroom in Freshman English." *College English* 37 (1976): 654–56.

Carnicelli, Thomas A. "The Writing Conference: A One-to-One Conversation." *Eight Approaches to Teaching Composition*. Ed. Timothy R. Donovan and Ben W. McClelland. Urbana, IL: NCTE, 1980. 101–31.

Cicourel, Aaron V. "Three Models of Discourse Analysis: The Role of Social Structure." *Discourse Processes* 3 (1980): 101–32.

Cooper, Marilyn M. "The Pragmatics of Form: How Do Writers Discover What to Do When?" *New Directions in Composition Research*. Ed. Richard Beach and Lillian S. Bridwell. New York: Guilford, 1984. 109–26.

Ducrot, Oswald, and Tzvetan Todorov. *Encyclopedic Dictionary of the Sciences of Language*. Trans. Catherine Porter. Baltimore: Johns Hopkins UP, 1979.

Dyson, Anne Haas. "Talking Up a Writing Community: The Role of Talk in Learning to Write." *Perspectives on Talk and Learning*. Ed. Susan Hynds and Donald L. Rubin. Urbana, IL: NCTE, 1990. 99–114.

Elbow, Peter. *Writing Without Teachers*. New York: Oxford UP, 1973.

Fitzgerald, Jill, and Carol Stamm. "Effects of Group Conferences on First Graders' Revision in Writing." *Written Communication* 7 (1990): 96–135.

Freedman, Sarah Warshauer, and Anne Marie Katz. "Pedagogical Interaction during the Composing Process: The Writing Conference." *Writing in Real Time: Modeling Production Processes*. Ed. Ann Matsuhashi. Norwood, NJ: Ablex, 1987. 58–80.

Freedman, Sarah Warshauer, and Ellen W. Nold. "On Budz and Grabar's 'Tutorial vs. Classroom' Study." *College English* 38 (1976): 427–29.

Freedman, Sarah Warshauer, and Melanie Sperling. "Written Language Acquisition: The Role of Response and the Writing Conference." *The Acquisition of Written Language: Response and Revision*. Ed. Sarah Warshauer Freedman. Norwood, NJ: Ablex, 1985. 106–30.

Galda, Lee, and A. D. Pellegrini. "Play Talk, School Talk, and Emergent Literacy." *Perspectives on Talk and Learning*. Ed. Susan Hynds and Donald L. Rubin. Urbana, IL: NCTE, 1990. 91–97.

Genishi, Celia, and Anne Haas Dyson. *Language Assessment in the Early Years*. Norwood, NJ: Ablex, 1984.

Gere, Anne Ruggles. "Talking in Writing Groups." *Perspectives on Talk and Learning*. Ed. Susan Hynds and Donald L. Rubin. Urbana, IL: NCTE, 1990. 115–28.

———. *Writing Groups: History, Theory, and Implications*. Carbondale: Southern Illinois UP, 1987.

Gere, Anne Ruggles, and Robert D. Abbott. "Talking about Writing: The Language of Writing Groups." *Research in the Teaching of English* 19 (1985): 362–85.

Gere, Anne Ruggles, and Ralph S. Stevens. "The Language of Writing Groups: How Oral Response Shapes Revision." *The Acquisition of Written Language: Response and Revision*. Ed. Sarah Warshauer Freedman. Norwood, NJ: Ablex, 1985. 85–105.

Grice, H. P. "Logic and Conversation." *Speech Acts*. Ed. Peter Cole and

Jerry Morgan. New York: Academic, 1975. 41–58. Vol. 3 of *Syntax and Semantics*. 24 vols. to date. 1972– .

Haraway, Donna. "Situated Knowledges: The Science Question in Feminism and the Privilege of Partial Perspective." *Feminist Studies* 14 (1988): 575–99.

Harding, Sandra. "Conclusion: Epistemological Questions." *Feminism and Methodology: Social Science Issues*. Ed. Sandra Harding. Bloomington: Indiana UP, 1987. 181–90.

Harris, Joseph. "The Idea of Community in the Study of Writing." *College Composition and Communication* 40 (1989): 11–22.

Harris, Muriel. *Teaching One-to-One: The Writing Conference*. Urbana, IL: NCTE, 1986.

Hawkins, Thom. *Group Inquiry Techniques for Teaching Writing*. Urbana, IL: NCTE, 1976.

Heritage, John, and J. Maxwell Atkinson. Introduction. *Structures of Social Action: Studies in Conversation Analysis*. Ed. J. Maxwell Anderson and John Heritage. Cambridge: Cambridge UP, 1984. 1–15.

Jacobs, Suzanne E., and Adela B. Karliner. "Helping Writers to Think: The Effect of Speech Roles in Individual Conferences on the Quality of Thought in Student Writing." *College English* 38 (1977): 489–505.

Levinson, Stephen C. *Pragmatics*. Cambridge: Cambridge UP, 1983.

Matsuhashi, Ann, Alice Gillam, Rance Conley, and Beverly Moss. *Writing and Response: Theory, Practice, and Research*. Ed. Chris M. Anson. Urbana, IL: NCTE, 1989. 293–316.

Mehan, Hugh. *Learning Lessons: Social Organization in the Classroom*. Cambridge: Harvard UP, 1979.

Miller, Susan. *Rescuing the Subject: A Critical Introduction to Rhetoric and the Writer*. Carbondale: Southern Illinois UP, 1989.

Mortensen, Peter L. "Authority, Discourse, Community." Diss. U of California, San Diego, 1989.

Murray, Donald M. "The Listening Eye: Reflections on the Writing Conference." *College English* 41 (1979): 13–18.

Newkirk, Thomas. "The First Five Minutes: Setting the Agenda in a Writing Conference." *Writing and Response: Theory, Practice, and Research*. Ed. Chris M. Anson. Urbana, IL: NCTE, 1989. 317–31.

North, Stephen M. *The Making of Knowledge in Composition: Portrait of an Emerging Field*. Upper Montclair, NJ: Boynton/Cook, 1987.

Nystrand, Martin. *The Structure of Written Communication: Studies in Reciprocity between Writers and Readers*. Orlando: Academic, 1986.

Nystrand, Martin, and Deborah Brandt. "Response to Writing as a Context for Learning to Write." *Writing and Response: Theory, Practice, and Research*. Ed. Chris M. Anson. Urbana, IL: NCTE, 1989. 209–30.

Odell, Lee, Dixie Goswami, and Anne Herrington. "The Discourse-Based Interview: A Procedure for Exploring the Tacit Knowledge of Writers in Nonacademic Settings." *Research on Writing: Principles and Methods*. Ed. Peter Mosenthal, Lynne Tamor, and Sean A. Walmsley. New York: Longman, 1983. 221–36.

Phelps, Louise Wetherbee. *Composition as a Human Science: Contributions to the Self-Understanding of a Discipline*. New York: Oxford UP, 1988.

Porter, James E. "Intertextuality and the Discourse Community." *Rhetoric Review* 5 (1986): 34–47.

Sacks, Harvey, Emanuel A. Schegloff, and Gail Jefferson. "A Simplest Systematics for the Organization of Turn Taking for Conversation. *Studies in the Organization of Conversational Interaction*. Ed. Jim Schenkein. New York: Academic, 1978. 7–55.

Shuy, Roger W., and David G. Robinson. "The Oral Language Process in Writing: A Real-Life Writing Session." *Research in the Teaching of English* 24 (1990): 88–100.

Sinclair, J. McH., and R. M. Coulthard. *Towards an Analysis of Discourse: The English Used by Teachers and Pupils*. London: Oxford UP, 1975.

Sternglass, Marilyn S. *The Presence of Thought: Introspective Accounts of Reading and Writing*. Norwood, NJ: Ablex, 1988.

Swarts, Heidi, Linda S. Flower, and John R. Hayes. "Designing Protocol Studies of the Writing Process: An Introduction." *New Directions in Composition Research*. Ed. Richard Beach and Lillian S. Bridwell. New York: Guilford, 1984. 53–71.

Taylor, Talbot J., and Deborah Cameron. *Analysing Conversation: Rules and Units in the Structure of Talk*. Oxford: Pergamon, 1987.

Tomlinson, Barbara. "Talking about the Composing Process: The Limitations of Retrospective Accounts." *Written Communication* 1 (1984): 429–45.

Toolan, Michael. "Ruling Out Rules in the Analysis of Conversation." *Journal of Pragmatics* 13 (1989): 251–74.

Walker, Carolyn P., and David Elias. "Writing Conference Talk: Factors Associated with High- and Low-Rated Writing Conferences." *Research in the Teaching of English* 21 (1987): 266–85.

Wertsch, James V. *Vygotsky and the Social Formation of Mind.* Cambridge: Harvard UP, 1985.

Wong, Irene B. "Teacher-Student Talk in Technical Writing Conferences." *Written Communication* 5 (1988): 444–60.

The Narrative Roots of the Case Study

In preparing this chapter I reread a case study I had written almost ten years ago and came across a sentence that disturbed me. In defending my focus on one student I wrote, "While Anne's experience is clearly not typical, it is at least possible that her case illustrates—in heightened and intensified form—the development of many freshmen writers" (133). I asked myself why I wrote this lame attempt to make this one account, by some circuitous route, representative of freshman writers. Perhaps it was in response to the editors who wondered about the other three people I interviewed but did not mention. Or it could have been my answer to a member of my tenure review committee who didn't want to send the study out to reviewers because "it was just about one student." Or it may have been my own way of justifying the value of case study research, and doing it the only way I knew how: by claiming that we can move (somehow) from a single case to a whole population.

This chapter deals with the same questions I faced when I wrote about Anne—what is the authority of case studies? In what sense can they claim to produce knowledge? Or, more colloquially, what makes them "work"? Even at the time, I rejected the traditional answer to these questions, the one given in the educational research textbooks we were required to read in graduate school. Information on case studies was usually sparse and discouraging: we were told that case studies were useful in isolating variables and suggesting hypotheses that could be examined through more rigorous methods of investigation (for a more recent version of this argument, see Lauer and Asher). Like a minor league of research, case study research could offer up a few promising ideas to the big leagues where the true professionals could give them a tryout.

This traditional rationale, with its explicit hierarchy of research, seemed fundamentally wrong. In the first place, experimental researchers, so far as I could tell, did not rely on case studies to develop hypotheses; they built their work on other experimental studies. And those who conducted case studies viewed the nature of their inquiries as fundamentally different from experimental research. I did not view the elements of my description of Anne as a set of extractable variables that could be pulled out, tested, and given a causative weight. Instead, these elements "transacted" (Harste, Woodward, and Burke); they were all necessary to create an adequate description of her progress in the course.

Early attempts to justify the case study (and qualitative research in general) were, as Stephen North has pointed out, schizophrenic. Researchers claimed to adhere to traditional standards of objectivity and methodological rigor, while at the same time pushing the narrative potential of the case study form. They were telling stories while pretending not to. For example, Donald Graves in his influential essay, "A New Look at Writing Research," seems to have a foot in both camps. He is sharply critical of attempts to turn educational research into a science that ignores context and produces "voiceless" prose and "faceless" data. Yet his break with traditional research is hardly complete for he claims that the contextualized case study approach he advocates is still "rigorous" and "objective":

> Writing process research can help the classroom teacher with writing. It's just that this research cannot pretend to be science. This does not mean that research procedures cease to be rigorous when describing the full context of human behavior and environment. The human faces do not take away objectivity when the data are reported. The face emerges from enormous amounts of

> time spent in observing, recording, and analyzing the data. When the face emerges in the reporting, it comes from tough selection of the incident that represents a host of incidents in context. (97)

It is striking how much of the scientific method remains in these recommendations. The human faces emerge not by becoming part of a narrative, but through the accumulation of an immense sample of descriptive information. The researcher objectively sorts through this data and, through a "tough" selection process, picks out the incident that "represents a host of other incidents." The process is strikingly parallel to that of experimentalists who rigorously sample the behavior of a population, only in Graves's case the population is a set of accumulated observations.

Central to Graves's vision is the idea of context—the writer at work in a community that shapes and constrains the writing process. But the researcher is apparently free of such constraints and is able to objectively account for the context in which the student writer works. If Graves were to be consistent with his claims for context, he would look reflexively at the discourse community the researcher works in and explore the ways in which narrative conventions predispose the researcher to account for data in a particular way.

According to North, case-study writers have diminished the power of their approach by straddling paradigms, as Graves did (and as I did). The strength of this mode of research is not in producing generalizable conclusions, guaranteed by rigorous and objective observation procedures; the strength, according to North, comes from the "idiographic" nature of case studies, their capacity for detailed and individuated accounts of writers writing. Then, by means of a process that North admits "we can only imagine," these particular studies will evolve a "richer canonical framework" and offer up "a far more powerful image of 'People Writing' than we have now" (237).

North is better at describing what the authority of the case study *is not* than at defining that authority. Why should authority come from the "idiographic" nature of the descriptions? Why should a reader pay attention to an account that is concrete, individual, and unique? Perhaps North is making a claim for the realism of case studies: as readers we get the gritty, day-to-day detail that is usually dismissed in a few dry sentences sometimes called the "Treatment," in traditional studies. We come to know Glenda Bissex's son Paul in a way that we never know the children in group-comparison research. We are made to feel that we are face-to-face with Reality itself, detailed, alive, recognizable.

But particularity, by itself, is no guarantee of acceptance by the reader. Any setting or subject provides a limitless source of detail, and pure particularity, even if it were a possibility, would overwhelm the reader. Parodoxically, we would reject the overly particular study as so unshaped as to be unreal (take, for example, the almost surrealistic excess of detail of Robbe-Grillet's fiction). So the answer to the question of how case studies work cannot rest, ultimately, on particularity. We can claim that experimental studies strip the context (e.g., Mischler), but in their own ways, so do case studies and ethnographies. Even those researchers who claim to account for the context must disregard or decline to report most of what they record. So the issue is not who strips and who doesn't strip but how each strips to create accounts, narratives that gain the assent of readers. The issue is not which is more Real, but how each creates, through selection and order-ing of detail, an illusion or version of Reality. The issue is not one primarily of methodology and objectivity, but of authoring and the cultural values embedded in various narrative plots.

This position will, no doubt, seem a dangerous one for a case-study researcher to take. After all, the consistent warning in the educational research textbooks is that researchers should not turn into storytellers, introducing cultural and personal bias into their work. The great god of Methodology is invoked to protect the researcher from charges of storytelling. Case-study research-ers set up coding procedures, establish inter-rater reliability, and adopt the format of the research report in order to appear rigorous (and not incidentally to get published). In this way the account appears as the almost inevitable output of a methodological machine. The researcher didn't write the study; the method did. To talk seriously of writing—to acknowledge the personal decisions of inclusion and exclusion—is to reveal a fallibility that is better hidden.

The Lens of the Case Study Writer

A more honest strategy—for both quantitative and qualitative researchers—is to admit, from the beginning, that we are all storytellers (Brodkey). Even the experimental research report follows a conventionalized narrative line: Background, Method, Results, Discussion. The narratives that experimentalists tell are, for the most part, incremental narratives, ones that report on fractional gains for large populations along a preestablished scale. The case-study researcher usually tells transformative narratives, ones in which the individual experiences some sort of conflict and undergoes a qualitative change in the resolution of that conflict. This view of human development is similar to that described by Lev Vygotsky in *Mind in Society:*

> Our concept of development implies a rejection of the frequently held view that cognitive development results from the gradual accumulation of separate changes. We believe that child development is a complex dialectical process characterized by periodicity, unevenness in the development of different functions, metamorphosis or qualitative transformation of one form into another, intertwining of external and internal factors, and adaptive processes which overcome impediments that the child encounters. Steeped in the notion of evolutionary change, most workers in child pyschology ignore those turning points, those spasmodic and revolutionary changes that are so frequent in the history of child development. (73)

Rejecting a linear view of progress and change, Vygotsky, writing only eighteen years after the storming of the Winter Palace, argues for a more dramatic perspective, in which impediments, struggle, and transformation are the central elements. It is this perspective that often orients the case-study writer.

Case-study writers try to focus this Vygotskian lens upon the subject; the case that works is the one that fits the dramatistic requirements. In my own case study, I conducted a series of interviews with four students, and of these four only two worked as case studies. The most accomplished student of the group, a young woman returning to school after spending two years in Wyoming working the lines for the phone company, could not come into focus for me. She began the course as a strong writer and ended it as a strong writer. The course did not pose a particular challenge to her; she did not reach any crisis points; and when I asked her about her writing she would often simply shrug her shoulders. Her experience in the course may have been just as representative as that of her classmate, Anne (the focus of my study), but because of the lack of impediment, struggle, and transformation she would not work as a case study.

To write a case study that works, the writer needs to see the data in terms of one of a variety of culturally grounded narratives. The writer "author-izes" the data, and in doing so faces the same problem that confronts the biographer or historian who, according to Scholes and Kellogg, "is looking for aesthetically satisfying patterns in the people or events he considers as potential subjects for his work" (217). To create these aesthetic patterns, the writer must also assign moral weight to the actions of characters, for as Hayden White has effectively argued, we cannot "narratize" without moralizing (27). Real events do not conclude as narratives do; and they could only seem to consummate in conclusions through the imposition of some moral framework that allows us to feel satisfied by the ending.

I am arguing, then, that the case-study writer draws on a core of mythic narratives—deeply rooted story patterns that clearly signal to the reader the types of judgments to be made (as Vygotsky drew on the historical narrative of the 1917 revolution). By using these narrative patterns, the account can move beyond the particular or "idiographic," and come to embody a set of cultural beliefs. Paradoxically, case studies and ethnographic narratives, despite their seeming radicalism in composition research, draw their authority from these enduring narratives that writers borrow to shape their accounts. In this sense, the research is profoundly conservative and conventional. As readers of these studies, we find them true or convincing, not because of careful methodology (important as that is), or because of wealth of detail, but, I would argue, because of the gratification we get from seeing cultural myths being reenacted.

To account for the power of case studies, then, we need to attend to the narrative conventions that writers employ and the cultural myths that they embody. I have chosen for examination three case studies that I admire—Stephen Doheny-Farina's "Writing in an Emerging Organization: An Ethnographic Study," Nancie Atwell's "A Special Writer at Work," and Denny Taylor and Catherine Dorsey-Gaines's *Growing Up Literate*. In addition to examining narrative conventions, I will discuss some of the major authoring decisions each researcher made.

The Tragedy of Kingship

Doheny-Farina studied the relationship between writing processes and the organizational structure in a small high-technology company. As the study begins the company was on the verge of bankruptcy; it had not generated any sales revenue because it had failed to create any marketable products. The initial venture capital was almost gone. The study focuses on the writing of the company's 1983 business plan that would be crucial for its survival.

Bill Alexander, the company's president, had written the initial business plan, and he assumed that he would write this one. But during a week when he was away on a business trip, the company's vice-presidents, concerned about possible bankruptcy, began writing their own plan. When Alexander returned he found a revolt on his hands; at an emotional meeting of the board of directors it was decided that the plan should be written collaboratively. This new approach signaled a different distribution of power in the company—one that Alexander was reluctant to accept.

When there were problems with the collaborative process (where individual vice-presidents would write sections), Alexander took over the task of writing as if nothing had changed: "I haven't changed the way I have put together the Business Plan. What has changed is others' attitudes towards the process. Their input is minimum, but their conception of their input is maximum. The process hasn't changed; they just think that it has changed" (168). The conflict between the vice-presidents and Alexander reflects two differing versions of reality. Alexander held a promotional view of reality. According to one informant: "[He] think[s] that what is, is what you can convince someone else it is, or what you can convince yourself it is, or what you can convince the bank to keep paying [for] to promote what it is" (169). The vice-presidents took a "production view of reality"; they believed that any projections for future productivity had to be based on present and past performance. There needed be an integrated and sequential set of steps connecting the past to the future.

The issue narrowed to the writing of one goal in the company report. Alexander had originally proposed "purchase of [a] sophisticated computer graphics lab to generate graphic frames used in laserdisc/microcomputer computer products (Graphic Systems Corporation Image Animation System)" (166). In effect he was committing the company to purchasing a large and expensive laboratory. During a tumultuous meeting to work out the business plan, the vice-presidents objected to what they saw as an unrealistic commitment:

DAVE: I mean we all have to believe in this 100% and
                   I don't believe in this.

BILL ALEXANDER: But we don't have to have every [expletive]
                   decision to be a compromise so that everybody
                   has to agree, otherwise it doesn't get down on
                   paper. That's what it's been up to this point
                   and I'm tired of it!!!

When Dave persists, Alexander threatens to quit: "And I'll say I'll
walk out the door right now and you can finish the Business Plan.
Raise the rest of the money among yourselves! See if [a major
potential investor] gets involved" (174). Eventually one vice-
president suggests a compromise and the goal statement is rewrit-
ten to state: "*Initial staged development* of sophisticated computer graphics production lab to generate graphic frames used in
laserdisc/microcomputer consumer products *(contingent upon
capital raising)*" (174; italics added). Alexander agrees to the
change, but the reader senses that the conflict is not at an end.

In my view Doheny-Farina succeeds in showing how the act
of writing a document can define and redefine the power relations
within a company. But what could have been a fairly tedious
cataloging of the uses of writing in a business environment becomes an absorbing narrative in which Doheny-Farina draws on
a narrative structure that we, as readers, have seen before—the
crisis of kingship. From the *Iliad* to *Macbeth* to *King Lear* to *All
the King's Men* to *All the President's Men,* we have seen writers
explore questions of the legitimacy of power, the abuse of power,
and the morally complex task of removing from power a leader
who has ceased to work for the public good. Typically such
rulers—like Bill Alexander—begin with good intentions and a
level of competence that wins the support of constituents. But
power corrupts the leader's judgment as he (and in the conventional narrative it is a "he") begins to see himself as indispensable.
This deterioration, paradoxically, is best seen by those closest to
him, and this group must make the difficult moral decision

whether to continue their support (risking the welfare of the country, company, etc.) or overturn the ruler (risking security and seeming to betray the person most responsible for their personal success). It is the oedipal tragedy of the son (or surrogate son) who must kill the father.

I am not suggesting that Doheny-Farina consciously modeled his account along the lines of Shakespearean (or Sophoclean) tragedy. But I am claiming this narrative pattern is part of the cultural equipment we use to make sense of human behavior. For example, we intuitively see problems when Alexander boasts about the earlier plan that he wrote: "It [the 1982 Business Plan] was everything. Without a product, without furniture, without machines, without anything, the Business Plan (was) it. That's your whole case for existence. That's what attracted money. That's what kept us in the [Start-Up] program. That's what got most of the Board members into it. That's what got a lot of employees into it. It did a lot of things" (170). In the moral world of kingship tragedy, we recognize the danger of this kind of pride. We expect a fall from power, and when it comes we are gratified at witnessing the punishment of arrogance.

As a writer, Doheny-Farina is himself in a difficult position; he is at the beginning of his career and writing for an academic audience, the readers of *Written Communication*. His chapter headings are almost identical to those that might be used for group-comparison research: Theoretical Assumptions, Procedures, Results (where the case study actually appears), Discussion, Implications for Theory Building, Implications for Teaching, Implications for Future Research. The case study itself takes up only eleven of the twenty-seven journal pages.

Given the richness of the data (collected in more than 120 visits to the company), it is easily possible to imagine an alternative version of the study. Doheny-Farina could have begun with an introduction to the company instead of citing Michael Cole and Sylvia Scribner on the need for studies outside the classroom. Secondary sources and theoretical references could have been embedded into the narrative. In this way, the entire piece (and not simply the results section) could focus on the power struggle in the company and the role writing played in this struggle. As it is written, the narrative seems to push against the research format in which it is boxed.

Doheny-Farina may have chosen this format in order to be taken seriously by the research community. He needed to precede his case study with a methodology section in order to convince some readers that his approach was as rigorous as quantitative research. To move too far away from the traditional model would risk the epithet "journalistic" (see for example Smagorinsky's comments on Donald Graves's research). Fortunately, many case-study and ethnographic researchers in the 1980s did begin to experiment with alternative, more fully realized narrative forms—Sondra Perl and Nancy Wilson in *Through Teachers' Eyes,* Lucy Calkins in *Lessons from a Child,* Glenda Bissex in *GNYS AT WRK,* and perhaps most compellingly, Mike Rose in *Lives on the Boundary.*

The Near-Tragedy of Mislabeling

Nancie Atwell's case study focuses on an eighth grader whom she calls Laura, a shy, overweight student who has been classified as "learning disabled." Just as she does in *In the Middle,* Atwell begins her narrative about Laura with a "conversion narrative" about herself:

> For a long time I looked at Boothbay's special ed students as walking packages of clinically defined disabilities. Batteries of tests administered by the school psychologist produced technical diagnoses that I wouldn't have dreamed of challenging—let alone reading. I didn't have to. Although I was an eighth grade English teacher, eighth graders identified by the tests as language disabled did not come to me for English. They were tracked into the junior high resource room and the school's reading lab. There I assumed they received the instruction specially designed to remedy their

particular disabilities. Each year I ignored the ghosts in my school, the eight or ten eighth graders who never came to my room. ("A Special Writer" 115)

But Atwell, influenced by the special education teacher in her school, came to doubt the effectiveness of the prescribed remedial work, the "mountain of worksheets and workbook exercises designed by the same people who designed the tests" (115). Appalled by the mindless dreariness of this approach, she successfully argued that Laura and other special education students be mainstreamed into her class.

Laura immediately responds to Atwell's approach to teaching reading, picking a favorite author, Judy Blume, and writing to Nancie—and to Judy Blume herself—about her response to the books. Her early letters, while not lengthy or exceptional, do *not* read like the work of a severely disabled student. The letter to Blume, for example, is that of an adoring fan:

Dear Mrs. Blume:

I am one of your greatest fans. I want you to know I have read all of your books. I have two things to ask of you.

First, are you part of the main character in your books? Second, do you plan to write more? I hope so.

The one book I liked was *It's Not the End of the World.* I liked it because my parents got a divorce, and it helped me learn about other people's feelings, even if it's not true.

I hope some day I would be able to meet you in person. One thing that got me interested in your books was your titles. It's been a pleasure having someone like you read this.(119)

Despite the competence that this letter demonstrates, Laura did not enter the class without deficiencies in writing. Atwell lists these on a chart and contrasts them with the deficiencies indicated on the diagnostic tests, and the contrast is dramatic. Atwell identifies precise (and correctable) problems that have surfaced in the writing—"where/were confusion," "apostrophe to show something belongs," "draft in paragraphs: guess and indent," and others. The list from the tests is more global, suggesting fundamental cognitive deficiencies—"grammar," "arranging words in sentences in their logical order," "classifying," and others.

In the latter part of the case study, Atwell shows how Laura, aided by the collaborative classroom environment, expands her reading interests to Robert Lipsyte, Susan Pfeffer, Robert Frost, E. E. Cummings; by the end of the year she has read thirty-one novels. Similarly, she has explored different genres of writing: an interview with her teacher (published in the school newspaper), a poem to commemorate the shuttle disaster, and a letter to Mikhail Gorbachev that went through three drafts and began with a quote from a Robert Frost poem, "A Time to Talk":

Dear Mikhail Gorbachev:

I also believe that Americans and Russians shall thrust down their hoes in the mellow ground and meet soon at a stone wall, for a friendly visit. (127)

Her letter won second prize in the Rotary Club contest.

Again, the plot of the case study is one that readers are familiar with: a member of a submerged group (racial, ethnic, socioeconomic, handicapped) is initially "invisible" to members of the mainstream culture—significantly Atwell refers to them as "ghosts." The label and associated stereotype define the limitations of everyone in that group until someone, often a teacher or someone in a teacher-like role, doubts or rejects the label and enables the individual to reveal himself or herself as competent—or even gifted. Atwell's narrative parallels well-known stories like *The Miracle Worker* in which Anne Sullivan defies the mislabeling of Helen Keller by her family, to be proven right in one dramatic moment by the water pump. It is an archetypal American story, touching, as it does, our distrust of class systems and our belief in individual potential.

Unlike Doheny-Farina, Atwell is writing as an open advocate

of a method for teaching; where Doheny-Farina ends with "Implications for Teaching," most advocacy case studies begin with a commitment to an approach, and the case study becomes a testimonial to the potential of the method. Case studies are told as success stories. Probably the classic case study of the writing process approach is Lucy Calkins's *Lessons from a Child*, which shows the extraordinary development of a young writer over a two-year period. The success story format, however, poses the obvious potential problem of creating such a unidimensionally positive picture of the learner that readers will reject it as unrealistic.

In my own book, *More than Stories*, I wanted to describe a classroom in which a variety of types of discourse were being used. I chose a second grade classroom and tried to interweave student texts, a physical description of the school and classroom, a description of a typical day, and commentary by the teacher. I thought this would be a chapter that would appeal to classroom teachers, but, in fact, many readers have found the chapter too good to be true. In it everything seems to work; the intentions of the teacher seem to be fully realized. While I was trying to be accurate in the chapter, I clearly was screening out much that was mundane—the student who never got down to work, another student's hastily written letter—in favor of what, to my mind, was more interesting and more persuasive. In the end, I probably lost some credibility.

Again there are examples of researchers willing to disrupt the success narratives in a way that enhances the authority of their accounts. In *Through Teachers Eyes*, Perl and Wilson create portraits of teachers in a school district in which they had been conducting intensive in-service work for years. The stories Perl and Wilson tell are, for the most part, success stories, yet they include one that is not. Ross Burkhardt, an eighth grade teacher, had a bad year. Though using the same general approach as the other teachers, his class does not form a cooperative unit, and his efforts to bring the group together seem to make the problems worse. By including this "counter narrative," one that runs against the grain of the other stories, the authors add to the credibility and complexity of their account.

Missing Voices

Growing Up Literate: Learning from Inner City Families (Taylor and Dorsey-Gaines) is a study of literacy learning in four inner-city families. In many ways the authors use the same narrative form Atwell uses in her case study. Like Atwell, they invoke the metaphor of invisiblility:

> In 1986, Tom Gralish photographed the homeless of Philadelphia; some of the photographs were published in the *Philadelphia Inquirer*. One of the photographs, of a man sheltering himself in a cardboard box, was republished in *The New York Times*. The caption under the picture read, "Now you see him," and the text began, "Most people don't. To many people Walter is invisible. They've trained themselves not to see him. They look the other way when Walter and other street people come into view." (xv)

The purpose of the book is to make this invisible class of urban dwellers visible, to create ethnographic images that will dispel stereotypical racist images of the pathologically dysfunctional inner-city families in which illiteracy is passed on from generation to generation.

The authors build these images of literacy in a number of compelling ways. They catalog the literacy activities of the parents, which covered a wide range of functions and included the complex negotiation of housing applications. They collected the writing and drawing of the children to demonstrate that the early literacy development of the children is strikingly similar to that of more economically advantaged children (e.g., Taylor, *Family Literacy*; Harste, Woodward, and Burke).

I will focus on Taylor and Dorsey-Gaines's chapter on schools, one that is significant both for what is said and what is left unsaid.

The major part of the chapter is devoted to one day in Shauna's second-grade classroom, and the shorter second section of the chapter is an account of an incident involving Danny, a seventh grader in one of the families the authors studied. In the second-grade classroom the researchers observed several full days of class and several half days, recording Shauna's activity in brief "snapshots." In the chapter these snapshots stretch on tediously, and the authors contend that this tedium is reflective of the child's day (although the flat, factual manner of reporting would probably make any class appear dull). They describe Shauna at work on a phonics worksheet:

> 9:37 Shauna continues to write. She writes each sentence and the words that go with them. She yawns and puts her hand over her mouth; then she continues.

> 9:40 Shauna is working on the third question. Children are quietly looking from the board to their papers. There is very little talk.

> 9:44 Shauna finishes the third problem. She gets up and takes it to her teacher's desk. She picks up a ditto on George Washington and returns to her seat. (105)

And so on for twelve pages of *Growing Up Literate*. Shauna's teacher is not given a name and is not asked to comment on the class—and neither, for that matter, is Shauna.

The incident involving Danny is considerably more dramatic and occured just after his father's death. According to Danny's mother Ieshea, the only informant the authors quote concerning this incident, Danny was severely beaten by his teacher for writing "Seventh Grade" instead of "Grade Seven" at the head of his paper. At first Ieshea thinks Danny was simply grabbed or given one "lick." But after a conference at the school Danny tells Ieshea that the beating was far more serious: " 'Momma, he didn't just hit me, he beat me with the stick.' So I looked at Danny. I said, 'He did what?' He said, 'He beat me with—' I said, 'What kind of stick?' So he said, you know, the pointer that you go to the chalkboard with. He said, 'He beat me with that stick, that—you know—pointer.' And he said, um, 'I have whips all over my body' " (117). A referral slip at the school shows that Danny had raised reddened areas on his right shoulder, right upper arm, right thigh, and right leg. The school's reaction to the incident was to recommend that Danny be classified as "emotionally disturbed."

These two incidents, each appalling in its own way, lead the authors to conclude at the end of the chapter that children like Shauna and Danny "move from the promise of their early years through an educational system that gradually disconnects their lives" (121). The implied message is even stronger: schools are places of pyschological and physical abuse. And as readers we are drawn to this conclusion both by the evidence that is presented and also by the narrative expectations that accounts like this activate. We expect conventional public schooling (with the exception of the classes taught by the special teacher—Marva Collins, Anne Sullivan, etc.) to be portrayed as repressive, blind to the giftedness of students. It is the image of schools in the novels of Dickens, in Joyce's *Portrait of the Artist as a Young Man,* in the critiques of public schooling written in the late 1960s—Kozol's *Death at an Early Age,* Holt's *How Children Fail,* Silberman's *Crisis in the Classroom.* As Mike Rose eloquently writes in *Lives on the Boundary:*

> The churches these children attended told them they were made in the image of God. But I began to wonder what images they were creating for themselves as they came to know their physical being was so vulnerable, that whatever beauty they bore could be dismissed by the culture and destroyed by the street. The schools could have intervened but instead seemed to misperceive them and place them at the margin. (101)

As readers, we cast our lot not with the teacher, but with the more knowing, more sensitive, more moral ethnographer who, while not a special teacher, clearly has the sensibility so lacking in the schools.

I do not want to act as an apologist for inner city schools—I taught in one for three years and know how poorly they provided for the education of students. My question, though, is this: does the "givenness" of this perspective restrict our capacity to account for the complexity of the situations that Shauna and Danny find themselves in? Does our tendency to write the drama in terms of victims (minority students) and victimizers (the schools and teachers) radically oversimplify the situation of students and teachers in inner city schools? Are we, in effect, trapped in our own narrative?

I remember going into my position as an English teacher in a Roxbury (Boston) High School (three years after *Death at an Early Age* was published) thinking I would be one of the special teachers who would transform the lives of my students. I soon found my influence far weaker than I ever imagined. I was challenged; students refused to work at the more interesting writing and reading activities I planned (though they would work at more routine activities like worksheets). Routine cruelty made walking the halls dangerous for many students. The attendance patterns made long-term planning a joke. I remember the numbing fatigue at the end of every day. And I remember how difficult it was to work with students like Danny who, in his own words, "like[s] to fool around." After three years I came to see all of us—teachers and students—as victims. We were all being ground down.

So, while moved by the literary and moral force of *Growing Up Literate*, I began to wonder about missing voices. We don't hear Shauna's account of her day; it is possible she found the day as tedious as the authors, but sometimes children appreciate the orderliness of such a classroom. Other children in the study are so taken with school literacy that they develop their own worksheets in their homes. We don't hear from Shauna's unnamed teacher to learn her reasons for what she does. Presumably the teacher who had allowed the researchers into class would have been willing to talk, and the researchers could easily have allowed her perspective to become part of their account. In the case of Danny, everything we learn about Danny's beating, we learn secondhand through his mother. This is not to condone the teacher's action, but to raise the question of whether we are getting the full story. Frankly, I am unconvinced that a teacher would severely beat a student for inverting the words on a heading—there must have been a greater provocation than that. I'm left feeling that there is another side I am not getting, that potential informants are not allowed to speak.

The authors of *Growing Up Literate* must reconcile two conflicting imperatives—the phenomenological imperative and the rhetorical imperative. The first is potentially disruptive, multivocal, and nonjudgmental; the second, the rhetorical imperative, is coherent and univocal, and it invokes a moral standard that allows us to assign blame. The force of the book comes, I believe, from the dominance of the rhetorical imperative; the authors so thoroughly identify with the families they describe that they dedicate the book to them. The moral world is clearly and cleanly divided between the heroism of these families and the evil of the social institutions that victimize them. This world is considerably less ambiguous than that depicted by many African American artists like Gloria Naylor in *The Women of Brewster Place* or Spike Lee in *Do the Right Thing*. Alternative perspectives that might complicate this narrative—those of teachers, social workers, parole officers—either were not sought or were screened out, in order to create a seamless moral fabric.

The issue is not, as positivistic researchers have argued, the problem of bias or the lack of objectivity. Rather it is one of polyvocality (Clifford; Tobin). To what extent should the ethnographer or case-study writer allow discordant voices into the account, voices that complicate the moral judgments readers will make? Or should the reader assume a stance of resistance and fill in the gaps with imagined narratives—as I did by imagining the other side in the incident of Danny's beating? For without some form of resistance, either in the construction of the text or in the act of reading, it is difficult to see how readers can avoid the seductiveness of deeply rooted and deeply satisfying narratives that place us in familiar moral positions.

Henry James, in his introduction to *Roderick Hudson,* elegantly defines the challenge that the writer of narratives faces:

> Really, universally, relations stop nowhere, and the exquisite problem of the artist is eternally to draw, by a geometry of his own, the circle in which they shall happily *appear* to do so. He is in the perpetual predicament that the continuity of things is the whole matter for him, of comedy and tragedy; that this continuity is never, by the space of an instant or an inch, broken, and that, to do anything at all, he has at once intensely to consult and intensely to ignore it. (5)

I was reminded of James's quote as I reread my case study of Anne and thought back to the writing problems we both had. Anne began the course with a cockiness that regularly crossed into arrogance. When I asked her how she evaluated her first paper, a chaotically disordered account of the creative process, she said it was an *A.* When I asked her why, she said all of her work (almost by definition) was *A* work. She maintained this pose for five weeks, but dropped it when she wrote, for the first time, about a topic she had an investment in—the way her father abused her mother.

In the conference I held with her on that paper, Anne was surprisingly disappointed in what she'd done. I asked her if it was a hard paper to write:

> Yeah, because there's so much I'm leaving out and there's so much more. I mean, we still get letters from him [her father]. I wanted to keep going but I couldn't. . . . There's so many little things you notice but when you sit down to write them out they don't have the significance they had at the moment. . . . And some of the

sentences were really hard for me to get the ideas into them, the actual feelings. It's like you don't have the words in your mind to say what you feel. The whole paper was like that. You know, looking for words. (138)

In her last paper for the course, she wrote, with stunning power, about the physical abuse she too received from her father. She slipped a copy of the paper under my door and missed her conference that day. Maybe she figured she had told me enough. But on that paper she left me a note: "I am dissatisfied with this because it lacks total honesty. There are some perspectives that I can't or am unable to express concisely on paper" (142). I never saw her again.

The difficulties she named were similar to the ones I experienced writing about her. After all the interviews were transcribed, all the drafts examined, all the revisions noted, after the methodological machine had come to a halt, I still had to find the narrative thread that led me through the material. I had to "intensely consult and intensely ignore," keeping the data I needed, putting aside the rest, grieving a bit for all I had to leave out.

It is a lonely feeling, and for a while an empty feeling. But I was not totally alone because I had patterns of other narratives to draw on. I could make new stories out of old ones.

Works Cited

Atwell, Nancie. *In the Middle: Writing and Reading with Adolescents.* Portsmouth, NH: Heinemann, 1987.

———. "A Special Writer at Work." *Understanding Writing: Ways of Observing, Learning, and Teaching.* Ed. Thomas Newkirk and Nancie Atwell. 2d ed. Portsmouth, NH: Heinemann, 1988. 114–29.

Bissex, Glenda. *GNYS AT WRK: A Child Learns to Write and Read.* Cambridge: Harvard UP, 1980.

Brodkey, Linda. "Writing Ethnographic Narratives." *Written Communication* 4 (1987): 25–50.

Calkins, Lucy. *Lessons from a Child*. Portsmouth, NH: Heinemann, 1983.

Clifford, James. "On Ethnographic Authority." *Representations* 1 (1983): 118–46.

Doheny-Farina, Stephen. "Writing in an Emerging Organization: An Ethnographic Study." *Written Communication* 3 (1986): 158–85.

Graves, Donald. "A New Look at Writing Research." *A Researcher Learns to Write: Selected Articles and Monographs*. Portsmouth, NH: Heinemann, 1984. 92–109

Harste, Jerome, Virginia Woodward, and Carolyn Burke. *Language Stories and Literacy Lessons*. Portsmouth, NH: Heinemann, 1984.

Holt, John. *How Children Fail*. New York: Pittman, 1964.

James, Henry. "Preface to *Roderick Hudson*." *The Art of Fiction*. New York: Scribners, 1934. 3–19.

Kozol, Jonathan. *Death at an Early Age: The Destruction of the Hearts and Minds of Negro Children in Boston*. Boston: Houghton, 1967.

Lauer, Janice, and J. William Asher. *Composition Research: Empirical Designs*. New York: Oxford UP, 1988.

Lee, Spike, dir. and pro. *Do the Right Thing*. videocassette. MCA Home Video, 1990.

Mischler, Eliot. "Meaning in Context: Is There Any Other Kind?" *Harvard Educational Review* 49 (1979): 1–19.

Naylor,Gloria.*The Women of Brewster Place*. New York: Viking, 1982.

Newkirk, Thomas. "Anatomy of a Breakthrough: Case Study of a Freshman Writer." *New Directions in Composition Research*. Ed. Lillian Bridwell and Richard Beach. New York: Guilford, 1984. 131–48.

———. *More Than Stories: The Range of Children's Writing*. Portsmouth, NH: Heinemann, 1989.

North, Stephen. *The Making of Knowledge in Composition: Portrait of an Emerging Field*. Portsmouth, NH: Heinemann, 1987.

Perl, Sondra, and Nancy Wilson. *Through Teachers' Eyes: Portraits of Writing Teachers at Work*. Portsmouth, NH: Heinemann, 1985.

Rose, Mike. *Lives on the Boundary*. New York: Viking, 1989.

Scholes, Robert and Robert Kellogg. *The Nature of Narrative*. New York: Oxford UP, 1966.

Silberman, Charles. *Crisis in the Classroom: The Remaking of American Education*. New York: Random, 1970.

Smagorinsky, Peter. "Graves Revisited: A Look at the Methods and Conclusions of the New Hampshire Study." *Written Communication* 4 (1987): 331–42.

Taylor, Denny. *Family Literacy: Young Children Learning to Read and Write*. Portsmouth, NH: Heinemann, 1983.

Taylor, Denny, and Catherine Dorsey-Gaines. *Growing Up Literate: Learning from Inner City Families*. Portsmouth, NH: Heinemann, 1988.

Tobin, Joseph. "Visual Anthropology and Multivocal Ethnography: A Dialogical Approach to Japanese Preschool Size." *Dialectical Anthropology* 13 (1989): 173–87.

Vygotsky, Lev. *Mind in Society: The Development of Higher Psychological Processes*. Cambridge: Harvard UP, 1978.

White, Hayden. "The Value of Narrativity in the Representation of Reality." *Critical Inquiry* 7 (1980): 2–27.

Ethnography and Composition

Studying Language at Home

WHEN, AS A GRADUATE STUDENT, I was faced with the task of choosing an area of research and—more specifically—a research question that would lead to a dissertation, I was, to say the least, a little intimidated. I realized that much of the research I had read seemed to have no real connection to me and where I came from, that a large gap existed between the people I knew and the people being described in that research. Much research in composition studies focused on novice and expert writers and on how one group (usually people from backgrounds similar to mine) didn't measure up to another group (expert writers, usually white, middle-class students). I knew then that I needed my scholarly life to have some real connection to my personal life, that I needed a bridge between what I saw as a rather large gap between academic research and real problems that affected the people where I came from.

So where did that discovery get me? It got me interested in the work of Shirley Brice Heath. In a very concrete way, Heath's work on communities in the Piedmont Carolinas touched me. As I read *Ways with Words,* I realized that I was reading about people and communities I knew. I was born and raised in the Piedmont Carolinas, and most of my relatives still live in that area. Heath's work validated my desire to do research that connected with me, and I became more and more interested in examining language use outside the classroom because I was convinced, as were Heath and others, that finding out what students did outside class was the key to helping them succeed in school.

Next, I needed a research problem and a method. Enter divine inspiration (literally). I was sitting in church one morning listening to the sermon when I was struck not only with what the minister was saying but how and why he was saying it and how the congregation reacted to it. The beginnings of a research project were stirring. More and more studies were being done on language use in the home and the work place, but I realized that various community institutions also played a prominent role in the lives of our students. In the African American community, one of the most prominent institutions is the church. While Heath had included the church in the study of Trackton and Roadville, it was only a minor part of her study. This community institution deserves more attention than it has received because its literate practices are powerful in the lives of its members, shaping, in part, their identities and ways of thinking, acting, and engaging in everyday discourse. So why not study literacy in the African American church?

The only way that I could even think about examining literacy in the African American church was through ethnography. This was the only research method I had been introduced to that allowed a researcher to tell a story about a community—a story told jointly by the researcher and the members of the community. In addition, this method allowed for, even demanded, that context be a part of the data. Ultimately, ethnography allowed me to be part of the research project in more than some abstract "researcher" way. It allowed me to take pictures of the community (through fieldwork) and be in the picture at the same time, something that other research methods frown upon.

However, this ethnographic project presented me with challenges and methodological questions: What did I, as a composition scholar, need to learn about ethnography in order to do the project? And what special problems did I face because I had chosen to do an ethnography in a community of which I was a member? These two questions are the central questions behind this essay. I first describe the goals of ethnography, including the principles that inform good ethnographic studies, and then I address the particular issues associated with studying one's own community, using my study of the African American church as illustration.

Conducting an Ethnography: Making the Strange Familiar

Ethnography is a qualitative research method that allows a researcher to gain a comprehensive view of the social interactions, behaviors, and beliefs of a community or social group. In other words, the goal of an ethnographer is to study, explore, and describe a group's culture (Agar 12–14; Spradley 3–10; Zaharlick and Green 205–6). Ethnographers tend to focus on the daily routines in the everyday lives of the communities being studied. They study what members of a community do, what they say, what they know, and what their physical artifacts are (Spradley 54). It is through examining such ordinary, daily routines of a community that ethnographers are able to accomplish their ultimate goal: to describe a particular community so that an outsider sees it as a native would and so that the community studied can be compared to other communities. Only through such careful comparisons can researchers start to develop a global picture of cultural groups.

Hymes, in "What Is Ethnography?" identifies three modes of ethnographic inquiry: comprehensive-oriented ethnography, topic-oriented ethnography, and hypothesis-oriented ethnography. Comprehensive-oriented ethnography seeks to document or describe a total way of life. Few ethnographers claim to have done totally comprehensive ethnographies. Time and space generally do not allow for describing everything about a community. Topic-oriented ethnography narrows the focus to one or more aspects of life known to exist in a community (see Heath's *Ways with Words* and Shuman's *Storytelling Rights*). Comprehensive and topic-oriented ethnographies lead to hypothesis-oriented ethnography, which can be done only when one has a great deal of general ethnographic knowledge about a community (Hymes, "What Is Ethnography?" 22–23). The mode of inquiry may influence the type of data collected, how data are collected, how long an ethnographer stays in the field, and what role she plays in the community being studied.

While ethnography in general is concerned with describing and analyzing a culture, ethnography in composition studies is generally topic oriented and concerned more narrowly with communicative behavior or the interrelationship of language and culture. Hymes describes this kind of ethnography as ethnography of communication ("Models of Interaction"; *Foundations*). Saville-Troike explains that ethnography of communication "is directed, on the one hand, at the description and understanding of communicative behavior in specific cultural settings, but it is also directed toward the formulation of concepts and theories upon which to build a global metatheory of human communication" (2). Given its goals and methods, it is not hard to see why ethnography has gained in popularity in composition research. This methodology not only allows for but emphasizes the context that contributes to acts of writing and written products. That is, ethnographers who study writing, literacy, and so on, study writing as it occurs in its specific cultural setting. A study that ignores the social context of language use is not an ethnography.

Ethnographers look to several principles to inform the research and guide them through its various stages. First, good ethnographies are theoretically driven, and due to the interdisciplinary nature of the field, composition scholars may make use of more than one theoretical perspective. The theoretical orientation of an ethnographer may not always be a conscious choice or even be made explicit, but it is usually evident. Ethnography is generally associated with a "phenomenological-oriented paradigm which embraces a multi-cultural perspective because it accepts multiple realities" (Fetterman 15). This or any other theoretical perspective necessarily orients researchers, leading them to focus on one aspect of cultural phenomena rather than another. For instance, a cognitive theory might orient a researcher to focus on what members of a social group say and do as a way of finding out what they think and what they believe. This researcher looks to make "cognitive maps and taxonomies." On the other hand, researchers who are influenced by cultural ecology or Marxist theory may focus on material resources within a community to determine social behavior patterns. The theoretical perspective that ethnographers adopt influences research questions, tools and techniques of data collection and analysis, and the conceptual framework of the study.

Because of the decisions ethnographers have to make before they even enter the field, such as choosing theoretical perspectives, they do not enter communities with blank slates. They gather some information on the history of the community (if appropriate), the participants, and the language. In spite of this previous knowledge, however, one important feature of ethnography is the open-mindedness of the ethnographer. While an ethnographer may begin with a set of research questions, new questions should emerge and old questions be reshaped as data are collected and analyzed. As much as possible, research questions and hypotheses are context-dependent and, therefore, should emerge from the social situation being studied.

At the root of most ethnographic research is the native's perspective (the emic perspective), usually accessible to ethnographers through fieldwork. Ethnographers allow the participants (along with artifacts from the community) to define the community for them. The object of ethnography is to provide what Geertz refers to as a "thick description" of the culture being studied (10–14). That thick description is based on how the members make meaning and explain and interpret social actions in their own communities; in short, how they define culture. One can gain such data only by immersing oneself in the community being studied.

An important prerequisite to this immersion is for ethnographers to negotiate both access into the community and the role the ethnographers will take on. How access to a community is gained can influence the ease or difficulty with which ethnographers can collect data. Just as there is no cookbook recipe for how to do ethnography, there is no best way to gain access to a community (Walters). There are countless ways to enter a community, and these depend on such variables as the type of community (village, school, bar, church, and so forth), the focus of the ethnography, the length of time the ethnographer plans to invest in the study, the relationship of the ethnographer to the community, and the role the ethnographer will play in the community. For many ethnographers, the first step toward gaining access is to have a contact person within the community who will introduce the ethnographer to or identify the key person(s) from whom the ethnographer must seek permission to conduct the study (if permission is needed). Ethnography in a school may require permission from several levels, from parents to a state board of education. An ethnography of shoppers in a mall may require no permission.

Once access is gained, the role the ethnographer takes in the community must be negotiated with participants and may determine the kind of data an ethnographer can collect. The goal in negotiating a role is to interfere as little as possible with the daily routines in the community. The teacher who studies his or her own classroom will run into difficulty here because the daily routines depend, in large part, on him or her. Since participant observation is the major data gathering technique in ethnography, the ethnographer's role in the community influences the level of participant observation in the field. Spradley explains that "the participant observer enters a social situation with two purposes: to engage in activities appropriate to the situation and to observe the activities, people, and physical aspects of the situation" (55). Holy stresses that actively participating allows the researcher to fully experience actions of the community, and that observation alone cannot be the main process through which data are gathered (22–29).

With a community or social situation located, a research question and mode of inquiry identified, a theoretical perspective and conceptual framework in mind, access to the community gained, and one's role negotiated, the ethnographer is ready to begin fieldwork, the major method of data collection for the ethnographer. The goal of fieldwork is to collect as much data as possible, data that will yield an understanding of the complex relationships that exist in a community. Fieldwork is characterized by participant observation, formal and informal interviews of informants, photographs, audio and video recordings of daily occurrences in a community, gathering of physical artifacts that are a part of the daily routine of a community (e.g., written documents produced and used in a community), and on rare occasions questionnaires distributed to members. Not all of these methods will be used in every ethnography, and no ethnography makes use of only one of these methods. However, participant observation and formal and informal interviews have traditionally yielded the richest fieldnotes. Through these methods, the ethnographer usually has her or his greatest contact with informants, and from these informants, the ethnographer gains an emic perspective (insider's view) of the culture. Zaharlick and Green go so far as to argue that "the members of the social group (e.g., classroom) become formal and informal collaborators in the research. That is, the researcher needs the support and cooperation of those members of the social group who hold 'cultural knowledge' about the meaning of the events, actions, objects, and behaviors the ethnographer observes as well as the beliefs, values, and attitudes of members of the group" (214). Any patterns or impressions that the ethnographer recognizes and forms throughout the ethnography are tested by comparing one source of information with other sources in order to eliminate alternative explanations and arrive at a valid interpretation (Fetterman 89). The ethnographer checks her notes against informants' explanations and vice versa to determine whether informants do what they say they do and to see if the ethnographer has recorded notes accurately. This verification is referred to as triangulation, a concept that is essential to every ethnography and that provides validity to data analysis (see also Grant-Davie, this volume, for a discussion of validity, reliability, and interpretation).

Data analysis consists of recognizing patterns and relationships that emerge from the fieldwork. Because of the cyclical nature of ethnography, data analysis takes place throughout the study. Early analysis can help the ethnographer become more focused and may contribute to refined research questions. The ethnographer who waits until all the data have been collected (anywhere from months to years) to start data analysis runs the risk of being totally overwhelmed by the amount of data collected as well as finding out too late that she has focused on one aspect of the community while patterns in the data indicate that she should have focused on another. The ethnographer develops a coding scheme that illuminates these patterns and turns them into categories. It is by establishing these categories that the ethnographer begins to make meaning of a community for an outsider. One of the flexibilities of ethnography is that data can be analyzed and reported in various ways. While ethnography is qualitative, qualitative and quantitative methods can often be combined (Jacobs). Depending upon the type of data collected and the focus of the ethnography, an ethnographer can make use of no statistics at all or use some of the most sophisticated statistical analyses available.

When the analysis (the process) is complete, the ethnographer's final step is to write the ethnography (the product). According to Van Maanen, how an ethnography is presented depends on several factors, such as the nature of the ethnographic study (comprehensive-oriented, topic-oriented, or hypothesis-oriented), its purpose, its audience (policy makers, other ethnographers, members of the community), and its style (critical, literary, realistic, impressionistic) (quoted in Zaharlick and Green

221). Linda Brodkey adds that in writing ethnographies, "The controversy specifically raised by ethnographic narratives is whether data are interpreted or analyzed, or, put another way, whether the researcher or the research methodology is telling the story" (26). She argues that we must recognize the role of narrative in all ethnographic reports, that "the single most important lesson to be learned from ethnographic fieldwork is that experience is not—indeed, cannot be—reproduced in speech or writing, and must instead be narrated" (26).

Studying One's Own Community: Making the Familiar Strange

When ethnographers study a community as outsiders, they must spend a significant amount of time gaining access to the community and learning the rules of the community well enough to gather and eventually analyze the data. In contrast, ethnographers who study their own community may already have access to almost all facets of that community's life, most likely have roles in the community that existed before the study, and consciously or subconsciously know the rules of behavior within the community. In composition studies, where ethnography is becoming valued as a way to explore problems in the field, more researchers are studying communities with which they have some prior experience and/or of which they are members. For example, a growing number of researchers are conducting ethnographies of their own classrooms or, as in my case, of social organizations to which they belong.

Are there special problems for ethnographers in composition who study their own communities? Consider the following excerpt from Gloria Naylor's *Mama Day:*

> Look what happened when Reema's boy—the one with the pear-shaped head—came hauling himself back from one of those fancy colleges mainside, dragging his notebooks and the tape recorder and a funny way of curling up his lip and clicking his teeth, all excited and determined to put Willow Springs on the map. . . .

And then when he went around asking us about 18 & 23, there weren't nothing to do but take pity on him as he rattled on about 'ethnography,' 'unique speech pattern,' 'cultural preservation'. . . . He was all over the place—What 18 & 23 mean? What 18 & 23 mean? And we told him the God-honest truth: it was just our way of saying something . . . but he done still made it to the conclusion that 18 & 23 wasn't 18 & 23 at all—was really 81 & 32, which just so happened to be the lines of longitude and latitude marking off where Willow Springs sits on the map. And we were just so damned dumb that we turned the whole thing around. . . . The people who ran the type of schools that could turn our children into raving lunatics—and then put his picture on the back of the book so we couldn't even deny it was him—didn't mean us a speck of good. . . . Naw, he didn't really want to know what 18 & 23 meant, or he woulda asked. . . . On second thought, someone who didn't know how to ask wouldn't know how to listen. (5–7)

If Reema's boy really wanted to know what "18 & 23" meant, he would have found out how to ask and who to ask (a function of fieldwork), as Naylor's narrator illustrates later in this opening section of *Mama Day*. The issue for Reema's boy was not only that he did not know how to ask (a problem any ethnographer may have), but that he assumed that by virtue of being born and raised in this community, he automatically had access to all facets of the community. As this quotation illustrates, he was mistaken. He also assumed that no matter how he approached people and "asked questions," he would gain the information for which he was searching. Again, he was mistaken. And finally, because he thought he had all the answers to his questions, he never realized that he was asking the wrong questions. It is important that Naylor portrays the ethnographer as a member of this community, not as a stranger. His preexisting relationship with the members of the community sets up, rightly or not, expectations for both the researcher and community. Community expectations for ethnographers who study their own communities must be addressed, as must the researchers' own expectations.

This previous example comes from fiction; yet, it is not an unreal situation. When Seteney Shami, an Arab anthropologist, conducted an ethnography in her native town, she had an experience similar to that of Reema's boy. She comments on the value she attached to data she received early on from older informants: "Having heard many of the stories before, I was neither interested nor stimulated. I was laying too much emphasis on getting what I wanted to hear and dismissing what they were telling me as somehow not being data, because it was not new" (120). Shami's previous experience in her community affected her judgment about what is important. In *Arab Women in the Field*, Soraya Altorki and Camilla Fawzi El-Solh point out, on the one hand, that some researchers believe ethnographers studying their own communities may be able to discern patterns and attach meanings to them more quickly and with less difficulty than outsiders. On the other hand, Altorki and El-Solh (7–9) and others (Ablon 70; Cassell 412–26; Aguilar 21) point out that insiders may also be more vulnerable to value conflicts because they are unable to maintain a safe emotional distance from the communities they research.

The move to study one's own community raises a number of questions: (1) What role does an ethnographer's degree of membership in a community play in successfully carrying out the study? (2) How does the role of the researcher affect the preexisting established relationships in this community; specifically, how does her or his role affect how he or she is perceived by the community and how he or she perceives the community? (3) Will the ethnographer make assumptions about what certain behaviors signify or how meaning is established in this community based on previous knowledge or on the actual data collected? (4) Would an outsider attach more significance to observed patterns than the insider, based on the degrees of distance? (5) What issues might an insider face when writing up the ethnography? These are just a few questions that I faced when doing my study of the African American church and that I will address in the remaining pages of this essay.

There are, of course, degrees of membership in a community. For instance, we may hold membership in the larger society (e.g., American society) as well as specific social institutions (e.g., the African American church, college composition teachers) and small groups (Ohio State University English professors). Within any of these communities, a member may be a more actively involved, full-fledged member than others who may operate on the boundaries of a community. Generally, the smaller the community, the fuller the degree of membership; and the degree of membership and size of the community influence the various stages of the ethnography. For instance, I collected ethnographic data in three African American churches in Chicago. Because I was a member of the African American church community, I was familiar in a general sense with how these fairly traditional African American churches operated. I knew how to enter this community and act in a manner that signaled my membership. However, I had little knowledge of two of the three churches. I needed someone within those churches to introduce me to the minister. Yet, in the third church, which I had been attending for more than two years, I needed no intermediary, no introductions. I just went in to see the minister and told him about my study. The third minister was far more accessible than the first two; he volunteered a great deal of references to me in my interviews and let me have free audiocassettes of his sermons (usually sold by the church). In the first two churches, I had to make my own tapes (one church did not record its services) or buy the tapes of the services (the other church recorded and sold tapes of its services). This difference in level of familiarity with the specific churches and the level of familiarity with African American churches in general influenced how I gained access to the churches and ministers and gathered data.

As I suggest in the second question, ethnographers must be concerned with how their previous roles and their new roles (that of researcher) will affect their perceptions of the community as well as the community's perception of them. Will informants talk more openly because they know the ethnographers, or less openly? Will they assume that the ethnographers already know everything about the community because of their membership? Will the ethnographers be more judgmental or attach more value to certain acts because of their knowledge of the community or their preexisting relationships with members of that community?

Obviously, Reema's boy was not a hit in Willow Springs when he came back to town running around with his tape recorder and notebooks. He consistently reinforced these skeptical feelings in the community because he was perceived as asking senseless questions and not really listening to the answers people gave him. Novelist Zora Neale Hurston, a trained cultural anthropologist who collected folktales in her community, initially ran into similar problems when she began her study. She explains that she returned to Eatonville from Barnard and began to ask people in her best "Barnardese" if they knew any folktales (49). She got virtually no response from these people whom she had known most of her life. When Hurston realized that she was then perceived as an outsider because of her Barnardese and her newly acquired urban manners, she was able to revise her approach. She went back into Eatonville some time later and reacclimated herself to the ways of her community and fit in to their way of life. She was then perceived as the insider she originally had been and was able to collect more folktales than she could use.

While Reema's boy and Hurston contributed to their community's perception of them, sometimes ethnographers have no control over how they are perceived. When I was interviewing three ministers (one whose church I was studying and two visiting ministers), they constantly relied on shared knowledge among the four of us about African American preaching and assumed a great deal of knowledge on my part. During the interview one of these ministers said to me in reference to a point he was making, "you know what I mean, you've grown up in southern black churches." I was put in the position of having to answer either "yes" and assume I did know what he was referring to (that was basically true) or saying "no, could you tell me what you mean" (or some variation). The problem with saying yes is that I may have assumed mistakenly; also, my object was to get the informants to be as explicit as possible. However, if I had said no, the informants may have questioned whether or not I was really a member of this community. If they questioned my community membership, it may have affected the easy relationship we had already established, due in part to my being a southern African American woman who had grown up in and gone to African American churches all her life. I chose to signal that I indeed did know what this minister meant and let the ministers continue to talk, which they did for two and one-half hours. At another point, one minister's expectations and perception led to great anxiety on my part. During an interview in the early stages of fieldwork, this minister explained that because of my joint memberships in the African American community, the African American church community, and the academic community, I had the knowledge and the opportunity to raise African American language to the high status it deserves, especially in the eyes of the academy. I found this minister's expectations overwhelming and a little scary. Consequently, for awhile, I found myself thinking about how skilled these ministers were with language instead of describing their language use.

Of course, my perceptions and expectations of the community also posed potential problems. I expected to find a great deal of similarity in the churches because they were, after all, three African American inner-city churches with well-educated African American male ministers and fairly well-educated congregations. I expected the smallest church, which was Pentecostal, to be like many southern African American Pentecostal churches, "stay in all day Sunday holy rollers." However, through my fieldwork, I found that, while there were similarities among the three churches, each church had its own distinct personality, and that the Pentecostal church was the most sedate church of the three churches studied. I learned the hard way that I shouldn't have so many expectations. My membership in the African American church community at large and in specific churches did not provide me with knowledge about every African American church and about all denominations.

There are other concerns for ethnographers who study their own communities: they must learn to think of all patterns that occur in the communities as important and informative. There is a tendency for insiders to overlook patterns because they are not unique or strange or new (as Shami did). After my first two weeks of fieldwork in the first church, I recognized that I had fallen into the same trap as Shami had. I reviewed my two weeks' worth of fieldnotes, which took less than an hour. Obviously, something was wrong. I knew I should have more than the few pages of fieldnotes. However, as I reviewed them again and reflected on why I had written some things down and not others, I found I had been looking for events that stood out. Since so much of what was happening during the church service was not new to me, I had either assumed that many of the routine events were unimportant or hadn't even noticed certain events. When I reminded myself and was reminded by my adviser that the routine "stuff" was the most important data, I then had to train myself to pay attention to as much detail as possible and to assume that everything was important until I had enough data and had done enough analysis to know otherwise.

Ethnographers may also have a tendency to rely on their own knowledge for a great deal of data. This is not to say that they must ignore everything they know about the community, but they must find a way to make explicit that implicit knowledge that is in their heads and that comes from membership (they cannot rely solely on that knowledge). Ethnographers must be careful to actually listen to and see the community, rely on informants, and draw conclusions from actual data collected during the study; basically, ethnographers should not be major informants. Triangulation is one of the keys to success here. For teachers who study their own classrooms, familiarity with their community is problematic because they are major informants in their own studies (see, for example, Herrmann's "Using the Computer"). How might teachers achieve triangulation? Vidoetaping may help here, or having another participant observer in the classroom might be most useful. Another key is to gather as much data as possible from as many different sources as possible (see also Ruth Ray's chapter on teacher research in this volume).

What do ethnographers do when faced with the issues raised above? Taylor and Dorsey-Gaines, in *Growing Up Literate,* remind us that, as outsiders, we must "deal on a daily basis with our own ethnocentrism and mental baggage. Reflection and introspection are continuous processes which must take place throughout the study" (xv). As insiders, we too must deal with our own ethnocentrism and the mental baggage we carry, precisely because of our memberships in the communities we study. And we must also be prepared to deal with the mental baggage and expectations of the other members of the community. That critical reflection and introspection which Taylor and Dorsey-Gaines speak of takes on greater importance than usual for ethnographers examining their own classrooms or neighborhoods. I contributed to my own introspection and reflection in two ways: I constantly asked myself questions such as, Where is my evidence for this or that claim? or Did I assume something? or Did my informants say or do this? And I discussed my findings with people who were familiar with ethnography and composition research but who were not members of the community I was studying. The latter proved to be a most valuable tool because I found myself looking to the data for answers to the questions that these outsiders would raise.

The final challenge that ethnographers face is writing the ethnography. When they are writing about their own communities, this challenge can be problematic. Most likely, ethnographers who write about communities that they aren't members of will have little, if any, contact with those communities once the ethnography is completed. However, ethnographers who write about communities to which they belong may spend unlimited amounts of time in or may indeed live in those communities. Consequently, they may face certain pressures: What pictures do their ethnographies paint of the communities? Have they been as accurate and fair as possible? Have they been overly critical? Not critical enough? How will the communities react to their studies? I faced all these questions in my study. I did not want to be unfair to any of the churches and ministers I studied. Like most ethnographers, I developed a strong sense of loyalty to the community I studied; I did not want anyone in the community to be dissatisfied with what I had written. I also knew that once the study was completed, I wanted to go back to these churches, particularly the one I had been attending, as a regular parishioner. At the same time, I wanted to be rigorous and thorough. These feelings led to anxiety as I was writing, yet they must be faced in the same way that getting through fieldwork and analysis are faced, through introspection, reflection, and triangulation. Most important, of course, ethnographers must be responsible to the community.

Many of the issues I have raised may, of course, concern ethnographers who are strangers to the communities they are studying. However, these issues seem to be paramount for the insider who has to make the "familiar strange." If those of us who study our own communities do not want to be caught in Reema's boy's shoes, that is, being denied by our own communities, then we must be aware of and prepared to deal with the baggage that membership brings. What kept me from being in Reema's boy's shoes was my willingness to learn as much about ethnography as I could before and during the study. Those of us who study our own communities have an obligation to understand as much as we can about ethnography. This knowledge will make us aware that our role in a community may provide us with insights that others do not have, but it can also blind us, just as it did Reema's boy. The goal of any ethnographer, whether insider or outsider, must be to guard against blindness, to drive instead toward increased insight into the ways in which language communities work. That is the excitement and the challenge of ethnography.

Note

I would like to thank Lisa Ede, Marcia Farr, Kay Halasak, Andrea Lunsford, and Carole Clark Papper for their comments on various drafts of this essay.

Works Cited

Ablon, Joan. "Field Methods in Working with Middle Class Americans: New Issues of Values, Personality and Reciprocity." *Human Organization* 36 (1977): 69–72.

Agar, Michael. *Speaking of Ethnography.* Newbury Park, CA: Sage, 1986.

Aguilar, John L. "Insider Research: An Ethnography of a Debate." *Anthropologists at Home in North America: Methods and Issues in the Study of One's Own Society.* Ed. Donald A. Messerschmidt. Cambridge: Cambridge UP, 1981. 15–26.

Altorki, Soraya, and Camilla Fawzi El-Solh. Introduction. *Arab Women in the Field.* Ed. Soraya Altorki and Camilla Fawzi El-Solh. Syracuse: Syracuse UP, 1988. 1–24.

Brodkey, Linda. "Writing Ethnographic Narratives." *Written Communication* 4 (1987): 25–50.

Cassell, Joan. "The Relationship of Observer to Observed in Peer Group Research." *Human Organization* 36 (1977): 412–16.

Fetterman, David. *Ethnography Step by Step.* Newbury Park, CA: Sage, 1989.

Geertz, Clifford. *The Interpretation of Cultures.* New York: Basic, 1973.

Heath, Shirley Brice. *Ways with Words: Language, Life, and Work in Communities and Classrooms.* Cambridge: Cambridge UP, 1983.

Herrmann, Andrea. "Using the Computer as a Writing Tool: Ethnography of a High School Writing Class." Diss. Columbia Teachers College, 1985.

Holy, Ladislav. "Theory, Methodology and the Research Process." *Ethnographic Research: A Guide to General Conduct*. Ed. Roy F. Ellen. New York: Academic, 1984.

Hurston, Zora Neale. *I Love Myself When I am Laughing . . . and Then Again When I am Looking Mean and Impressive: A Zora Neale Hurston Reader*. Ed. Alice Walker. Old Westbury: Feminist, 1979.

Hymes, Dell. *Foundations in Sociolinguistics*. Philadelphia: U of Pennsylvania P, 1974.

———. "Models of the Interaction of Language and Social Life." *Directions in Sociolinguistics: The Ethnography of Communication*. Ed. John J. Gumperz and Dell Hymes. New York: Holt, 1972. 35–71.

———. "What Is Ethnography?" *Children In and Out of School: Ethnography and Education*. Ed. Perry Gilmore and Allan A. Glathorn. Washington: Center for Applied Linguistics, 1982. 21–32.

Jacobs, Evelyn. "Combining Ethnographic and Quantitative Approaches: Suggestions and Examples from a Study in Puerto Rico." *Children In and Out of School: Ethnography and Education*. Ed. Perry Gilmore and Allan A. Glathorn. Washington: Center for Applied Linguistics, 1982. 124–47.

Moss, Beverly J. "The African-American Sermon as a Literacy Event." Diss. U of Illinois at Chicago, 1988.

Naylor, Gloria. *Mama Day*. New York: Tichnor, 1988.

Saville-Troike, Muriel. *The Ethnography of Communication*. New York: Basil Blackwell, 1982.

Shami, Seteney. "Studying Your Own: The Complexities of a Shared Culture." *Arab Women in the Field*. Ed. Soraya Altorki and Camilla Fawzi El-Solh. Syracuse: Syracuse UP, 1988. 115–38.

Shuman, Amy. *Storytelling Rights*. Cambridge: Cambridge UP, 1986.

Spradley, James. *Participant Observation*. New York: Holt, 1980.

Taylor, Denny, and Catherine Dorsey-Gaines. *Growing Up Literate: Learning from Inner City Families*. Portsmouth, NH: Heinemann, 1988.

Walters, Keith. "Initiation Rites and Responsibilities." Unpublished essay, 1990.

Zaharlick, Amy, and Judith Green. "Ethnographic Research." *Handbook of Research in Teaching the English Language Arts*. Ed. James Flood, et al. New York: Macmillan, 1991. 205–25.

Composition from the Teacher-Research Point of View

IN THIS CHAPTER, I examine a general movement—teacher research—rather than a particular method in composition studies. In doing so, I am emphasizing that "what matters for teacher-researchers is less their learning of a method than their understanding of a *point of view about observation* that holds regardless of method and that also validates certain methods" (Knoblach and Brannon 22; emphasis mine). There is already a large body of research that discusses the methods of teacher research, most of which which are taken from anthropology, the social sciences, and linguistics; they include journal keeping, participant observation, interviews, surveys, questionnaires, and discourse analyses of student texts (see Mohr and Maclean; Myers; Odell; and Lytle and Cochran-Smith for detailed descriptions of these methods in teacher research). There has been much less discussion, however, of the teacher-research *perspective*—the philosophical and epistemological assumptions underlying the practice of teacher research—and even less consideration of the potential of teacher research to alter composition theorizing and teaching. My intention in this chapter is to name the beliefs and assumptions underlying teacher research and to demonstrate, through discussion of several teacher-research projects, including my own, that teacher-researchers differ from other composition teachers, that their inquiry differs from other composition research, and that their work could potentially change the field of composition studies.

The term *teacher research* was first used in the 1960s by British educator Lawrence Stenhouse, the originator of the teacher-research movement, to describe classroom-based inquiry involving both schoolteachers and university researchers. The American version sometimes involves collaboration between teachers and researchers, but more often it entails work initiated and conducted by teachers alone. As such, teacher research has been characterized in the United States as "any study conducted by teachers of their school system, school, class, groups of students, or one student, either collaboratively or individually" (Myers 5). A good working definition of teacher research is "systematic and intentional inquiry carried out by teachers," where systematic implies methodical data gathering, analyzing, and reporting; intentional means planned rather than spontaneous activity; and inquiry implies a questioning, reflective stance toward teaching and learning (Cochran-Smith and Lytle 3).

Teacher research in the United States has been conducted primarily in K–12 classrooms and has been supported in part through grants, seminars, and workshops offered by the National Council of Teachers of English, the U.S. Department of Education's Office of Educational Research and Improvement, the National Writing Project, and the teacher-research special interest group of the American Educational Research Association. Because of its growing popularity among teachers in Great Britain, Australia, and the United States, as well as its potential for initiating significant change in classrooms and schools, teacher research is referred to as a movement and has even been called a quiet revolution (Bullock; Britton).

The revolutionary nature of teacher research has to do with its emphasis on change from the inside out—from the classroom to the administration, rather than the other way around, as is typical in most educational institutions. It is a response to a conformist educational system based on a strong belief in the separation of powers. In this system, administrators, curriculum specialists, university researchers, school boards, parents' groups, and taxpayers have primary control over educational policy making, and teachers have little influence. Teacher research challenges the conventional belief in the separation between researchers (those who make knowledge) and teachers (those who consume and disseminate it). Stenhouse believed that school systems, by privileging university research and dismissing teachers' experiential knowledge, are creating "a majority [of teachers] who are ruled by knowledge, not served by it—an intellectual, moral and spiritual proletariat characterized by instrumental competencies rather than autonomous power" (Rudduck and Hopkins 3). He argued that teachers need to move out of a system in which "knowledge is tyranny" and into a system in which they themselves are responsible for the production of knowledge. Thus, the teacher-research movement seeks to engage teachers in research and to demystify and democratize knowledge making. Teacher research is, in short, an emancipation proclamation that results in new ownership—teachers' *own* research into their *own* problems that results in modification of their *own* behaviors and theories; this personally owned research replaces the concept of research as residing "elsewhere" in universities and other traditional sites of inquiry (Boomer). By conducting their own research and communicating their results to other teachers, teacher-researchers "present a serious challenge to current and traditional education and to the public's definition of what teachers are and do"; most importantly, they demonstrate their "power to take control of their subject and their profession" (Bullock 22–23).

The teacher-research movement attempts not only to redress the imbalances between researchers and teachers, but also the imbalances between quantitative and qualitative research paradigms, and between theory and practice in education. Teacher-researchers assert that much university-based research results in counterintuitive findings that are inappropriately applied to the classroom. One of the reasons they cite for the many inadequacies in educational research is an overemphasis on quantitative, "scientific," theory-driven approaches and an underemphasis on qualitative, interpretive, practice-oriented approaches. Teacher-researchers challenge a number of assumptions underlying the traditional (positivist) paradigm in education: that research should be objective, controlled, and decontextualized; that the researcher should be distanced and uninvolved; that research is always theory-driven and must be generalizable in order to perpetuate theory building; and that knowledge and truth exist in the world and are found through research. In direct contrast to the assumptions underlying the positivist paradigm are the assumptions underlying teacher research: that research should account for context (of the classroom, school, and community) in all its complexity; that researchers are active participants in this context; that research should be conducted primarily to inform and improve practice as well as to advance theory; that some research can profitably focus on the detailed and the particular—on one classroom, even one student—in the search for insights into specific learning environments; and that knowledge and truth in education are not so much found through objective inquiry as socially constructed through collaboration among students, teachers, and researchers.

It is their belief in the social construction of knowledge and their actions based on this belief that set teacher-researchers apart from other teachers and that distinguish their kind of research from other kinds of inquiry. Successful teacher research is usually conducted by an open-minded, inquiring teacher who sees the classroom as an egalitarian community in which he or she is but one of many learners. Peter Elbow perhaps best describes this perspective: "Even though we are not wholly peer with our students, we can still be peer in [the] crucial sense of also being engaged in learning, seeking, and being incomplete. Significant learning requires change, inner readjustments, willingness to let go. We can increase the chances of our students being willing to undergo the necessary anxiety involved in change if they see we are also willing to undergo it" (quoted in Kantor 65). Students are not merely subjects whom the teacher-researcher instructs and assesses; they are co-researchers, sources of knowledge whose insights help focus and provide new directions for the study. Examples of this kind of teacher-student relationship at work in composition research include Marilyn Cooper's discussion of first-year English students' development of critical reading and thinking abilities; Jeffrey Schwartz's study of collaborative learning between two high schools using a computer network; and Art Young's description of his college students' collaborative work on a computer manual.

The Cooper study, though not explicitly presented as teacher research, illustrates some key features of this type of inquiry: it grows out of a classroom problem (in this case, how to teach the research paper as a form of critical inquiry that is personally meaningful to students); it makes use of narrative to re-create the classroom context (the first fourteen pages tell the story of a course based on analysis of Herbert Marcuse's *One Dimensional Man*); and it emphasizes the collaborative nature of learning and teaching. Cooper describes how she collaborated with her students to negotiate the meaning and significance of a text:

> My students and I brought different resources and perspectives to bear on the task of making sense of Marcuse's theories in today's world. I brought Freud and Marx and a reflection in popular culture of some of Marcuse's ideas—the movie *The Terminator*. They brought a more immediate knowledge of certain scientific and technological information than I had, and certainly more familiarity with not only *The Terminator* . . . but also other movies that exemplified Marcuse's critique of technology. I came to understand better the limitations of Marcuse's ideas in critiquing the present relations between technology and society (*One-Dimensional Man*, after all, was published in 1964); they came to understand better that some of Marcuse's ideas could help them explain their own experiences in the technological society . . . and in their classes in science and technology. Collaboration assumes an exchange. . . . It assumes that differences among people are a resource, not something to be eliminated in the name of education, remediation, socialization. (45)

The passage is significant because it illustrates the teacher-research point of view—that learning and knowing are collaborative, and that teachers learn as much from their interaction with students as students learn from teachers.

In another study, Schwartz describes two teacher-research projects he conducted that rely even more on what he calls shared inquiry between teacher and students. For the first project, Schwartz worked with two high school students to determine how an electronic network helped create a writing community among students at different high schools. The student-researchers shared the responsibility with Schwartz for collecting and analyzing classroom data. For the second project, Schwartz made his entire class research partners by encouraging them to study and report on aspects of local history to students at a high school in another city. Through his first project, Schwartz learned "three things about shared inquiry: (1) students discovered information I wouldn't have seen, (2) they acted responsibly as peer readers, and (3) when raising questions and analyzing data, we all learned about language together" (154). Through his second project, Schwartz learned that he "had to give up the traditional authority [he] was used to in the classroom" (166) and that some students and fellow colleagues felt uncomfortable with this restructuring. Ultimately, however, he concludes that the benefit of collaboration between teacher and students is that "it makes students responsible for their own learning. It redistributes the power of the class, not equally, but so that it's not exclusively in the hands of the teacher" (166).

Such redistribution of authority often affects the direction of the research, as well as the teaching and learning that occur. Young's research on his college technical writing class illustrates this point. His study entails a description of the discourse community that developed within his class as the students—English majors and students of science and technology at the graduate and undergraduate levels—learned about a computer system and collaboratively wrote a manual to explain its use. Young acknowledges that the entire focus of his research changed as a result of one student's response to an early draft of his article. The student wrote:

> I think you should focus on storytelling and collaboration—in light of how we collaborated to form a group that produced a good product, and how, to collaborate and form that group, we used stories. . . . [T]he class as a whole had (has) a common experience about which we can tell stories—and you are now doing so—but all of the individual stories told in class or at night meetings and at Nick's Tavern help make up the final product and collaboration—and the stories therefore colored the manual— sometimes overtly (the ordering of sections, how to be user-friendly) and sometimes subtly (personal relationships that very likely influenced give-and-take in discussions and decisions about the final product). (184)

Because he found it valuable to see the class and his own research from the students' perspective, Young revised the article. His published work, entitled "Storytelling in a Technical Writing Class: Classroom-Based Research and Community," emphasizes that "one important concept that emerged from this research and my analysis of it was the essential role that storytelling played in developing and sustaining our collaborative community. . . . In many ways, this chapter is the story of those stories" (168).

The distinguishing feature of all these teacher-research studies is that the teachers gave up their attempts to control students' learning, and in the process students helped teachers to see, think, respond, and even write in different ways. Other forms of collaboration, such as those between teachers and those between teachers and university researchers, are equally important aspects of the teacher-research movement.

The philosophy underlying teacher-teacher collaboration is best articulated by Ann Berthoff, who asserts that what teachers need is "not what is called 'research,' but the kind of theory that is generated in dialogue among teachers" (29). In a much-quoted passage from "The Teacher as REsearcher," Berthoff asserts that educational research, if it is to have any significance at all, must be created by, for, and among teachers: "Educational research is nothing to our purpose, unless we [teachers] formulate the questions; if the procedures by which answers are sought are not dialectic and dialogic, that is to say, the questions are not continually REformulated by those who are working in the class-room, educational research is pointless" (30). Berthoff sees teacher research as a means of changing the nature of research, which she says should be pronounced so as to emphasize its purpose: "Research, like REcognition, is a REflexive act. It means looking—and looking again. The new kind of REsearch would not mean going out after new 'data,' but rather REconsidering what is at hand. REsearch would come to mean looking and looking again at what happens in the English classroom" (30). This kind of research is being conducted among groups of K–12 teachers in various school districts across the United States (see the 1988 special issue of the *Carolina English Teacher,* as one example) and, increasingly, among groups of community college faculty, as described at the 1990 National Conference on College Teaching and Learning. In an introduction to the teacher-research issue of the *Carolina English Teacher,* the volume editor attests to the importance of collaboration among teachers across the state as well as within individual school districts. The editor emphasizes that "sharing—the active exchange of ideas—has become the real point of teacher research" ("Letter from the Editors" i).

Among the few examples of teacher-teacher collaboration in research at the university level is the ongoing work in composition of Basham, Ray, and Whalley. As a member of this teacher-research team, I can speak from experience about the excitement, the frustration, and the inevitable change that occurs in one's research perspective as a result of conducting inquiry with other teachers. In our work, we originally set out to address a set of broad questions: How does social context—students' language, culture, and community of origin—affect their interpretations of writing tasks? Further, do students' cultural orientations lead them to interpret writing tasks differently from their teachers? If so, what is the impact of these differences on students' attitudes toward writing? As teachers, we were interested in these questions because we had observed that our bicultural and bilingual students often responded to writing assignments, especially those based on reading passages, differently from other students and that college faculty often judged their responses negatively. As researchers, we were interested in studying these questions because they have not been fully addressed in the literature on social constructionism and academic literacy and because they raise significant issues for all educators seeking ways to respond to student diversity. One way to study the questions is to compare the writing of different student populations. We decided to conduct a collaborative project, with each of us giving the same assignment and collecting the same data from different cultural groups. Basham, a professor at the University of Alaska, conducted her research with Alaskan native students, including Eskimos and Athabaskan Indians; Whalley, a professor at San Francisco State University, conducted her research with Asian students; and I, a professor at Wayne State University in Detroit, conducted the study with Hispanic students.

One thing we have learned so far from this project is that a stimulating dialectic occurs when teachers get together to plan and conduct research and to analyze their collective data. For example, through independent analysis of my own data, I had come to the conclusion that my Hispanic students did not "read" the text of an assignment in the same way I "read" it, and this accounted for the differences between their responses to readings and those I expected. I attributed this difference to the fact that I was an experienced reader of academic texts and my students were not; I saw my students' responses as having little to do with their language and culture. However, I was forced to reconsider this interpretation when I began to analyze the data collaboratively with my partners—both trained ESL teachers and applied linguists—who saw cultural influences on my students' responses that I had not considered significant, such as my students' willingness to "talk through" the topic at length on tape and their many references to family, religious beliefs, and rituals. As a teacher trained in literature and composition, I needed to REsearch, in Berthoff's terms, the data from their perspective. Similarly, my partner from Alaska had to reconsider some of the conclusions she had drawn about her data when she saw similarities between Eskimo and Hispanic responses that called into question the cultural influences she had attributed solely to Alaskan native students.

Through this study we also gained an appreciation for the enormous amount of effort students had put into the interpretation of our writing task—effort that was often not at all apparent in their writing. As we listened to taped protocols in which Chinese students agonized over the assignment and attempted to understand the reading passage on which it was based, we perceived a central conflict between our students' assumptions that there was a "correct" meaning, which was to be "found" in the text, and their own experience of reading, which revealed that the meaning was in fact negotiable and that much of their interpretation relied on their experiences with prior texts. As a result of these protocols, we are planning to follow up our initial study with a more focused analysis that requires us to reformulate our research questions and look again at the data we have collected. In the next study, we will examine, following reader-response theory, how the three groups of students define "text" differently and how they create different roles for themselves in the construction of meaning. We are convinced that the directions in which our research is moving and the enthusiasm we have for continuing it are largely a result of our collaborative efforts and the intellectual and personal challenges they pose.

Another kind of collaboration that often results in a rethinking and revision of one's perspective is that between the classroom teacher and the university researcher. Ken Kantor, a university researcher, illustrates the change that has occurred for him through his work with middle-school teachers:

> In a more conventional sense I am observing in classrooms and interviewing the teachers, but we are also sharing journal entries, responding to students' writing, and discussing problems and possibilities in teaching writing. Later in the school year I plan to do some team-teaching with them. The project involves research, yes, but also teacher education, curriculum development, and above all collaborative inquiry. It is compelling me to redefine my relationships with my colleagues, and to reevaluate and broaden my conceptions of research. (66)

Kantor has learned through interacting with teachers and reading their journals that they are often observant, perceptive, reflective, and analytical; they raise theoretical questions, and they address them effectively in terms of their own practical wisdom. As a result of his collaborative efforts, and in response to teachers' critiques of his previous research, Kantor has revised his definition of research and reconsidered the false hierarchies his earlier work established between researchers and teachers. He offers, at the end of his article entitled "Learning from Teachers," a "better way of looking at the world of teaching and research"—one that questions the value of current definitions of research that require "a hierarchy of preferred and less-preferred modes, with university-sponsored investigations published in 'prestige' journals considered as superior to studies conducted by classroom teachers" (69). Instead, he proposes that research be "regarded as a quintessential human endeavor, with people of all ages, backgrounds, occupations, interests, and talents collaborating in processes of inquiry and constructing meaning" (69). In other words, Kantor himself has come to the realizations that fuel the larger teacher-research movement: research is a valuable form of knowledge making that teachers can and should engage in; interaction and collaboration are crucial to this type of research; and good teacher research requires a willingness to question assumptions, challenge beliefs, and initiate change in the classroom.

By now it should be clear that teacher research is a specific kind of inquiry, and that not all composition research is teacher research, even though most composition researchers are also teachers. It is important to distinguish between teacher research and research on teaching (Cochran-Smith and Lytle). The latter type of inquiry may use the same methods as teacher research, but it does not emphasize the teacher's role in the generation of knowledge, nor does it acknowledge the collaborative nature of this knowledge making. In most research on teaching, "teachers are the objects of researchers' investigations and then ultimately are expected to be the consumers and implementors of their findings. Missing . . . are the voices of the teachers themselves, the questions that teachers ask, and the interpretive frames that teachers use to understand and improve their own classroom practices" (Cochran-Smith and Lytle 3). What distinguishes teacher research from other composition research is its collaborative spirit; its emphasis on the interrelationship between theory and practice; and its interest in bringing about change—in the teacher, the student, the school system, the teaching profession, the field of study, and the practice of research—*from within the classroom.*

Of course, change through teacher research does not come easily. At this point I want to emphasize that I am speaking about the *potential* of the movement; teacher research, as yet, has had few far-reaching effects on educational practice or theory. One of the reasons is that teacher research, like other forms of inquiry, has its detractors. Critics point to the following as limitations: (1) teachers, as participant-observers, may lack the perspective necessary to see and interpret their own classroom environment; (2) teachers conduct research that does not always meet the expectations of the established research community; (3) teachers do not always frame their findings in terms of theory, and thus their research has little relevance beyond their own classrooms; and (4) teacher research creates a tension in the classroom between researching and teaching, dividing the teacher's attention between data gathering and instruction.

The first three critiques are the same ones that face the ethnographer: they challenge the credibility of socially constructed knowledge that is presented in genres not recognized as strictly academic, namely narratives and case studies. The third critique also assumes that theory is something that exists "out there" in the research community and needs to be "applied" to teacher research when it is "written up." However, another way to view theory is in terms of function rather than form—as a way of seeing and questioning rather than as a body of already existing knowledge. Robert Scholes refers to this alternative view of theory in *Textual Power;* he describes it as the willingness to step outside patterned ways of thinking and behaving, to make strange the familiar in order to see where change is needed in the classroom.

The fourth critique assumes that research and teaching are mutually exclusive, or even competing, enterprises. Teacher-researchers, however, proceed on the alternative premise that teaching and researching are interactive—that they form a dialectic relationship in which they continually inform each other. Teacher-researchers know that there is always a theory underlying their practice; the purpose of classroom-based research is to make that theory explicit and to examine and question it.

Additional critiques of teacher research question the logistics and politics of its introduction in schools: For example, teachers need to be specially trained to do classroom inquiry; most teachers lack the time and energy to add research to their already heavy workloads; and teacher research in some cases may cause tension between researching and nonresearching teachers because teacher-researchers "model professional behavior through seizing authority for their subject matter and activities" rather than looking to the "experts"—administrators and university researchers—for that authority (Bullock 23).

All of these critiques of teacher research are legitimate in the sense that they call into question the epistemological assumptions underlying the movement. Teacher-researchers need to learn to address these questions directly and articulate their beliefs—to themselves as well as to their critics. In so doing, they will begin to see the significance of their own work within the larger field of composition and be better able to represent it to others. What, then, might teacher-researchers say about the effect of the movement on composition studies?

Surely, in its emphasis on the classroom as the locus of change, teacher research has the potential to alter the field significantly. The movement successfully argues for the validity of teachers' knowledge, for the necessity of empowering teachers to conduct their own inquiries, and for teachers' abilities to make their own informed decisions about what and how they teach writing; it also argues against the valorization of university-based research that currently prevails in composition studies (see North). As the teacher-research movement grows, fewer K–12 teachers will be looking to university-based composition specialists for answers to their questions about the teaching of writing. Instead, they will be looking within their own classrooms and gaining confidence in the practical sources of their own knowledge. Already, teacher-researchers are becoming more critical readers of others' composition research. Increasingly, they will be challenging the relevance of existing composition studies, questioning the meaning of composition theory and their role in making it, and calling for a much closer relationship between composition theory and the teaching of writing. These challenges, from my perspective as a university-based teacher-researcher, can only revitalize and improve the field.

It is my contention, too, that teacher research at the K–12 level has the potential to change the way writing and researching are taught in graduate programs at the university. Practicing teacher-researchers returning to the university for additional courses and advanced degrees will bring with them a greater awareness of their potential as agents for change and a more critical perspective on the research-based knowledge of the academy. These students will propose teacher-research projects for their master's essays and dissertations and will challenge assumptions underlying the more traditional research paradigms promoted in graduate schools. Graduate faculty in English departments will need to reassess their traditional views of teaching as a form of transmission and a mere service to the institution, reconsidering it as an intellectual enterprise and a dynamic form of inquiry. Programs in composition theory will need to adopt new perspectives on the teaching process, as well as the composing process (Petersen), explaining the methods involved in classroom-based inquiry and providing opportunities for students to conduct studies in collaboration with other students and faculty.

Perhaps most importantly, as graduate faculty read more and more classroom-based dissertations, they will find themselves questioning, as did Kantor, their assumptions about the nature and purpose of research and their criteria for judging its value. Some of the most interesting work in education is now being done by university faculty who are training new teachers and confronting the possibility that teacher research is a new "genre" that cannot be evaluated in terms of traditional research paradigms. The following questions, which have important implications for redefining academic inquiry, will need to be addressed in terms of the teacher-research movement: What counts as research? What are the different purposes and audiences for academic research? Where and to what extent are classroom narratives an appropriate means of research? What is an appropriate stance for a researcher to take in describing his or her findings, and how does this stance relate to the epistemology underlying the methods used? (Often teacher-researchers assume a personal, tentative voice in reporting their findings. What does this voice suggest about their attitudes toward knowledge making? What are the implications of attempting to change this voice to a more traditional, authoritative one?) What is the place of theory in teacher-research and how is it best articulated? How does one distinguish between successful and unsuccessful teacher research? That is, if teacher research relies on classroom narrative, what constitutes an authentic story? And how does the teacher establish her authority to tell this story and call it research? Should teachers be involved in judging the value of teacher research? (See Threatt; Hollingsworth; Cochran-Smith and Lytle; Lytle and Cochran-Smith; and Ray for more detailed discussion of these issues.)

My predictions for the influence of teacher research on higher education may be optimistic. However, my own involvement in the movement and my observations of K–12 teachers who have "reclaimed the classroom" (Goswami and Stillman) lead me to believe that teachers are going to demand more in the future from composition research. Teachers will not continue to allow themselves to be categorized as mere "practitioners" whose knowledge is nothing more significant than "lore" (North). My most optimistic prediction is that teacher research will force composition studies to come to terms with its ambiguous relationship to teaching. It will offer a new point of view—one that sees teaching as equal to research in its intellectual rigor and intent and envisions full collaboration between teachers and researchers as central to the maturing of composition studies as a field.

Works Cited

Basham, Charlotte, Ruth Ray, and Elizabeth Whalley. "Cross-Cultural Perspectives on Reading-to-Write." *Reading in the Composition Classroom: Second Language Perspectives.* Ed. Joan Carson and Ilona Lecki. Rowley, MA: Newbury House, forthcoming.

———. "Text, Task and Topic: A Cultural Comparison of Reader Orientations." Wyoming Conference on English. University of Wyoming, Laramie, 25 June 1990.

Berlin, James. "The Teacher as Researcher: Democracy, Dialogue, and Power." Daiker and Morenberg 3–14.

Berthoff, Ann. "From Dialogue to Dialectic to Dialogue." Goswami and Stillman 75–86.

———. "The Teacher as REsearcher." Goswami and Stillman 28–39.

Bissex, Glenda L. "Small is Beautiful: Case Study as Appropriate Methodology for Teacher Research." Daiker and Morenberg 70–75.

Bissex, Glenda L., and Richard H. Bullock. *Seeing for Ourselves: Case-Study Research by Teachers of Writing*. Portsmouth, NH: Heinemann, 1987.

Boomer, Garth. "Addressing the Problem of Elsewhereness." Goswami and Stillman 4–13.

Britton, James. "A Quiet Form of Research." Goswami and Stillman 13–19.

Bullock, Richard H. "A Quiet Revolution: The Power of Teacher Research." Bissex and Bullock 21–27.

Carr, Wilfred, and Stephen Kemmis. *Becoming Critical: Education, Knowledge, and Action Research*. London: Falmer, 1986.

Cochran-Smith, Marilyn, and Susan L. Lytle. "Research on Teaching and Teacher Research: The Issues That Divide." *Educational Researcher* 19.2 (1990): 2–11.

Cooper, Marilyn M. "Unhappy Consciousness in First-Year English: How to Figure Things Out for Yourself." *Writing as Social Action*. Ed. Marilyn M. Cooper and Michael Holzman. Portsmouth, NH: Heinemann, 1989. 28–60.

Daiker, Donald A., and Max Morenberg, eds. *The Writing Teacher as Researcher: Essays in the Theory and Practice of Class-Based Research*. Portsmouth, NH: Boynton/Cook, 1990.

Elbow, Peter. "Embracing Contraries in the Teaching Process." *College English* 45 (1983): 327–39.

Goswami, Dixie, and Peter Stillman, eds. *Reclaiming the Classroom: Teacher Research as an Agency for Change*. Upper Montclair, NJ: Boynton/Cook, 1987.

Hollingsworth, Sandra. "Coming to View Teaching as Research: A Feminist Perspective on an Epistemological Pedagogy for Teacher Educators." American Association of Colleges of Teacher Education. Chicago, 24 Feb. 1990.

———. "Teachers as Researchers: Writing to Learn about Ourselves—

and Others." *The Quarterly of the National Writing Project and the Center for the Study of Writing* Fall 1990: 10–18.

Kantor, Ken. "Learning From Teachers." Daiker and Morenberg 61–69.

Knoblach, C. H., and Lil Brannon. "Knowing Our Knowledge: A Phenomenological Basis for Teacher Research." *Audits of Meaning: A Festschrift in Honor of Ann E. Berthoff.* Ed. Louise Z. Smith. Portsmouth, NH: Heinemann, 1988, 17–28.

"Letter from the Editors." *Carolina English Teacher,* Special Issue, 1988, i–iii.

Lytle, Susan L., and Marilyn Cochran-Smith. *Learning from Teacher Research: A Working Typology,* forthcoming.

———. "Teacher Research: Toward Clarifying the Concept." *The Quarterly of the National Writing Project and the Center for the Study of Writing* Apr. 1989: 1–3, 22–26.

Mohr, Marian, and Marion S. Maclean. *Working Together: A Guide for Teacher-Researchers.* Urbana, IL: NCTE, 1987.

Myers, Miles. *The Teacher-Researcher: How to Study Writing in the Classroom.* Urbana, IL: NCTE, 1985.

North, Stephen. *The Making of Knowledge in Composition: Portrait of an Emerging Field.* Upper Montclair, NJ: Boynton/Cook, 1987.

Odell, Lee. "Planning Classroom Research." Goswami and Stillman 128–60.

Peterson, Jane. "Valuing Teaching: Assumptions, Questions, and Possibilities." Conference on College Composition and Communication. Chicago, 22 Mar. 1990.

Ray, Ruth. *The Practice of Theory: Teacher Research in Composition,* forthcoming.

Rudduck, Jean, and David Hopkins, eds. *Research as a Basis for Teaching: Readings from the Work of Lawrence Stenhouse.* London: Heinemann, 1985.

Scholes, Robert. *Textual Power.* New Haven: Yale UP, 1985.

Schwartz, Jeffrey. "On the Move in Pittsburgh: When Students and Teacher Share Research." Daiker and Morenberg 153–66.

Threatt, Susan. "When Teachers Do Research . . . What Do They Do and Where Do They Belong?" Wyoming Conference on English. U of Wyoming, Laramie, 26 June 1990.

Young, Art. "Storytelling in a Technical Writing Class: Classroom-Based Research and Community." Daiker and Morenberg 168–87.

Connecting Cognition and Context in Composition

THE LAST THREE DECADES have been an exciting time for research in composition. The rise of interdisciplinary work in the area has enabled scholars in composition to look at old questions with different lenses and has helped to raise many new questions. The last thirty years have produced a corpus of research about reading and writing, particularly about the cognitive dimensions of these constructive activities. More recently, scholars in composition have been calling for research focused on readers and writers as they are situated in context. In the past decade, a hybrid line of inquiry has been emerging: research that explores the complex interplay between cognition and context. In this essay, I discuss the growing body of research on composition that connects cognition and context, highlighting the questions researchers are asking and reflecting on the assumptions and tensions that underlie their inquiry.

In the past, many composition researchers tended to concentrate their attention on issues of cognition or of context. The stereotype of the researcher interested in cognition is the positivist who makes reductive statements about human behavior or who confirms the obvious. The stereotype of the researcher concerned with context is the naturalistic observer who creates sweeping generalizations about human behavior or who argues the impossibility of drawing any generalizations at all. Fortunately, stereotypes about methods are beginning to fade not only in composition scholarship but throughout the research community in the human sciences.

At this point, composition researchers (as well as scholars in literacy studies more generally) are working on conceptualizing the goals for their inquiry into cognition and context. (See, for example, the collection of essays on research directions in literacy studies in the forthcoming book edited by Beach et al.) Such ground-clearing discussions serve an important heuristic function for framing future studies in the area, stressing the importance of interdisciplinary rhetorical research. Debates about the future of literacy studies motivate invention in research and provoke scholars to examine their assumptions and articulate their agendas more precisely.

The Evolution of Cognitive Approaches to the Study of Composition

Cognitive approaches in composing, which emerged in the early 1970s, focus on identifying the thinking processes of individuals and on describing the ways in which those processes are organized and carried out. Researchers who study cognition in writing—from rhetoric, English, psychology, or education—do so for a variety of reasons. Some study cognition with the very practical and immediate goal of helping writers, at school or at work, to improve their writing. Others see the study of the cognition of composing as basic research into the more general processes of thinking and creating. Most see their research efforts as combining basic and applied aims, integrating theoretical and applied knowledge to validate both. Although those who study the cognitive dimensions of composing differ in their particular research thrusts, they share beliefs about what is important to study. At its most general level, the cognitive research agenda in composition is motivated by a concern for what goes right and what goes wrong when people try to communicate in writing. In *When a Writer Can't Write,* Mike Rose puts it this way:

No one writes effortlessly. Our composing is marked by pauses, false starts, gnawing feelings of inadequacy, crumpled paper.

Many of these dead ends are necessary; they occur when we've come up short on information or hit a knotty conceptual problem, when we can't quite arrive at the most effective way to organize material or we're trying to go beyond staid and stereotypic phrasing. Would that more writers understood such tangles for what they are: signs they've hit a critical moment in composing. And would that more writers honored these moments—took time to struggle with the conceptual or rhetorical challenge they present. Our reading would be made sweeter by their efforts. (ix)

Since the earliest studies of cognition and composing, researchers have tried to provide writers with a sense of what they may face during composing (Emig; Hayes and Flower; Matsuhashi; Bereiter and Scardamalia). The effect has been not only to generate knowledge about reading and writing, but to empower teachers with detailed accounts of writers at work that both support and challenge their intuitions about composing processes. A few of the questions that guided some of the early research on cognitive dimensions of writing include:

- In what ways do writers represent composing tasks to themselves?
- How do writers construct an image of readers or of an audience?
- How do writers formulate and act on their intentions?
- What options do writers consider in solving rhetorical problems?

Cognitive researchers in the 1970s and early 1980s typically studied such questions by describing writers as they composed in classroom contexts or in the quiet space of the research lab. Early research produced compelling narratives about the experience of writing—the thinking, the difficulties, the self-doubt that writers share—whether young or old, student or professional. Such renderings of individual writers' day-to-day struggles quickly dispelled the once popular assumption that anybody who can talk can write. Composing could no longer be viewed as simply writing down what one was thinking. By the mid 1980s, more researchers in composition were attempting to study the contextual influences on cognition than ever before. During this period, questions such as those mentioned above were reframed to include:

- In what ways does context—e.g., the context of school, of work, of home—influence writers' task representations?
- How do writers' constructions of readers and of audiences depend on their social, political, and cultural experiences?
- What role does context play in inhibiting or enabling writers to formulate and act on their intentions?
- How does the context constrain or empower writers to recognize and act on their options for solving rhetorical problems?

Although much of the early research in writing provided vivid details about the context in which writers were observed (e.g., Shaughnessy), there were few studies that explored the mutual embeddedness of cognition, context, motivation, and affect. Theorists and researchers are now trying to characterize how these dimensions of composing interact (Green). A gradual reorientation in the ways cognitive researchers explore composing can be seen in the questions they ask and in their approaches to building theories about how people learn to write.

Over the last decade or so, cognitive researchers have been evaluating how well the theories that have guided their work characterize what is involved in learning to write. For example, researchers have questioned the assumptions that underlie the Piagetian model of cognitive development—a model that influenced a great deal of early theorizing about how and when people learn (Brown; Stein and Trabasso). When it was applied to composing behavior, the Piagetian model led some researchers to construe the problems that children face in learning to write as determined rather rigidly by their developmental stage. The teacher's role was viewed as guiding learners to move to the next stage, to cross the next developmental hurdle. When children performed poorly in writing, they were sometimes viewed as lacking the "right mental stuff" and were labeled as having cognitive deficits. The implication was that such children probably could not be helped by instruction. Additionally, a writer's inability to adapt his or her prose to an audience was often characterized as a problem of cognitive egocentricism. Although work that grew out of the Piagetian model provided many valuable insights about the development of literate behaviors, it seemed to encourage researchers to pay more attention to "sites of failure" than to "possibilities for improvement."

A great deal of writing research is still focused on important issues related to how students develop writing abilities, but it often takes a different rhetorical stance, positing that students "are not so much trapped in a private language as they are shut out from the privileged languages of public life" (Bartholomae 139). Some researchers are applying Vygotskian ideas, which emphasize the teachers' role in scaffolding instruction, in creating "zones of possibilities," and in identifying the contexts and situations that make literate practices engaging (Cazden; Dyson; Moll and Greenberg). Others, particularly researchers outside of composition studies, are pointing out that even Vygotsky did not go far enough in articulating how intimately context and cognition are related (Saxe).

Early cognitive research in composition tended to focus on the "context-independent" dimensions of writing. The goal was to understand the aspects of writing abilities that could readily transfer to new situations, more or less independent of the context for composing or people's attitudes about writing. An assumption was that if a writer acquired heuristics for composing, using them would prepare the writer for many rhetorical situations, and indeed, often they did. For example, researchers who studied planning in writing found that effective writers construct elaborate optional plans for composing, reflect critically on these plans, resolve conflicting plans, use goal conflicts to foster invention, and monitor their progress toward acting on their plans (Flower,

Schriver, Carey, Haas, and Hayes). Experienced writers appear to rely on these useful ways of proceeding across writing contexts. Even so, however, the role of the writer's domain-specific and situation-specific knowledge—topical, personal, social, contextual—is crucial to effective composing within any given context. Teaching methods that grow out of such research (e.g., collaborative planning) try to make these rhetorical problem-solving activities explicit and show how they can be adapted across situations.

The cognitive research agenda has been expanding to investigate the context-dependent dimensions of writing. There is now more interest in exploring how an individual writer's ability to access relevant prior knowledge and to use heuristics for writing interacts strongly with the unique features of a given rhetorical situation. Teachers and researchers want to know how to help writers value and use their prior knowledge (Ackerman; Stein). For example, Peck's study of college students who were training to become public policy advocates for at-risk inner city neighborhoods shows that students who draw on their "insider social and rhetorical knowledge of the community" compose more effective written arguments than do other students. Student advocates who wrote the most persuasive arguments, in this case about "hunger in America," had been encouraged to draw on their prior knowledge to invent, structure, and elaborate ideas. Cognitive research on instruction, whether in composition or in other domains, has shown consistently that children and adults learn best when there are "appropriate relationships between their existing knowledge and the instructional material presented to them" (Siegler and Klahr 206), between the context for learning and the culture of learning (Brown, Collins, and Duguid).

If once they did so, researchers with a cognitive orientation no longer represent literate activities as comprised of bundles of discrete and neutral context-free skills. Rather they view them as complexly interrelated cultural practices that "fluctuate as a function of the situation" (Rogoff and Lave 1). A central concern lies in knowing what aspects of cognition in writing are more or less situation-specific or domain-specific than others. The goal is to understand how cognition and context interact, particularly *with what effects, at what levels, and to what extent.* Anthropologist Frederick Erickson argues this issue persuasively:

> People's abilities to reason appear to be domain-specific rather than generalizable across task domains that differ in surface form. This is a fundamental point. ... All "literacies" are radically constituted by their contexts of use. ... [A]n individual's ability to think is dialogically defined, that is, constituted by (a) other people in particular forms of social relationship, (b) the physical objects (utensils, tools) and symbols (words, numbers) with which the individual interacts, directly or vicariously, in doing the thinking. Change the physical form of the tools and symbols, or change the social forms of relations among people with whom the individual is learning the practice (or is performing it once learned) and one has profoundly changed the nature of the interaction—the nature of the learning task. (209–10)

In making a similar point, Rogoff and Lave describe the interaction between domain-specific knowledge and knowledge that is generalizable across situations as follows:

> Cognitive activities are [not] completely specific to the episode in which they were originally learned or applied. In order to function, people must be able to generalize some aspects of knowledge and skills to new situations. Attention to the role of context removes the assumption of broad generality of cognitive activity across contexts and focuses instead on determining how generalization of knowledge and skills occurs. The person's interpretation of the context in any particular activity may be important in facilitating or blocking the application of skills developed in one context to a new one. ... A broader view of context requires that task characteristics and cognitive performance be considered in light of the goal of the activity and the interpersonal and cultural context in which the activity is embedded. (3–4)

Scholars in composition want to know how people generalize their knowledge of writing and how transfer of writing ability from one rhetorical context to another occurs. Currently, researchers believe that transfer may depend heavily on the writer's representations of:

- The audience (e.g., the reader's needs, values, and expectations)
- The topic (e.g., the writer's understanding of and point of view on the subject matter)
- The nature of the text (e.g., the genre, text conventions, and the intertextual context)
- The social situation (e.g., the writer's sense of authority over the text as expressed through tone, voice, or persona)
- The technological environment (e.g., how computers or multimedia may facilitate or constrain composing)
- The constraints (e.g., issues of time, length, or format).

In addition, writers' attitudes about writing shape their use of the knowledge they may possess. Connecting cognition and context means more than studying people's thinking processes; it also means studying the role of affect and motivation in writing (Brand). Individuals differ greatly in their feelings about writing, both generally as well as in particular contexts. For example, Bloom, who studied graduate students in English, found they were positive about writing in most situations, but in the context of writing their dissertations, they were often paralyzed by a fear of failure. Feelings not only help set writers' goals for composing, but figure prominently throughout the writing process.

Even as scholars try to understand the uniqueness of contexts, they are not abandoning the enterprise of trying to find out what is common across writing situations. This has been and will continue to be one of the major emphases for research in writing. Researchers with a cognitive orientation are heavily invested in constructing knowledge that may be useful in diverse situations. In studying patterns across learning contexts, they find, for example, that "performance improves with time on task." This finding has been observed across tasks as different as writing expository prose, riding a bicycle, playing a piano, or learning a foreign language.

In carrying out research, cognitive researchers are guided by the "one mind principle" (Hayes), which captures the idea that when humans approach the world, they do so with a mind that adapts the same underlying processes—representation, perception, comprehension, memory, decision making, search, and so on—to do many tasks. The assumption is that the mind that writes is the same mind that reads, converses with friends, absorbs cultural traditions, learns to play music, and so on. Thus, the discoveries made about the mind in each of these contexts may to some important extent be used by the people who study writing. For example, researchers in composition are finding that what is known about planning and revision in other domains such as graphic design may be helpful to teachers of composition (Bernhardt; Kostelnick; Schriver, "Document Design").

The evolution of approaches to the study of composition has influenced researchers' thinking and the manner in which they reflect on their findings. Researchers are trying to develop theories about the relations between cognition and context—theories that go beyond perspectives suggesting that learners are simply reproductions of their culture, with nothing to say, nothing to contribute, because they are nothing more than social products. Such overdetermined social theories erase the individual and deny individual creativity in the composing process.

The last several decades of composition studies have provided consistent evidence that individual choices matter. Teachers and researchers have striven to increase writers' awareness of the complexity of their choices, both those shaped by the context and those made by the individual. A better understanding of the dynamics of cognition and context may provide the groundwork for developing pedagogies that demonstrate to students their opportunities for becoming agents of change within contexts. To do so, teachers and researchers need a much more detailed view of how choices in writing occur. It is too simple to assume that either individual cognition weighs most heavily in the choices people make during composing or that context is the more potent force. Individual agency is likely to be more possible in some contexts than in others. The relative balance between cognition and context is a complex empirical issue that warrants sustained attention from the research and teaching community. For such reasons, studies that help to unpack the relations between cognition and context will play a central role in the future of writing instruction.

Approaches to Studying Cognition and Context

Researchers in our sister fields, reading and psychology, have also been intrigued with connections between cognition and context, but unlike scholars in composition, they have been conducting work in the area for some time. For example, in *Remembering: A Study in Experimental and Social Psychology*—one of the earliest demonstrations of relations between cognition and context—Frederick C. Bartlett shows how readers' remembrance of stories is culturally mediated. His classic studies examining the factors that influence readers' recall of prose passages provide dramatic evidence of the social construction of knowledge and memory (although he did not refer to it as such). From 1917 until 1927 Bartlett studied readers' recall and reconstruction of a series of folktales, of descriptive and argumentative prose passages, and of picture materials.

In his "War of the Ghosts" study, Bartlett demonstrates how social and cultural factors dramatically influence readers' reconstruction and retelling of a tale. British readers in his study were asked to read "The War of the Ghosts," a North American folktale, and to retell it. Bartlett studied their retelling at various time intervals after reading—from fifteen minutes up to ten years later! He found that even after fifteen minutes readers consistently omitted major story elements, made up elaborate rationalizations for parts of the tale they couldn't understand, updated the language (names, phrases, and events) of the tale in their own vernacular and social group, reduced the complexity of the main characters to fit stereotypes within their culture, shortened the story and changed the order to fit a narrative structure they were familiar with, embellished details they liked, and made the story more coherent and organized from their cultural point of view (Bartlett 64–127). Bartlett's theory of remembering, an early schema theory, grew out of his interest in the "constructive character of remembering" (204). Surprisingly, his work seems much like a present-day study of cognition and context. Bartlett asserts that the data

> have repeatedly shown that both the manner and the matter of recall are often predominantly determined by social influences. In perceiving, in imagining, in remembering proper, and in constructive work, the passing fashion of the group, the social catch-word, the prevailing approved general interest, the persistent social custom and institution set the stage and direct the action. There is no doubt whatever about the operation of these social influences, they have been pointed out and illustrated by many writers. But the exact ways in which they work have never, I think, been given sufficiently detailed consideration. (244)

Bartlett's call for a more thorough examination of relations between cognition and context has resonance for researchers studying reading and writing as constructive activities (see Spivey for a review of constructivist perspectives in reading). Scribner and Cole's *Psychology of Literacy* and Heath's *Ways with Words* are among the more recent studies to examine these relations. Scribner and Cole's study of the Vai of Liberia as well as Heath's study of poor and middle-class Appalachians show in dramatic ways how the thinking that underlies the creation of oral and written texts, as well as the ways texts are valued, varies according to the language community to which individuals belong. Purves points out that studies such as these illustrate how context influences:

- The content and the conventions of oral and written discourse
- The perceived functions of oral and written discourse
- The cognitive demands associated with generating oral or written discourse
- The reading and writing activities people engage in and how they represent and value literate practices (*Writing Across Languages* 11–12)

So far, most composition researchers interested in studying how cognition is contextually mediated have been investigating one of two very broad contexts. On the one hand, they are examining classroom contexts both in the United States and abroad, and their effects on learning about writing. On the other hand, researchers are going beyond the classroom context to explore the nature of writing in nonacademic settings—its discursive practices and rhetorical formations.

Classroom Contexts and Cognition

As Durst points out in his recent survey of the composition literature, less than 10 percent of the published research between 1984 and 1989 was carried out with the intent of studying the contexts of the classroom (395). Studies of composition classrooms in the ethnographic tradition, although few to date, have the potential to sensitize teachers to the values, ideologies, norms, and expectations for literate practices that are cultivated in school contexts. Researchers want to play a significant role in refocusing writing pedagogy for students from diverse backgrounds (e.g., social, economic, ethnic, racial, or national) and in making the classroom a more encouraging site of literate activities and productions. Researchers motivated by these concerns are refuting the idea that classrooms have been providing meaningful literate experiences and opportunities for all students. Instead, researchers with a vision of wedding cognition and context are designing studies to investigate the multiple literacies students bring to the classroom, the multiple ways of using language—oral and written, visual and verbal. By building on the cultural capital students bring to the writing classroom, teachers can better enable students to become more flexible in using language as a symbol system and as a cultural tool. The research and teaching goal is to find ways to provide more students with better chances for active participation in the multiple discourses of society.

Of the existing work on the writing classroom at the elementary level, Dyson's corpus stands out. Her research details the various sorts of knowledges first- and second-graders in the United States bring to the act of learning to write. Dyson portrays a web of interrelationships among drawing, talking, and writing in young children—showing how students learn to negotiate the language arts curriculum. Through the narrative of participant observation, she provides a lens for teachers to view the difficulties children encounter in "doing school." Her studies show that the methods of sense making children bring to bear in the "often messy, noisy, and colorful process of becoming literate" (408) are diverse, multidimensional, and often difficult to differentiate. She finds substantial individual differences in children's ways of weaving together pictures and talk, thus suggesting that the resources and the tensions these media create vary in identifiable ways for different children (407). Her work responds to the growing concern from people in composition about the need to pay more attention to understanding the literacies involved in creating and thinking visually. Researchers who study adult writing suggest that much of the planning adult writers do takes the form of images, pictures, and other nonverbal representations (see Witte, for example). Dyson's studies of early literacy development underscore the need for teachers and researchers in composition to enlarge their object of inquiry beyond the making of verbal text and to investigate the links among multiple literacies.

Another approach traces how classroom contexts influence

students' interpretations of writing tasks, especially how school settings shape the knowledge students use, the conventions they invoke, and the texts they produce. Studies by Flower and her colleagues of how college freshmen learn about academic discourse show that the context of schooling and the cognition of argumentative discourse may conspire to make academic writing a difficult, painful, and mysterious process. Research on classroom contexts is presenting teachers with a perplexing picture of students' representations of teachers' goals in assigning writing tasks. Nelson, for example, finds that the culture of undergraduate lecture courses in college may foster a "blow off" attitude toward the academic writing tasks teachers design to engage students in critical thinking. She interviewed college freshmen and asked them to keep diaries of their writing experiences for college classes over the course of a semester. Students reported that most of their writing assignments were "dumb busy work" and "a waste of time" instead of the kind of learning experience their professors had designed the assignments to promote. Nelson found that some students who "blew off" their writing assignments typed their papers directly into the computer the day they were due ("right before class"). Others spent a total of four hours researching, planning, writing, word processing, and revising their semester papers. On the other hand, students who were intellectually engaged started researching their term papers up to six weeks before the paper was due, went to the library several times, collected background information on their topics, wrote and revised extensively. Although researchers have focused much of their attention on the kinds of writing tasks that promote metacognition and higher order reasoning, few studies offer a perspective on writing tasks that turn students off, disable, or shut down thinking. (See, for example, Hull and Rose's sociocognitive approach to rethinking remediation.) As Brand puts it, compositionists need to understand more about the "why of cognition" within classroom contexts.

Several studies investigate the classroom ecologies of cross-national contexts as influences on the why of cognition. For example, Stevenson and his colleagues found remarkable similarities in the cognitive abilities of Chinese, Japanese, and American children. They have been investigating why American children do much more poorly than Asian children in achievement tests in mathematics and science. In a study of eighth graders from twenty countries, they report that Japanese children receive the highest scores in arithmetic, algebra, geometry, statistics, and measurement. The average scores for American children on these tests range from the eighth to the eighteenth position (154). To uncover clues regarding the possible bases of these striking cross-national differences in children's levels of achievement, Stevenson and his colleagues examined the educational practices surrounding the teaching of language arts and mathematics in the first and fifth grades in China, Japan, and the United States. They suggest that a possible basis for difference in academic achievement may be that American children spend too little time engaged in academic activities related to science. They conclude that for American students to improve their achievement in math and science, they may need to spend considerably more time on task as well as be exposed to more teacher-led instruction in the classroom. Their work is a striking example of how researchers can obtain a broad yet detailed understanding of an issue by focusing on both cognitive and contextual variables.

Purves provides additional cross-national data on cognitive and contextual factors of the classroom, finding significant differences between American and European high school students in regard to time spent in class on writing. Writing sessions in the United States, for example, typically last from thirty-seven to fifty-two minutes, while sessions in European countries may last as long as three hours. Such differences in time on task may seriously affect students' abilities to move from generating content to revising for structure, tone, and style ("Research" 106).

Time on task is only one issue in the constellation of cognitive and contextual dimensions of classroom writing experiences, however. Researchers are observing important differences between American students and their British counterparts regarding the kind of writing teachers emphasize in high school (Freedman and McLeod; Squire and Applebee). In most American writing classrooms, audience sensitivity is taught through engaging students in analytic and expository writing aimed at getting students to think for themselves and to take a position. In contrast, British teachers tend to ask students to write imaginative essays illustrating their personal experience. Such findings suggest that American students may be somewhat better prepared to write for an audience. But more to the point here is that the context of the classroom may engender particular kinds of thinking about writing, authorize certain rhetorical stances, and reward some authorial voices, while silencing or ignoring others.

In characterizing the context of the Japanese classroom at the elementary level, for example, Kitagawa and Kitagawa describe "sekatsu tsuzurikata," an expressive writing model in which students write narratives and poetry based on detailed observations and introspection about their personal lives. Much like American teachers who use journal writing to help students find a voice, Japanese teachers who use sekatsu tsuzurikata believe that the writing process and the writer's inner growth are the most important parts of the method. In terms of anticipating readers' needs, student writers are encouraged in the following manner:

> Readers can be rewarded by the writer's generosity with details and careful attention to organization. ("Write so that we can all understand how it was" is a commonly expressed injunction.) But the readership is not the sort of audience that requires impressing or entertaining. Its attention is assumed. It is an audience whose primary function is to break through the text barrier in order to appreciate the writer's perspective. That is, the reader is not to stop at appreciation of the product, but should strive to understand more about the writer's connection to experience, a perspective that happens to be accessible only through the text. (16)

Empathizing more with the writer's point of view than one's own (even if one does not comprehend the writer's message) appears to be the reader's responsibility in classrooms using this model. Such classroom-cultivated attitudes toward reader-writer relations are likely to have lasting influences on students' abilities to consider readers' needs (compare this pedagogy with the audience-centered method evaluated in Schriver, "Teaching Writers"). Classroom experiences may figure prominently in students' ability to transfer their rhetorical talents from one situation to the next, particularly from school writing to the kinds of writing required in the world of work.

Beyond the Classroom—Cognition and Context in Nonacademic Settings

Although the classroom context is an extremely important kind of context to study, it is only *one of the many kinds that need to be explored* to understand literate practices fully. Teachers need to understand reading and writing activities as they take place at home (Heath), on the job (Diehl and Mikulecky), in the community (Peck), in the professions (Barabas; Doheny-Farina; Spilka), or in other social institutions such as the church (Moss). Researchers who study writing beyond the classroom are concerned with how discourse is employed and valued in the range of out-of-school contexts. The goal is to understand the ways that nonacademic contexts vary in informing, reproducing, or constituting individual and collaborative literate practices.

In "Moving Beyond the Academic Community," for example, Anson and Forsberg describe the transitional stages of professional writers as they move from the college classroom to the world of work. They show that writers who leave the academy to take up professional internships experience frustration and confusion about what to do and how to adapt to the discourses of corporate environments. Writers in their study were unprepared for the culture of the corporation with its rituals for communication and with the territoriality that accompanies what gets what done, who gets to do it, and for what ends. They argue for more research about how writers adapt to new professional contexts, particularly with respect to issues of gender and class.

While some researchers concerned with connecting cognition and context focus on what happens to students after instruction in school, others look at what happens before students get there. For example, Moll has investigated Latino communities and the literacies that develop within the contexts of households, communities, or workplaces. He characterizes the social and cultural practices that can serve as resources for children's schooling, especially for the development of literacy. Some of these resources for Latino children, for instance, include knowledge about agriculture (e.g., crops, rodents, and insects like crickets or cockroaches), marketing (e.g., labor laws, building codes, federal regulations), construction (e.g., carpentry, bricklaying, plumbing), childcare (e.g., caring for siblings or adults), and religion (e.g., catechism, bible reading, or cosmic information). Through combining qualitative and quantitative research methods such as participant observation, questionnaires, checklists, audiotapes, videotapes, and archival materials, Moll identifies these resources and then develops practical ways to harness them for use in literacy instruction. Teachers and researchers, he argues, need to be concerned with studying multiple literacies and with helping students to take over and appropriate their learning about reading and writing.

The study of multiple literacies in nonacademic contexts is just beginning to produce interesting results. For example, when Spilka investigated the composing processes of engineers in a large electric company, she found that writing was strictly secondary to speaking. Writing served to record settlements already reached orally. An important value within the corporate environment was that writing should provide no surprises. Planning a written text was done by talking, negotiating, and gaining agreement. Similarly, Haas and Funk, who studied the literate practices of Japanese engineers, observed that the Japanese corporate culture is highly collaborative, with oral concensus-building strategies far outnumbering written ones.

A rarely studied dimension of the context of work is the role of composing constraints on cognition. Schumacher and his colleagues, for example, in studying journalists, report that the day-to-day writing environment for news story writers is one of tight linguistic, rhetorical, and time constraints. Stories are composed under the rules of the Associated Press and the United Press International style books which function as arbiters of form, style, and structure. Some genres—such as news stories, case reports, and obituaries—are so restrictive that most experienced journalists can produce them by going on "automatic pilot," bypassing extensive planning and goal setting (405). The work of Schumacher and his colleagues emphasizes the importance of studying the range of genres that are produced in particular nonacademic contexts, for they appear to have dramatic influences on writers' thinking, planning, and doing.

The rise of the process movement in the 1970s tended to deemphasize the importance of providing students with practice across written genres, but as Matsuhashi's work shows, genres such as exposition are cognitively more difficult than genres such as narration. Without sufficient practice in the more demanding genres, students may be unprepared to write them. In Japan, for example, expository writing is not taught at the high school or college level. There are no advanced writing courses at the high school level as well as no equivalent to freshman English or upper division writing courses in college. Although high school students receive intensive practice in writing Japanese and English sentences, they do not gain practice in whole-text planning and revising of expository text. Consequently, when Japanese students leave college, many still have difficulties with writing the sorts of prose required in the professional world, either in Japanese or in English (Kinosita). The lack of teaching expository writing and document design in the schools in Japan has had a pronounced impact on the ability of writers in corporate contexts to recognize and meet the needs of readers. The writing that is produced for consumers of Japanese high-tech products is not always intelligible, even for Japanese readers.

In my own ongoing research into the processes of writing within Japanese computer and consumer electronic companies, managers report that employees who write about technology have significant difficulties in taking the reader's point of view ("The Role of the Reader"). Japanese writers tend to produce narratives about how they engineered the product rather than expositions about how to use the product. But Japanese managers are not certain how to evaluate this problem because they believe that American and Japanese consumers may view the rights of readers somewhat differently. Americans expect consumer information about products such as VCRs to be easy to understand. When documents are badly written, Americans have a greater tendency to complain and take back products. For example, the American company, Coleco, suffered a major setback after introducing the Adam, a computer designed for children. When the product was released, parents who bought it found they could not decipher the instruction guides and were unable to help their children use the machine. So many parents returned the Adam computer that it had to be withdrawn from the market (see "Hundreds of Coleco's Adams Returned"). Japanese managers find this story somewhat surprising because it would not happen in their country. When Japanese consumers purchase a major product, the after-the-sale service from the store personnel is so extensive that reading the instruction manual is not necessary. After buying a VCR, for example, an employee from the store is assigned to come to the purchaser's home, set it up, and show the buyer how to use it. If the buyer is leaving for vacation and wants to tape a few shows while gone, the store employee will come to the purchaser's home and tape the shows. Clearly, the context makes a difference in how and if written texts get used. Composition teachers and researchers are just beginning to uncover the ways that context influences readers' thinking about written texts.

A Note on the Future

Relating cognition and context is proving to be a methodological challenge. Because such inquiry is so recent in composition studies, researchers are still searching for methods that are sensitive to their questions. Many feel that it is essential to combine quantitative and qualitative approaches to inquiry and that the distinctions between these approaches have been overemphasized. Unfortunately, the tendency of some individuals within the composition research community has been to focus on the distinctions between these approaches—waging epideictic war against one another rather than promoting scholarship in the area (Schriver, "Theory Building"). Although methodological differences are not trivial and must be articulated and understood, we must not ignore the benefits of blending qualitative and quantitative approaches (Patton). We need to embrace the growing number of studies that fuse "fieldwork and observation with quantitative analysis and statistical inference" (Purves, *Writing Across Languages* 15). My purpose here was to show that although many complicated methodological issues still remain, even a few examples of recent research illustrate that the study of cognition is not incompatible with the study of context.

Even so, researchers' focus on methods and technology for research has in some ways obscured the more substantive problems associated with attempts to blend cognitive and contextual research. In particular, discussions of the relations between the observer and the observed, the author and the text need to be considered more seriously. Researchers who work primarily in the cognitive tradition as well as those who work in the contextual tradition have become more rhetorically self-conscious, questioning their conception of the research act itself. Cognitive researchers have been worrying about their language for describing what they do. They seek to avoid language such as "objects of study" and "subjects." Contextual researchers are also more reflexive about the language of their writing. According to Geertz, there has been a shift from the "primitive, tribal, traditional, or folk" to the "emergent, modernizing, peripheral, or submerged," from the "colonial subject to the sovereign citizen" (131–32). In describing the dilemma of writing about ethnography, Geertz observes:

> The difficulty is . . . of constructing texts ostensibly scientific out of experiences broadly biographical. . . . The signature issue [the relation between the author and text], as the ethnographer confronts it, or as it confronts the ethnographer, demands both the Olympianism of the unauthorial physicist and the sovereign consciousness of the hyperauthorial novelist, while not in fact permitting either. The first brings the charges of insensitivity, of treating people as objects, of hearing the words but not the music, and of course, of ethnocentrism. The second brings charges of impressionism, of treating people as puppets, of hearing music that doesn't exist, and of course, ethnocentrism. Small wonder that most ethnographers tend to oscillate uncertainly between the two, sometimes in different books, more often in the same one. Finding somewhere to stand in a text that is supposed to be at one and the same time an intimate view and a cool assessment is almost as much of a challenge as gaining the view and making the assessment in the first place. (10)

As more researchers in composition undertake studies that explore cognitive and contextual relations, these problems of language, subject-object relations, author-text relations will need to be addressed in detail. Recent research is helping to make the study of "situated cognition" more than just a slogan, showing how literate practices are both socially constructed and individually situated. Moreover, the assumptions that underlie such work are evolving—refocusing our research questions, redirecting our attention to competing representations of problems, and reconceptualizing the ways in which we reflect on observation and experience. More sustained research into connecting cognition and context may lead to a critique of current theories of composing as well as to a critique of researchers' rhetoric of inquiry. Those who take up the study of cognition and context inherit the difficult but necessary project of reconsidering where composition has been and of charting a course for the future.

Works Cited

Ackerman, John M. "Reading, Writing, and Knowing: The Role of Disciplinary Knowledge in Comprehension and Composing." *Research in the Teaching of English* 25 (1991): 133–78.

Anson, Chris M., and L. Lee Forsberg. "Moving Beyond the Academic Community: Transitional Stages in Professional Writing." *Written Communication* 7 (1990): 200–31.

Barabas, Christine. *Technical Writing in a Corporate Culture: A Study of the Nature of Information.* Norwood, NJ: Ablex, 1990.

Bartholomae, David. "Inventing the University." *When a Writer Can't Write: Studies in Writer's Block and Other Composing-Process Problems.* Ed. Mike Rose. New York: Guilford, 1985. 134–65.

Bartlett, Frederick C. *Remembering: A Study in Experimental and Social Psychology.* London: Cambridge UP, 1932.

Beach, Richard, Judith Green, Michael Kamil, and Timothy Shanahan, eds. *Multidisciplinary Perspectives on Literacy Research.* Urbana, IL: National Conference on Research in English, in press.

Bereiter, Carl, and Marlene Scardamalia. "From Conversation to Composition: The Role of Instruction in a Developmental Process." *Advances in Instructional Psychology.* Ed. Robert Glaser. 3 vols. 1978–87. Hillsdale, NJ: Erlbaum, 1982. 2: 1–64.

———. *The Psychology of Written Composition.* Hillsdale, NJ: Erlbaum, 1987.

Bernhardt, Stephen A. "Seeing the Text." *College Composition and Communication* 37 (1986): 66–78.

Bloom, Lynne Z. "Anxious Writers in Context: Graduate School and Beyond." *When a Writer Can't Write: Studies in Writers' Block and*

Other Composing Problems. Ed. Mike Rose. New York: Guilford, 1985. 116–33.

Brand, Alice. "The Why of Cognition: Emotion and the Writing Process." *College Composition and Communication* 38 (1987): 436–43.

Brown, Ann L. "Knowing When, Where and How to Remember: A Problem of Metacognition." *Advances in Instructional Psychology*. Ed. Robert Glaser. 3 vols. 1978–87. Hillsdale, NJ: Erlbaum, 1978. 1: 77–165.

Brown, John Seely, Allan Collins, and Paul Duguid. "Situated Cognition and the Culture of Learning." *Educational Researcher* 18.1 (1989): 32–42.

Cazden, Courtney. *Classroom Discourse: The Language and Teaching of Learning*. Portsmouth, NH: Heinemann, 1988.

Diehl, William A., and Larry Mikulecky. "The Nature of Reading at Work." *Journal of Reading* 24 (1980): 221–28.

Doheny-Farina, Stephen. "Writing in an Emerging Organization: An Ethnographic Study." *Written Communication* 3 (1986): 158–85.

Durst, Russell. "The Mongoose and the Rat in Composition Research: Insights from the RTE Annotated Bibliography." *College Composition and Communication,* 41 (1990): 393–408.

Dyson, Anne Haas. "Transitions and Tensions: Interrelationships between Drawing, Talking, and Dictating of Young Children." *Research in the Teaching of English* 20 (1986): 379–409.

Emig, Janet. *The Composing Processes of Twelfth Graders*. Urbana, IL: NCTE, 1971.

Erickson, Frederick. "School Literacy, Reasoning, and Civility: An Anthropologist's Perspective." *Perspectives on Literacy*. Ed. Eugene R. Kintgen, Barry M. Kroll, and Mike Rose. Carbondale: Southern Illinois UP, 1988. 205–26.

Flower, Linda, Karen Schriver, Linda Carey, Christina Haas, and John R. Hayes. "Planning in Writing: The Cognition of a Constructive Process." *A Rhetoric of Doing*. Ed Stephen Witte, Neil Nakadate, and Roger Cherry. Carbondale: Southern Illinois UP, in press.

Flower, Linda, Victoria Stein, John Ackerman, Margaret Kantz, Kathleen McCormick, and Wayne Peck. *Reading-to-Write: Exploring a Cognitive and Social Process*. New York: Oxford UP, 1990.

Freedman, Sarah W., and Alex McLeod. "National Surveys of Successful Teachers of Writing and Their Students: The United Kingdom and the United States." *Technical Report 14*, U of California at Berkeley and Carnegie Mellon U: Center for the Study of Writing, 1987.

Geertz, Clifford. *Works and Lives—The Anthropologist as Author.* Stanford, CA: Stanford UP, 1988.

Green, Stuart. "Toward a Dialectical Theory of Composing." *Rhetoric Review* 9 (1990): 149–72.

Haas, Christine, and Jeffrey Funk. "Shared Information: Some Observations of Communication in Japanese Technical Settings." *Technical Communication* 36 (1989): 362–67.

Hayes, John R. "A Cognitive Perspective on Composition Research." *Multidisciplinary Perspectives on Literacy Research.* Ed. Richard Beach, Judith Green, Michael Kamil, and Timothy Shanahan. Urbana, IL: National Conference on Research in English, in press.

Hayes, John R., and Linda Flower. "Identifying the Organization of Writing Processes." *Cognitive Processes in Writing: An Interdisciplinary Approach.* Ed. Lee Gregg and Erwin R. Steinberg. Hillsdale, NJ: Erlbaum (1980): 3–30.

Heath, Shirley Brice. *Ways with Words: Language, Life, and Work in Communities and Classrooms.* Cambridge: Cambridge UP, 1983.

Hull, Glynda, and Mike Rose. "Rethinking Remediation: Toward a Social-Cognitive Understanding of Problematic Reading and Writing." *Written Communication* 6 (1989): 139–54.

"Hundreds of Coleco's Adam's Returned: Firm Blames Manuals." *Wall Street Journal* 30 Nov. 1983, eastern ed.: 4.

Kinosita, Koreo. "On the Need to Teach Expository and Technical Writing in Japan." Plenary Address. Conference on Document Design for Japanese Academics and Industrialists. Carnegie Mellon U, Pittsburgh, 17 May, 1986.

Kitagawa, Mary M., and Chisato Kitagawa. *Making Connections with Writing: An Expressive Writing Model in Japanese Schools.* Portsmouth, NH: Heinemann, 1987.

Kostelnick, Charles. "Process Paradigms in Design and Composition: Affinities and Directions." *College Composition and Communication* 40 (1989): 267–81.

Matsuhashi, Ann. "Pausing and Planning: The Tempo of Written Discourse Production." *Research in the Teaching of English* 15 (1981): 113–34.

Moll, Luis C. "Literacy Research in Community and Classrooms: A Socio-Cultural Approach." *Multidisciplinary Perspectives on Literacy Research.* Ed. Richard Beach, Judith Green, Michael Kamil, and Timothy Shanahan. Urbana, IL: National Conference on Research in English, in press.

Moll, Luis C., and J. Greenberg. "Creating Zones of Possibilities: Combining Social Contexts for Instruction." *Vygotsky and Education.* Ed. Luis C. Moll. New York: Cambridge UP, in press.

Moss, Beverly. "Being Literate in Three Black Churches." Responsibilities for Literacy: Communities, Schools, and Workplaces, MLA Convention. Pittsburgh, 15 Sept. 1990.

Nelson, Jennie. "This Was an Easy Assignment: Examining How Students Interpret Academic Writing Tasks." *Research in the Teaching of English* 24 (1990): 362–96.

Patton, Michael Quinn. *Qualitative Evaluation and Research Methods.* 2nd ed. Newbury Park, CA: Sage, 1990.

Peck, Wayne C. "Community Literacy: Composing for Action." Diss. Carnegie Mellon U, 1991.

Purves, Allen. C. "Research on Written Composition: A Response to Hillocks' Report." *Research in the Teaching of English* 22 (1988): 104–8.

———, ed. *Writing Across Languages and Cultures: Issues in Contrastive Rhetoric.* Newbury Park, CA: Sage, 1988.

Rogoff, Barbara, and Jean Lave. *Everyday Cognition: Its Development in Social Context.* Cambridge, MA: Harvard UP, 1984.

Rose, Mike. Preface. *When a Writer Can't Write: Studies in Writer's Block and Other Composing-Process Problems.* Ed. Mike Rose. New York: Guilford, 1985: ix–xiii.

Saxe, Geoffrey B. *Culture and Cognitive Development: Studies in Mathematical Understanding.* Hillsdale, NJ: Erlbaum, 1990.

Schriver, Karen A. "Document Design from 1980 to 1990: Challenges That Remain." *Technical Communication* 36 (1989): 316–31.

———. "The Role of the Reader in Writing and Document Design: Differences between Japan and the United States." Unpublished ms., 1991.

————. "Teaching Writers to Anticipate the Reader's Needs: Empirically-based Instruction." *DAI* 50/01A (1989): 8905259. Carnegie Mellon U.

————. "Theory Building in Rhetoric and Composition: The Role of Empirical Scholarship." *Rhetoric Review* 7 (1989): 272–88.

Schumacher, Gary, Byron Scott, George Klare, Frank Cronin, and Donald Lambert. "Cognitive Processes in Journalistic Genres." *Written Communication* 6 (1989): 390–407.

Scribner, Sylvia, and Michael Cole. *The Psychology of Literacy*. Cambridge: Harvard UP, 1981.

Shaughnessy, Mina. *Errors and Expectations*. New York: Oxford, 1977.

Siegler, Robert, and David Klahr. "When Do Children Learn? The Relationship Between Existing Knowledge and the Acquisition of New Knowledge." *Advances in Instructional Psychology*. Ed. Robert Glaser. 3 vols. 1978–87. Hillsdale, NJ: Erlbaum, 1982. 2: 121–211.

Spilka, Rachel. "Studying Writer-Reader Interactions in the Workplace." *The Technical Writing Teacher* 15 (1988): 208–21.

Spivey, Nancy Nelson. "Construing Constructivism: Reading Research in the United States." *Poetics* 16 (1987): 169–92.

Squire, James R., and Arthur R. Applebee. *A Study of the Teaching of English in Selected British Secondary Schools* (Contract No. IEC 3–7–001849). Washington, DC: U.S. Department of Health, Education, and Welfare, 1968.

Stein, Nancy, and Tom Trabasso. "What's in a Story: An Approach to Comprehension and Instruction." *Advances in Instructional Psychology*. Ed. Robert Glaser. 3 vols. 1978–87. Hillsdale, NJ: Erlbaum, 1982. 2: 213–67.

Stein, Victoria. "Elaboration: Using What You Know." *Technical Report 25*, U of California at Berkeley and Carnegie Mellon U: Center for the Study of Writing, 1989.

Stevenson, Harold W., et al. "Classroom Behavior and Achievement of Japanese, Chinese, and American Children." *Advances in Instructional Psychology*. Ed. Robert Glaser. 3 vols. 1978–87. Hillsdale, NJ: Erlbaum, 1987. 3: 153–91.

Witte, Stephen P. "Pre-Text and Composing." *College Composition and Communication* 38 (1987): 397–435.

Experimental and Descriptive Research Methods in Composition

DURING THE FIFTIES, sixties, and early seventies, most of the composition research conducted was empirical, generally featuring experimental method *A* versus method *B* designs. As Anne Herrington argues in her review of research during the first twenty years of *Research in the Teaching of English,* this prevailing preference for experimental research reflected the prescriptive rhetorical methods of teaching generalizations about appropriate rhetorical modes and grammar. The textbooks of the era were filled with model essays and endless grammar exercises that served to illustrate what was presumed to be "good writing." There was little attention given to the specific ongoing processes of writing within the particular, unique social contexts of the classroom. It was assumed that if teachers in all classes taught the "five paragraph theme" and grammar rules, that students would learn to write. Given the teacher-centered nature of this approach, researchers therefore were primarily interested in determining whether certain kinds of direct instruction worked.

Traditional method *A* versus method *B* experimental research reflected the limitations of this prevailing paradigm. It focused primarily on the value of general instructional methods, for example, teaching transformational versus traditional grammar or teaching the topic sentence versus no instruction. Researchers were particularly concerned about controlling for contaminating variables that would prevent them from generalizing from their results to instruction in general. Such research and attempts to generalize ignored the particulars of writing and the diversity of writers, as well as the fact that students have unique abilities, perceptions, attitudes, and needs in various classroom situations.

More recently, as composition theory has focused more on particular writing contexts and on differences among writers, methods of experimental and descriptive research have changed. As they move toward social-constructionist perspectives of composing, many empirical researchers have abandoned traditional positivist and realist assumptions to embrace these social conceptions of writing. The question that remains is whether the methodological procedures of empirical research can remain consistent with social-constructionist assumptions about writing. Given this question, it is important, as Kirsch (this volume) argues, to examine the assumptions underlying empirical research methods.

For example, many empirical researchers no longer adopt the traditional realist assumption that it is possible to explain phenomenon in terms of direct cause and effect relationships in which one factor (instruction in sentence combining) may cause a single effect (improved writing quality). More current realists assume that events and behaviors are shaped by many different phenomena—individual abilities, histories, attitudes, intentions, and various aspects of the context—rendering it difficult, if not impossible, to isolate any one cause of phenomenon (Gere). Thus, experimental researchers employ multivariate designs in order to examine the effects of a range of different variables on writing. And, they are increasingly concerned with their study's ecological validity—whether its design accounts for or captures writing in authentic contexts.

At the same time, empirical methodological approaches rest on certain assumptions that differ from those held by other approaches such as ethnographical, rhetorical, or poststructuralist. Their procedures typically assume that one needs to understand writing according to collective, aggregate patterns both within and across writers' composing. For example, in finding that, as a group, beginning writers' revising processes consist primarily of minor wording changes, researchers assume that writers think according to a defined collective pattern or norm.

In discussing empirical experimental and descriptive research, I am discussing research that is "data-based" (Flower), that involves some systematic observation and analysis of composing. My belief in the value of using "empirical" in this sense to mean systematic observation and analysis does not necessarily mean that I subscribe either to empiricism, which is often used to mean that research should be quantitative, or to positivism or behaviorism, which posit, among other things, that unless a phenomenon can be measured, it is not worth studying. While empirical research typically involves some sort of quantitative analysis, it may also include qualitative analysis. It is also important at the outset to distinguish between parametric and nonparametric empirical research. Parametric research employs statistical analyses to generalize from samples to larger populations. In contrast, nonparametric research examines groups of writers as they are, without attempting to generalize to larger populations.

Empirical research differs from ethnographic research in that it often assigns tasks or creates rhetorical situations rather than studying writing as it occurs as part of natural events shaped by social or cultural meanings, meanings that generally cannot be captured by empirical analysis. For example, based on two years of observation at a suburban Detroit high school, Pamela Eckert learned that the meaning of students' experiences were shaped by two opposing social categories—"jocks" and "burnouts." The jocks, largely middle-class "good students," valued behaviors, dress, and school-sponsored activities that the burnouts, largely working-class, antischool, marginal students, opposed and resisted. Eckert could only have understood the influence of these social categories by careful observation of high school students within the culture of this high school.

At the same time, as empirical research in composition has moved away from the artificial rhetorical contexts of the laboratory or contrived experiment in order to study writing within relatively authentic settings, the distinction between descriptive empirical research and ethnographic research is blurring. In observing events and behaviors, some ethnographic researchers may include some systematic analysis of a particular phenomenon. As a small part of her study, Eckert used empirical analysis to compare the syntactic patterns of the speech of jocks and burnouts.

The value of empirical experimental research. Educators are continually confronted with the question of whether what they do makes a difference. They want to know whether peer conferencing, collaborative writing, teacher modeling, or reader-based feedback serve to improve writing ability. In order to determine the effects of certain instructional methods, researchers may conduct studies utilizing experimental treatments. These studies examine the effects of certain instructional methods on writing ability or quality to prove or disprove a hypothesis that there will be or will not be (a negative or null hypothesis) a difference between the groups receiving a treatment versus a group not receiving a treatment.

Consistent with social-constructionist perspectives, experimental research can be used to test the validity of generalizations about social aspects of writing. Take, for example, the use of electronic mail and computer bulletin boards to foster teacher-student and student-student social exchanges. In order to determine whether such computer networking resulted in more social interaction than was the case with face-to-face classroom conferencing or written feedback, Hartman et al., compared the effects of instruction relying on electronic mail with instruction using classroom-based methods. They found that students in the electronically based classroom interacted significantly more with their teachers and with each other than did students in the regular classes. Moreover, by using a multivariate design, the researchers were able to determine that the teachers communicated electronically more often with less able students than with able students. Generalizations such as these serve a useful purpose in justifying approaches that are consistent with current pedagogical theory.

At the same time, such generalizations need to be qualified according to the limitations of the research methods employed, a point I will return to later in this chapter.

Empirical research is also useful because it can be replicated with some degree of consistency. By replicating studies of the effects of grammar instruction on writing ability and generating a consistent pattern of results, researchers may develop some degree of confidence in arguing that, for example, grammar instruction has little effect on improving writing quality. The fact that researchers can achieve the same results with different populations further strengthens the validity of those results.

Or, researchers may use meta-analysis to combine the results of different studies (Hillocks). However, because there is no widely agreed-upon taxonomy regarding different writing types, it is often difficult to combine studies (Applebee, "Musings"). While this points to the need for clearly defined or even operational definitions to develop knowledge in the field (Stotsky), theorists often object to reducing the complexity of terminology.

The value of descriptive empirical research. Descriptive empirical research differs from experimental research in that it focuses on phenomena without attempting to manipulate the effects of variables. Because reports of such research are often less technical than reports of much experimental research, they are accessible to a wider range of educators than are most experimental research reports. In reading Donald Graves's or Anne Dyson's highly concrete, often data-based descriptions of the attempts of young children to make meaning through their writing, a reader gains insights into these processes. The very activity of reading the descriptive analyses in these reports may itself serve to foster change in instruction.

Teachers may also have less difficulty conducting descriptive research than experimental research, employing techniques to address practitioners' concerns (see Goswami and Stillman; Cochran-Smith and Lytle; Myers; Olson; Ray (this volume) for a discussion of teacher research). For example, one of my seventh grade teachers wanted to examine the value of teacher-student dialogue journals in her classroom. Based on reading other research on dialogue journal writing (Staton, et al.; Peyton and Seyoum), she developed a set of questions: To what degree did the students become involved in keeping the dialogue journals? To what degree did the students elaborate on their entries? What kinds of teacher feedback (evaluative-judgmental versus dialogic self-disclosure) were most likely to engage students? What topics were the students most likely to write about? She then used these questions to devise some interview questions, attitude scales, and categories for analyzing the journal exchanges. From her analysis of the results, she learned that her use of more dialogic, self-disclosure responses resulted in more student elaboration. Thus, by conducting this study she learned that certain kinds of responses are more useful than other kinds.

Procedures Involved in Conducting Empirical Research

In this section, I will discuss some of the procedures typically employed by experimental and descriptive research, along with the limitations and assumptions associated with these procedures (see Daly and Hexamer; Hilgers; Lauer and Asher; Kamil, Langer, and Shanahan).

Formulating research questions. Essential to the success of conducting empirical research is the ability to formulate clear, concise research questions. In order to formulate questions in a manner that guides the development of a design, researchers need to specify the variables and the methods to be included in the study. For example, the question, How do students revise? while not unimportant, does not provide much direction in terms of setting up a study. In contrast, the more specific question, What is the effect of a teacher's between-draft feedback on the number and level of changes in drafts as determined by judges' ratings?

serves to imply a research design. The question names the variables—the independent variable of a teacher's between-draft feedback and the dependent variables of number and level of changes in drafts—as well as telling how the dependent variables would be measured (as determined by judges' ratings). The question also implies a particular type of design. If the questions imply the need to examine the influence or effects of instruction or a factor such as grade or age level on writing quality, then a researcher would opt for an experimental design. On the other hand, if the questions involve examining characteristics of or relationships between variables, then a researcher would opt for a more descriptive design. In order to determine the effects of teacher feedback on students' revisions, a researcher may select an experimental design with two groups of students—a group that did receive versus a group that did not receive teacher feedback. In contrast, in order to examine the relationships between types of teacher feedback (personal versus impersonal) and level of revision (substantive versus surface-level), a researcher may select a descriptive design.

Researchers may derive questions from their own intuitive perceptions about writing. In reading our students' dialogue journals from a number of different classes, Chris Anson and I noted that the more students developed their social relationships through inviting their partners' responses, sharing experiences, and disclosing themselves, the more they encouraged each other to reflect on the course material. In noting this, we wondered if our own intuitions were valid. That is, while we might announce to our colleagues that social engagement seems to be related to reflective thinking, we wanted to test out empirically our intuitive perceptions, particularly because we suspected that students' journal writing is influenced by a lot of other factors—for example, their purpose, attitude, and perception of audience or context. If students are using the journals to rehearse material in preparation for an objective test, they may not do much reflecting, regardless of social engagement with their partners.

Researchers also use reviews of related research to define questions not previously addressed in that research. Researchers identify assumptions that need to be further examined or challenged. Or, in some cases, researchers verify their initial hunches. Once Anson and I developed an interest in dialogue journals, we turned to the research to find much of the pedagogical justification for dialogue journals at the college level assumes that a high degree of knowledge exploration may be fostered by a high degree of social or interpersonal involvement (Fulwiler; Yinger and Clark). However, analysis of teacher-student dialogue journal exchanges at the elementary school level (Peyton and Seyoum; Staton, et al.) and college level (Roderick and Berman; Schatzberg-Smith) indicates that students vary considerably in the degree to which they use journals to think reflectively—the extent to which they go beyond simply rehearsing course content to examine critically or to elaborate on connections between the course content and their own lives or prior knowledge. And they vary in their willingness to enter into and create a social relationship with their partners through acts of sharing experiences, self-disclosure, questioning, and inviting or reacting to partners' responses (Peyton and Seyoum; Staton et al.). Reviewing this research served to raise the question of whether the level of interpersonal exchange is positively related to the level of reflective thinking. It may be the case that partners are highly involved interpersonally but may simply be rehearsing course content.

Reviewing the related research may also suggest other contingency or subject variables that may influence the primary question. For example, students' attitudes toward the journal may be related to their degree of reflective thinking. Or, such variables as differences in age, sex, ability, previous writing experience, attitudes, interest, knowledge, apprehension, genre familiarity, cognitive complexity, and social status may influence not only their reflective thinking but also their relationship with their partners. For example, the more positive students' attitudes towards their journal writing, the more likely they were to use the journal to explore knowledge (Beach and Christensen). Given the skepticism about realist assumptions of direct cause and effect relationships between independent and dependent variables, researchers opt for multivariate designs that incorporate the influences of these subject variables.

Once researchers have identified relevant variables, they may classify those variables according to type. In conducting an experiment, independent variables consist of an instructional method, subject characteristics, or the mode or type of writing that a researcher applies to the dependent or outcome variables—for example, writing quality or amount of revision. In posing a question regarding the effects of variable A on variable $B,$ a researcher knows that the variable A is the independent variable and the variable B is the dependent variable. In conducting a descriptive study, a researcher, having identified the different variables, may want to define the nature of relationships between these variables. For example, in the dialogue-journal study, we were not considering the effects of using the dialogue-journal writing on any outcome variables. Rather, we were interested in simply examining the relationship between the level of partners' interpersonal involvement and the level of reflective thinking.

Note that we use the word level to imply the type of data analysis that will be used. In this case, level implies category or nominal data, low (1) versus high (2). Nominal numbers such as 1 or 2 simply represent types of categories or levels. In contrast, had we used the word degree, we may have implied an interval or ordinal data type, that is, an actual range of scores or real numbers based on a scale or test.

Each of these different types of data requires a different type of test to determine if relationships or group differences are statistically significant. By defining variables according to the type of data analysis in the questions, researchers can then select the appropriate type of statistical test. If they are using category or nominal data resulting in frequencies or percentages, they would use chi-square analyses to determine relationships between variables. If they are using interval or ordinal data to determine relationships between or among variables, they would use correlations or multiple regression. If they are using interval data to compare differences between groups, they would use a t-test or an analysis of variance. In our own study, because we were using only category data to examine the relationship between level of interpersonal involvement (low versus high) and level of reflective thinking (low versus high), we employed chi-square analyses.

None of this should imply that all variables in a study need to be quantifiable. Take, for example, students' sense of purpose for writing a dialogue journal, something we believed may influence their propensity to reflect. It would be difficult if not impossible to quantify our intuited sense of the students' unique purposes for journal entry. Rather than try to quantify the nature or types of purposes, we decided to simply note instances of statements of purpose in the entries. We then compared the statements of purpose in entries categorized according to low level versus high level of social involvement. By citing verbatim examples of statements of purpose, we could then discuss how purposes varied according to level of social involvement, even though we didn't conduct the statistical analysis that allowed us to generalize to a larger population.

Review of related research. In order to build a case for the validity and value of their methods, researchers draw on what could be defined as a rhetorical tradition associated with empirical research reports (Hayes). Within that rhetorical tradition, researchers conventionally build a case for the significance of their own study—whether or not the phenomenon is really worth studying. The significance of a study is often established in terms of the track record of previous research. Moreover, in building the case for a study, researchers argue that their questions and procedures address or rectify the limitations of previous research.

Sample size and description of subjects. In selecting subjects for a study, researchers need to be concerned with selecting an appropriate sample size (see Kraemer and Thiemann). In order to obtain statistically significant results, the number of subjects in each group needs to be large enough so that a statistical comparison of the range of scores in each group is possible (Lauer and Asher). For example, in comparing a treatment group and a control group, researchers should include at least twenty-five subjects in each group. In order to examine the interaction effects of a number of different independent variables, researchers may also employ a random stratified sample by randomly selecting a certain number of subjects from the population being studied to assign to each cell—defined as the groups involved with the independent variables. For example, in using a "2 x 2" design to examine the effects of an instructional treatment (experimental group versus control group), and mode of writing (personal versus impersonal), researchers may randomly select and assign students to each of the four cells in this design: an experimental/personal, an experimental/impersonal, a control/personal, and a control/impersonal group.

It is also important that researchers clearly and concisely describe the characteristics of their subjects. Providing information about the size of the groups, age or grade level, socioeconomic status, number of males and females, as well as the nature of the subjects' school, business, or institutional affiliations provides readers with information to make their own interpretations of the results or to replicate the study.

In order to eliminate the potential effects of differences in such characteristics as ability, background, or attitudes on posttest performance, researchers randomly assign subjects to treatment and control groups. In a study of the effects of between-draft teacher feedback, I randomly assigned high school students to one of three groups: those who received between-draft teacher feedback and completed a self-assessment form; those who completed only a self-assessment form; and those in a control group who did nothing between drafts.

Designing research studies. Researchers need to select a research design that best addresses the kinds of questions they are asking. Researchers may use more than one treatment group in order to compare the effects of different types of instruction. For example, James Marshall was interested in the effects of writing extended essays versus short answer questions on high school students' interpretations of literature. In this study, students in the three treatment groups wrote either extended analytic essays, extended personal essays, or short answers, while students in the treatment group wrote nothing. By using three instructional groups and a control group, Marshall was able to determine that both forms of extended writing resulted in higher levels of interpretation than did either the short answers or no writing. And he was able to determine that the no-writing control group did better than the short-answer group, suggesting that the short-answer experience may have been more detrimental than not writing anything.

In an experimental design, a researcher attempts to control for or eliminate the effects of any other variables on a certain phenomenon. Subjects in both the experimental and control groups should have the same instructors and the same materials and spend the same amount of time during the instructional period (see Pressley, El-Dinary, and Brown for a discussion of problems in experimental designs).

Quasi experiments differ from true experiments in that quasi-experimental designs employ intact groups rather than randomly assigned groups. Because it is often difficult for researchers to randomly assign subjects or administer different treatments within intact classes, they need to employ intact classes as treatment and control groups. The problem with using intact groups is that the differences within the groups themselves may affect the outcome of the experiment. Researchers therefore employ a pretest of writing quality (similar to the posttest) to determine the degree to which the groups are initially equivalent. (However, even if there are no significant differences between initial pretest mean scores, that does not necessarily eliminate all potential between-group differences that are eliminated through randomization.) If the groups are not equivalent, researchers could randomly eliminate high- or low-scoring students from a group. However, such elimination often creates another problem with intact groups—a regression towards the mean that results in a smaller range of scores.

In a study of the effects of instruction involving the use of a self-assessment form, Sara Eaton and I used four intact freshmen composition classes as groups. Two of the classes served as experimental groups and two as control groups; each of two teachers taught an experimental group and a control group. In order to determine if the groups were initially similar in their ability to assess themselves, we compared the groups' performance on the self-assessment forms used with a pretest essay.

In analyzing mean posttest rating scores in a pre- and posttest design, researchers should use analysis of variance (ANOVA) with repeated measures. (ANOVAs with repeated measures result in larger F-ratio scores, which means that the differences between means are more likely to be significant than the differences between means obtained using a regular ANOVA). Or researchers can use an analysis of covariance, a measure that takes into account the effect of the pretest score on the posttest score.

Researchers may also want to examine the interaction between the treatment and students' characteristics such as reading ability, attitudes towards writing, learning style, and writing apprehension. In this way, a researcher may determine how an instructional treatment may interact with a certain characteristic. It may be that students with certain characteristics or abilities may benefit more from a particular type of instruction than other students would. In an experiment designed to determine the influence of reading and writing instruction regarding the organizational structure of essays, Barbara Taylor and I found that the instruction benefited the less able readers more than the better readers. Based on a measure of reading ability, we selected students who were "better" readers, and, using what is called a 2 x 2 design, we examined the main effects for reading (high versus low readers) and treatment (experimental versus control), as well as the interaction effects (reading level by treatment) on the outcome measures. The fact that no interaction effect occurs is itself an important finding in that it means the instruction works equally well for the different subject variable levels in a study. (In studying the effects of subject variables, researchers often divide the overall group into low, middle, and high groups in order to compare the low and high groups as extremes without the middle group.)

One limitation of experimental research is that subject variables such as sex, grade level, reading ability, and apprehension serve only as gross, collective measures of individual differences. For example, comparing the writing of males and females may provide little understanding of the range of gender attitudes within each of these groups (Keroes). In order to determine the influence of individual perceptions, researchers may also want to conduct follow-up interviews that capture subjects' unique perceptions of their writing experience. For example, rather than simply comparing the writing of males and females, researchers could interview male and female subjects in order to determine differences in their cultural attitudes. It may be the case that some males and females adopt a more distanced, absolutist stance associated with a "masculine" cultural perspective, as distinct from a more engaged, contextually sensitive stance associated with a "feminine" cultural perspective (Flynn).

And outcome measures need to be reliable; that is, they must measure performance in the same consistent manner. Reliability is determined by interjudge agreement; if the agreement is too low (below .70), then the measures are too insensitive to measure experimental effects. The more training judges receive, the higher their agreement; researchers therefore need to provide ample training for their judges. In using quality ratings, three or more judges should be used, with reliability determined by Cronbach Alpha using the SPSS (Statistical Package for the Social Sciences) computer programs.

Defining relationships. Using correlations or regression analysis and a relatively large number of writers, empirical researchers may determine which of several factors is the most related to or best predicts writing quality. For example, in an analysis of a range of reading and writing experiences in fifty-seven eighth grade classrooms, Martin Nystrand ("Making It Hard") determined that writing more than a page was the best predictor of the ability to interpret texts. Consistent with other experimental research (Langer and Applebee; Marshall), he found that answering short-answer questions on worksheets or quizzes was negatively related to interpretative ability. In my own research, I found that the ability to elaborate in writing on related experiences or intertextual links correlates positively with the ability to interpret literary texts. While correlational research should not be perceived as establishing cause and effect relationships, it does provide teachers with some indication of the value of particular teaching activities.

Descriptive research studies may also define relationships by comparing groups of writers representing two divergent orientations. For example, I ("Responding") noticed that my students often differed considerably in their use of the journal. Some used their journals to explore ideas and draw connections between their reading and experiences. Others used the journals primarily to summarize or rehearse course readings. Because I suspected that these differences represented differences in learning styles, I gave my students the Schmeck Inventory of Learning Processes. Two of the scales on that inventory distinguish between students' propensity to abstract and to draw connections. I then selected individual students representing the extremes on these scales and interviewed them about their journal writing and their responses to my comments to their journals. By making this comparison, I learned that, given differences in their preferred learning orientation, students use their journals in quite different ways, ways I need to take into account in responding to their journals.

Piloting procedures. In devising an experiment, it is important to conduct pilot studies prior to the actual study. In their comparison of test makers' and test takers' intentions for either devising or taking a writing assessment test, Ruth and Murphy found that the test takers intuited a totally different set of intentions from those of the test makers. By testing the directions for an assignment or task on a comparable group of writers, a researcher can determine potential problems or misunderstandings prior to the actual study. For example, differences in writers' knowledge about an assignment topic or interest in the topic may influence their performance (Hilgers; Hoetker and Brossell). In some cases, the difference in one word in a set of directions can influence students' performance. In one study, Newell, Suszynski, and Wingart compared the effects of a personal and an impersonal version of an assignment on high school students' literary interpretation. The more personal version, which varied primarily in terms of addressing the students as "you," resulted in significantly higher levels of interpretation than the impersonal version.

Limitations of Experimental Designs

There are a number of limitations associated with experimental designs. They often assume that instruction consists of an input-output process, an assumption that masks the complexities and difficulties inherent in writing instruction (see Taylor for a discussion of "complexity theory"). Educators are more likely to implement new programs according to a model—for example, a writing process approach, whole-language learning, or a "Nancie Atwell" program—rather than in terms of a specific instructional method such as peer conferencing, cooperative learning, or computer-assisted instruction (Slavin) that might serve as a treatment factor. (At the same time, as Applebee found in studying teacher implementation of "writing process" models, these models may be so ill-defined that students still may not demonstrate improvement in writing.) Moreover, conceiving of instruction in terms of treatments tends to reify a more teacher-centered conception of the classroom. Educators also often assume that experimental research will provide them with definitive answers as to what works. However, questions about what works should often be answered from a theoretical perspective. As Hartwell argues, the question of the effects of grammar instruction on writing quality should be addressed primarily as a theoretical question regarding the validity of different theories of grammar rather than as an empirical question. If researchers become enraptured with the technical aspects of a design, they may ignore the theoretical assumptions underlying a study. For example, in studying the effects of word processing on revising, researchers may assign pre- or posttest writing tasks in which writers have little or no interest, failing to recognize that interest in the topic, in addition to the facility to revise provided by the word processing, may influence propensity to revise. Or, researchers may fail to examine the assumptions underlying their questions. Much research indicating that sentence combining had little effect on writing quality was based on questionable assumptions about the relationships between syntax and writing quality. Had the researchers more carefully examined these theoretical assumptions, they might have employed different outcome measures, for example, students' attitudes towards revision.

In conducting experiments, researchers must also be concerned about what is called a maturation effect. That is, if the experiment is conducted over a long period of time, students may simply improve due to their own growth or maturation, regardless of the instruction they receive. Or students may begin to drop out of the study, particularly less able students who may lose interest in participating. As a result, the final experimental and control groups may bear little resemblance to the initial makeup of the groups. Given these concerns, researchers may limit their study to a short period of time—often a matter of days. These "one-shot" studies often fail to recognize that learning composing strategies requires extensive practice over a relatively long period of time (Purves). And experiments that focus on the effects of a single strategy (for example, the use of mapping, guided imagery writing, or tagmemic heuristics) assume that when they write, writers may simply employ only one strategy rather than a range of different strategies (Pressley, El-Dinary, and Brown).

Experimental researchers also assume that by randomly selecting samples of writers, texts, or text aspects, they can use statistical analysis to test generalizations that can apply to entire populations. For example, using an analysis of variance, a researcher may claim that a certain instructional treatment employed with a specific group had a significant effect on students' writing with a probability level of p less than .01. This means that, given the sample size and the difference between the experimental and control group means, there is a probability of one in a hundred that this result would not occur for the larger population from which the sample was drawn. Researchers argue that the probability of correctly accepting or rejecting a hypothesis depends on an experiment's "power" which, in turn, depends on the sample size, the variance of scores, and the internal validity of the design (Hilgers; Daly and Hexamer). For example, a treatment may have had an effect on writing quality, but if an experiment had low power, that effect may not have been detected. Thus, in order to achieve generalizability, a relatively large number of writers need to be studied and various aspects of the context need to be controlled. This means that researchers often cannot study the complexities of composing by descriptive or case-study research with smaller numbers of writers. And attempts to control the rhetorical context—the nature of the task, time allotted, topic, and audience assignment—ironically serve to undermine the validity of understanding writing as a specific "literacy event" (Bloome and Bailey; Nystrand, "Sharing"). As Robert de Beaugrande argues, in controlling for factors that influence writing,

"These same controls can also make the context dissimilar to ordinary language activity. Psychology hopes to attenuate the problem of context by multiplying the number of persons and experimental events and thereby restricting the relative weight of situation-specific factors. But it is still uncertain why a cross-section of artificial contexts should necessarily distill out the same general factors as a cross-section of natural contexts" (4).

Moreover, in order to determine treatment effects on mean scores, researchers often use writing tasks and quality ratings that may not be valid or sensitive outcome measures (Charney). Holistic ratings are assigned according to performance within a particular group—so that there must be a range of scores. What this means is, based on the perceived group norms, good writers do well and poor writers do poorly, often regardless of the instruction they received. As a result, studies determining the effects of short-term instruction on quality often find that the instruction had no effect, when, in fact, there might have been some effect for less able writers who, relative to group norms, still performed poorly.

All of this points to the problem of relying solely on a single measure such as writing quality rather than on a range of different measures. In studying the writing of freshman composition students to determine those characteristics that distinguished high- versus low-quality writing, Cooper et al. analyzed a range of features, including specific linguistic features, cohesion ties, thinking strategies, and ideological assumptions. They found that the differences in quality were more pronounced for the higher-level aspects of thinking and valuing than for the more specific linguistics features. By comparing writers' performance across a range of features, a researcher can determine that these features may vary according to differences in such factors as instruction, attitude, or background knowledge.

Again however, as Cooper et al. acknowledge, the basic comparison between high- and low-quality writers was based on an analysis of one paper for the same one-shot assessment task. All of this points to a limitation of much empirical research: in its attempt to define similar, collective phenomena, it is often insensitive to the fact that writers vary across different tasks or contexts. Given differences in such factors as their prior knowledge, interest, experience, and social and cultural background, they may perform well with certain kinds of writing, but less well with others. In conducting descriptive studies, researchers could use a portfolio approach to gathering different kinds of writing composed in relatively authentic contexts (Tierney, Carter, and Desai). Rather than focusing on how writers gravitate to the norm, researchers could then determine the ways in which writers deviate from norms. They could also determine how individual writers vary across different types of writing.

Another alternative to analyzing only writing quality involves focusing on discourse practices (Cooper) or thinking processes at work within and across different types of writing and the activities associated with that writing. For example, Lee Odell developed a set of categories for analyzing secondary students' journal writing, drafting, small-group discussions, peer-conferences, and role play: (1) selecting and encoding, (2) creating/acknowledging dissonance, (3) drawing on prior knowledge, (4) seeing relationships, (5) considering alternatives, and (6) using metacognition. In addition to analyzing types of thinking, researchers can develop categories for analyzing the topics, themes, or kinds of knowledge writers typically include in their writing. For example, in order to determine differences between high school and college students' inferences in their writing about a short story, judges clustered students' responses according to similarity of content (Beach and Wendler). By defining common clusters, the judges then named these categories according to a composite title. Thus, in inferring characters' goals, some students inferred short-term goals, while others inferred long-range goals. In a study comparing autobiographical essays of seventh graders, college freshmen, and teachers, I ("Differences") analyzed the extent to which writers referred to certain identity themes consistent with their level of social development.

One limitation of content analysis categories is that in order to achieve agreement with other judges, a judge must consider only the surface meaning. As soon as judges attempt to intuit underlying intentions or motives, their agreement goes down. For example, in a transcript of a peer conference, one student may state, "Your opening paragraph contains a lot of information." In order to categorize that statement as either descriptive or judgmental, a judge needs to intuit the student's underlying intention. Did the student intend the statement to be taken as descriptive or judgmental? In order to achieve reliability, content analysis therefore often fails to capture the meaning of language as constituted by the motives or intentions inherent in any social context (see Grant-Davie, this volume, for further discussion of coding categories).

In order to gain further insight into composing processes, researchers can also ask writers to describe their conception of writing in general, for example, using a process log (Faigley, Cherry, Jolliffe, and Skinner), or metaphors (Tomlinson), or their perceptions of their role, attitude, audience, and situation in a particular rhetorical context. Because the meaning of particular literacy events are constituted by the particulars of their own history, intertextual relationships, consequences, and roles (Bloome and Bailey) unique to that particular event (Nystrand, "Sharing"), researchers need to reconstruct the meanings shaping that event. In order to help writers reconstruct these particulars, researchers can point to specific parts of the writing or revisions and ask the writer to discuss how their perceptions of the context shaped those parts or revisions (Odell and Goswami). They can also use individual writers to construct case-study portraits representing divergent orientations or patterns in the data.

Presenting and interpreting results. Researchers need to clearly and concisely present their results, employing tables, figures, and charts whenever possible. And researchers need to report honestly the fact that they found negative results, which, in many cases, is just as significant as achieving positive results.

In explaining and interpreting results, researchers need to link their results back to their review of related research in order to note ways in which the results serve to confirm or contradict previous findings. And researchers need to avoid the temptation to manipulate and interpret the data in order to find what they were looking for. Rather than simply attempting to confirm or deny hypotheses, researchers need to be willing to interpret data from a number of different, even contradictory, theoretical and disciplinary perspectives. The fact that Chris Anson and I found a significant relationship between the level of reflective thinking and the level of interpersonal involvement in dialogue journals could be interpreted from a range of different perspectives, perspectives that might highlight particular slices of the data. While an applied linguist might examine instances of the conventional rules established that serve to promote reflective thinking, a sociologist might focus on the students' perceptions of their institutional roles that serve to foster or limit their involvement with other students in a class.

Researchers also need to discuss the limitations of the study, noting problems in the design and procedures that could be rectified in future research. In stating implications for further research, researchers need to entertain the possibilities of a range of different types of research that could further illuminate the phenomenon under study. As Kirsch argues, this may include ethnographic or case-study approaches that yield the kinds of understanding not afforded by experimental procedures. And, while it is often a *pro forma* add-on at the end of a research report, researchers should carefully define implications for instruction that are consistent with the study results.

In summary, empirical experimental and descriptive research can yield important insights into the composing process. Rather than perceiving the validity of research methods as an either-or debate between advocates of empirical methods and nonempirical methods, researchers have recently began to combine these methods, for example, employing both experimental designs and case studies (Herrington). At the same time, researchers need to continually question the underlying assumptions guiding their research, assumptions shaping their perceptions of the writer's essential goal of formulating meaning through discourse. By adopting a self-reflexive mode and making these assumptions explicit, researchers can move away from letting a rigid adherence to technical procedures govern their understanding of writing.

Works Cited

Anson, Chris, and Richard Beach. *Journal Writing in the Classroom.* Manuscript in preparation.

Applebee, Arthur. *Contexts for Learning to Write.* Norwood, NJ: Ablex, 1985.

———. "Musings." *Research in the Teaching of English* 22 (1988): 6–8.

Beach, Richard. "The Creative Development of Meaning: Using Autobiographical Experience to Interpret Literature." *Beyond Communication.* Ed. Stan Straw and Deanne Bogdan. Portsmouth, NH: Boynton/Cook, 1990.

———. "Differences in Autobiographical Narratives of English Teachers, College Freshmen, and Seventh Graders. " *College Composition and Communication* 38 (1987): 56–69.

———. "The Effects of Between-Draft Teacher Evaluation versus Student Self-Evaluation on High School Students' Revising of Rough Drafts. *Research in the Teaching of English* 13 (1979): 111–19.

———. "Responding to Journal Writing." *Encountering Students' Texts.* Ed. Susan Sterr and Bruce Lawson. Urbana, IL: NCTE, 1990. 183–98.

Beach, Richard, Deborah Appleman, and Sharon Dorsey. "Students' Use of Intertextual Links to Understand a Story." *Developing Discourse Practices in Adolescence and Adulthood.* Ed. Richard Beach and Susan Hynds. Norwood, NJ: Ablex, 1990. 224–45.

Beach, Richard, and Mark Christensen. *Discourse Conventions in Academic Response Journals.* ERIC, 1989. ED 304 691.

Beach, Richard, and Sara Eaton. "Factors Influencing Self-assessing and Revising of College Freshmen. *New Directions in Composition Research*. Ed. Richard Beach and Lillian Bridwell. New York: Guilford, 1984. 149–70.

Beach, Richard, and Linda Wendler. "Developmental Differences in Responding to a Short Story." *Research in the Teaching of English* 21 (1987): 286–98.

Bloome, David, and Francis Bailey. "From Linguistics and Education: A Direction for the Study of Language and Literacy." *Multidisciplinary Perspectives on Literacy Research*. Ed. Richard Beach, Judith Green, Michael Kamil, and Timothy Shanahan. Urbana, IL: National Conference on Research in English, in press.

Charney, Davida. "The Validity of Using Holistic Scoring to Evaluate Writing: A Critical Overview." *Research in the Teaching of English* 18 (1984): 65–81.

Cochran-Smith, Marilyn, and Susan Lytle. "Research on Teaching and Teacher Research: The Issues That Divide." *Educational Researcher* 19 (1990): 2–11.

Cooper, Charles, et al. "Studying the Writing Abilities of a University Freshman Class." *New Directions in Composition Research*. Ed. Richard Beach and Lillian Bridwell. New York: Guilford, 1984. 19–52.

Cooper, Marilyn. "The Answers are Not in the Back of the Book: The Development of Discourse Practices in Freshmen Composition." *Developing Discourse Practices in Adolescence and Adulthood*. Ed. Richard Beach and Susan Hynds. Norwood, NJ: Ablex, 1990. 65–92.

Daly, John, and Anne Hexamer. "Statistical Power in Research in English Education." *Research in the Teaching of English* 17 (1983): 157–64.

de Beaugrande, Robert. "Writing and Meaning: Contexts of Research." *Writing in Real Time*. Ed. Ann Matsuhashi. Norwood, NJ: Ablex, 1987. 1–33.

Dyson, Anne. *The Multiple Worlds of Child Writers*. NY: Teachers College P, 1990.

Eckert, Pamela. *Jocks and Burnouts*. New York: Teachers College P, 1990.

Faigley, Lester, Roger Cherry, David Jolliffe, and Anna Skinner. *Assessing Writers' Knowledge and Processes of Composing*. Norwood, NJ: Ablex, 1985.

Flower, Linda. "Cognition, Context, and Theory Building." *College Composition and Communication* 40 (1989): 282–311.

Flynn, Elizabeth. "Composing 'Composing as a Woman': A Perspective on Research." *College Composition and Communication* 41 (1990): 83–89.

Fulwiler, Toby, ed. *The Journal Book.* Upper Montclair, NJ: Boynton/Cook, 1987.

Gere, Anne. "Empirical Research in Composition." *Perspectives on Research and Scholarship in Composition.* Ed. Ben McClelland and Timothy Donovan. New York: MLA, 1985. 110–24.

Goswami, Dixie, and Peter Stillman. *Reclaiming the Classroom.* Upper Montclair, NJ: Boynton/Cook, 1987.

Graves, Donald. *Writing: Teachers and Children at Work.* Portsmouth, NH: Heinemann, 1983.

Hartman, Karen, et al. "Patterns of Social Interaction and Learning to Write." *Written Communication* 8 (1991): 79–113.

Hartwell, Patrick. "Grammar, Grammars, and the Teaching of Grammar." *College English* 47 (1985): 105–27.

Hayes, John. "A Psychological Perspective Applied to Literacy Studies." *Multidisciplinary Perspectives on Literacy Research.* Ed. Richard Beach, et al. Urbana, IL: National Conference on Research in English, 1991.

Herrington, Anne. "The First Twenty Years of *Research in the Teaching of English* and the Growth of a Research Community in Composition Studies." *Research in the Teaching of English* 23 (1989): 117–38.

Hilgers, Thomas. "Experimental Control and the Writing Stimulus." *Research in the Teaching of English* 16 (1982): 381–90.

Hillocks, George. *Research on Written Composition.* Urbana, IL: National Conference on Research in English, 1986.

Hoetker, James, and Gordon Brossell. "The Effects of Systematic Variations in Essay Topics on the Writing Performance of College Freshmen." *College Composition and Communication* 40 (1989): 414–21.

Hunt, Russell, and Douglas Vipond. "First Catch the Rabbit: The Methodological Imperative and the Dramatization of Dialogic Reading." *Multidisciplinary Perspectives on Literacy Research.* Ed. Richard Beach, Judith Green, Michael Kamil, and Timothy Shanahan. Urbana, IL: National Conference on Research in English, 1991.

Kamil, Michael, Judith Langer, and Timothy Shanahan. *Understanding Reading and Writing Research*. Boston: Allyn, 1985.

Keroes, Jo. "But What Do They Say? Gender and the Content of Student Writing." *Discourse Processes* 13 (1990): 243–57.

Kraemer, Helena, and Sue Thiemann. *How Many Subjects? Statistical Power in Analysis of Research*. Beverly Hills, CA: Sage, 1987.

Langer, Judith, and Arthur Applebee. *How Writing Shapes Thinking*. Urbana, IL: NCTE, 1987.

Lauer, Janice, and J. William Asher. *Composition Research: Empirical Designs*. New York: Oxford UP, 1988.

Marshall, James. "The Effects of Writing on Students' Understanding of Literary Texts." *Research in the Teaching of English* 21 (1987): 30–63.

Myers, Miles. *The Teacher-Researcher: How to Study Writing in the Classroom*. Urbana, IL: NCTE, 1985.

Newell, George, Karen Suszynski, and Ruth Wingart. "The Effects of Writing in a Reader-Based and Text-Based Mode of Students' Understanding of Two Short Stories." *Journal of Reading Behavior* 21 (1989): 37–57.

Nystrand, Martin. "Making It Hard: Curriculum and Instruction as Factors in the Difficulty of Literature." *The Idea of Difficulty in Literature and Literature Learning*. Ed. Alan Purves. Albany: State of New York at Albany P, 1991.

———. "Sharing Words." *Written Communication* 7 (1990): 3–25.

Odell, Lee. "Analyzing Students' Thinking Strategies." National Council of Teachers of English Convention. Baltimore, November 20, 1989.

Odell, Lee, and Dixie Goswami. "Writing in a Non-academic Setting." *Research in the Teaching of English* 16 (1982): 201–23.

Olson, Mary. *Opening the Door to Classroom Research*. Newark, DE: International Reading Association, 1990.

Peyton, J. K., and M. Seyoum. "The Effect of Teacher Strategies on Students' Interactive Writing: The Case for Dialogue Journals." *Research in the Teaching of English* 23 (1989): 310–33.

Pressley, Michael, Pamela Beard El-Dinary, and Rachel Brown. "Is Good Reading Comprehension Possible?" Wisconsin Seminar on Reading Research 8 June 1990.

Pressley, Michael, et al. "A Methodological Analysis of Experimental

Studies of Comprehension Strategy Instruction." *Reading Research Quarterly* 24 (1989): 458–70.

Purves, Alan. "Commentary: Research on Written Composition." *Research in the Teaching of English* 22 (1988): 104–08.

Roderick, J., and L. Berman. "Dialoguing about Dialogue Journals: Teachers as Learners." *Language Arts* 61 (1984): 686–92.

Ruth, Leo, and Sandra Murphy. "Designing Topics for Writing Assessments: Problems of Meaning." *College Composition and Communication* 35 (1984): 412–42.

Schatzberg-Smith, Kathlee. *Dialogue Journal Writing and the Study Habits and Attitudes of Underprepared College Students.* Diss. Hofstra U, 1988.

Slavin, Robert. "On Making a Difference." *Educational Researcher* 19 (1990): 30–34, 44.

Staton, Jana, et al. *Dialogue Journal Communication: Classroom, Linguistic, Social and Cognitive Views.* Norwood, NJ: Ablex, 1988.

Stotsky, Sharon. "On Planning and Writing Plans—Or Beware of Borrowed Theories!" *College Composition and Communication* 41 (1990): 37–57.

Taylor, Barbara, and Richard Beach. "The Effects of Text Structure Instruction on Middle Grade Students' Comprehension and Production of Expository Text." *Reading Research Quarterly* 19 (1984): 134–46.

Taylor, Denny. "Teaching Without Testing: Assessing the Complexity of Children's Literacy Learning." *English Education* 22 (1990): 4–74.

Tierney, Robert, Mark Carter, and Laura Desai. *Portfolio Assessment in the Reading-Writing Classroom.* Norwood, MA: Christopher Gordon, 1991.

Tomlinson, Barbara. "Tuning, Tying, and Training Texts: Metaphors for Revision." *Written Communication* 5 (1988): 58–80.

Yinger, Ralph, and C. M. Clark. *Reflective Journal Writing: Theory and Practice. Evaluative Report.* Center for the Study of Teaching. East Lansing: Michigan State University, 1981.

Part II

Research Problems and Issues

Methodological Pluralism

Epistemological Issues

As the chapters in this collection illustrate, research in composition studies and rhetoric, by virtue of its interdisciplinary nature, draws from a variety of research traditions, among them literary studies, history, education, linguistics, psychology, sociology, and anthropology. These research traditions carry with them a set of assumptions that have remained largely unexamined in composition studies. Scholars in rhetoric and composition have just begun to question research methodologies in light of their practical, epistemological, and ideological implications. Moreover, while the proliferation of scholarship in composition over the last two decades strongly suggests that composition has emerged as a research discipline, interdisciplinary diversity has made it difficult for practitioners to forge an identity as a research community. During plenary sessions of the recently formed CCCC Research Network, for example, scholars questioned whether methodological pluralism is possible or whether different research methodologies might not be incompatible and in direct conflict with each other. They asked questions like these: What philosophical and epistemological assumptions guide different research methods? How are different methods related to each other? Do multiple methods build upon one another, producing cumulative knowledge? Or do various methods stand in conflict with each other, producing contradictory results? These questions carry a new importance as the field of composition studies and rhetoric grows: Only by understanding the nature and assumptions of various research methodologies can scholars and teachers in composition make informed decisions about the relevance, validity, and value of research reports. And only through shared, critical reflection on various research practices can composition researchers come to define the emergent discipline of composition studies for themselves.

In this chapter, I review recent debates about methodological pluralism, using arguments advanced by Carl Bereiter and Marlene Scardamalia, William Irmscher, and Stephen North as examples. I argue that methodological pluralism is possible if researchers bring a critical self-awareness to their studies and explicate—rather than gloss over—the epistemological issues implied by their research methods.[1] Such a critical self-awareness reveals that all methodologies are culturally situated and inscribed, never disinterested or impartial. I suggest that methodological pluralism demands a rethinking of *all* methodologies and new ways of conducting and interpreting research. New approaches to research will not necessarily produce a coherent or unified body of knowledge but, instead, may reveal contradictions, fissures, and gaps in our current knowledge of composition. The strength of new approaches will lie in the ability to invite new questions, to encourage dialogue and inquiry, and to define knowledge making as a continuously changing enterprise. I review work by scholars in women's studies who have articulated several principles that contribute to a more self-reflective use of methodology and have important implications for composition research. I conclude the chapter by illustrating how these principles have begun to inform recent research studies.

The Debate about Methodological Pluralism

On one side of the debate about methodological pluralism are scholars like Bereiter and Scardamalia who argue that research studies using different methodologies can contribute to the building of a coherent, cumulative body of knowledge. Bereiter and Scardamalia develop a framework that classifies research methodologies into "six levels of inquiry" and propose that diverse methods can work in a complementary fashion, one building upon another and leading to the next level of inquiry. The six levels of inquiry are characterized as follows: "Reflective inquiry" (level 1) identifies writing problems and phenomena through "informal observation, introspection, and literature reviews." Level 2 leads to "empirical variable testing"; researchers test assumptions and relationships between various factors involved in writing by using "surveys, correlation analysis, and factorial analysis of variance." Level 3 focuses on "text analysis"; researchers use "error analysis, story grammar analysis, and thematic analysis" to study "what rules the writer could be following." Level 4, "process description," tries to account for "patterns or systems revealed in the writer's thoughts while composing" and draws, among other methods, on "thinking aloud protocols and clinical-experimental interviews." Level 5 calls for "theory-embedded experimentation"; researchers ask questions like "What is the nature of the cognitive system responsible for observations? Which process model is right?" They address these questions by using "experimental procedures tailored to [their] questions." Finally, level 6 calls for "computer simulation and simulation by intervention"; researchers ask, for example, "What range of natural variations can the model account for?" (all quotes from table 1, p. 4). Bereiter and Scardamalia explain that "the successive levels of inquiry are marked by movement that is (1) further and further away from the natural phenomena of writing that are observed in their full context and (2) closer and closer to the psychological system viewed as a theoretical construct" (3–4). Their framework was developed with an egalitarian gesture in mind: "We think that in this era of competing methodologies there is a special need to promote tolerance and a free spirit of inquiry" (3). They state that the term level is misleading, and they do not wish to imply that work at any one level is more intellectually worthwhile than work at another level, insisting that we can only increase our knowledge of writing processes by engaging in research at all levels. Although Bereiter and Scardamalia claim that different methods contribute equally to knowledge in composition studies, they eventually show a preference for experimental research, stating that "a holistic ideology . . . poses an actual threat to writing research [because of its] opposition to any research (or instruction) that deals with less than the full act of writing carried out under natural conditions" (21). Ultimately, their framework reifies a hierarchy of research that privileges experimental over naturalistic methodology and endorses the quantitative research paradigm. Their assumption that we can arrive at a "right process model" (4) reflects a belief in a single, verifiable truth, and their notion that methodologies are "competing" suggests that there will be a "victor."

Bereiter and Scardamalia's framework raises several questions: Can different research methodologies add to a coherent and cumulative body of knowledge? Are studying and modeling cognitive processes involved in writing the most important kinds of composition research (represented as the highest level in Bereiter and Scardamalia's framework)? Can we advance our knowledge of writing by isolating features of composing processes or written texts in "esoteric laboratory procedures" (21)? By placing simulation at the highest level of inquiry and discussing simulation in reference to computer models, Bereiter and Scardamalia suggest a view of mind as a "neutral zone," separate and distinct from political, social, and cultural forces, or, if not distinct from such forces, then at least affected in a predictable, homogeneous way. Furthermore, simulation presupposes that researchers can build universal models of composing, at least models that apply to vast populations and warrant generalizations about writing activities. As scholars studying models of composing have noted, there is a "constant tension between the desire to simulate writing behaviors (necessarily abstracting from data in the quest for global descriptions) and the desire to achieve accuracy through close descriptions of individual writers (necessarily limiting the application of such findings to idiosyncratic cases)" (Pemberton). In recent years, many composition researchers, particularly social constructionists, have become critical of model building because it tends to reflect the cultural and social biases of researchers, not universal ways of thinking and writing. Bereiter and Scardamalia realize that different research methods are based on different epistemological assumptions, but they argue that "various methodologies, ranging from naturalistic observation to esoteric laboratory procedures, can be combined into a coherent effort to understand how human minds actually accomplish the complete act of writing" (21). They visualize research methods as working together in a linear and orderly fashion: case studies will lead researchers to form hypotheses that will lead to more controlled, experimental studies that will, in turn, confirm or refine hypotheses.

Much of the empirical research employing different methodologies, however, does not produce such symbiotic relationships. Case studies, for example, are rarely designed for hypothesis building, as Thomas Newkirk argues in this volume. Many case studies focus on unusual patterns of development or idiosyncrasies of writers, not on patterns common to a large number of writers. Importantly, case studies function rhetorically in a different way than experimental research; they set out to persuade readers not only with the depth of understanding gained through close observation of individual writers but also with the narrative strategies used to describe the development of writers. The effectiveness of a case study relies as much on its culturally rooted narrative structure—the rhetorical stance—as it does on the evidence presented.[2]

Furthermore, case studies often follow—rather than precede—experimental studies. When empirical researchers find themselves dissatisfied with the information gathered in experimental studies, they may turn to case studies as a means of following up on their experimental work. For example, researchers interested in composing processes of experienced writers may use interviews and stimulated recall in order to learn more about the motivations and goals shaping writers' decisions, while researchers interested in the effectiveness of pedagogical strategies may conduct not only pretests and posttests but also interview students about their motivations and engagement with course materials.

Most research in composition studies is opportunistic; researchers choose the methodology that will best address their questions. Research frequently begins with the urgency to understand events in the classroom or with a dissatisfaction with teaching methods. Instructional methods that work for one group of students may not work for another group. Mina Shaughnessy's seminal work, *Error and Expectations,* for example, grew out of the need to understand the new student population entering New York City colleges after the open admissions policy was introduced. Researchers like Bereiter and Scardamalia, who describe naturalistic research methods, including case studies, as mere prerequisites to experimental research, presuppose a linear relationship between research methods that rarely exists in actual, everyday practice.

On the other side of the debate about methodological pluralism are scholars who argue that composition studies should endorse a single methodology because different methodologies are likely to produce conflicting knowledge. William Irmscher's argument in "Finding a Comfortable Identity" is one such example. He argues for the importance and exclusive use of naturalistic inquiry, contending that any other research methodology is likely to distort observations about writers' composing processes and will fail to capture diverse contexts for writing. Irmscher develops a list of operating assumptions for researchers in which he privileges observations in natural settings over experimental procedures, attention to writers' idiosyncrasies over the study of patterns common to many writers, and description of the "fullness of experience" (87) in writing over the description of discrete features of writing activities or written texts. Irmscher claims that "research in composition has become identified with one kind of research—controlled experimental studies producing statistical evidence" (82) and advocates a holistic approach instead: "We need to reassert the humanistic nature of our own discipline, which in this context means its concern for the individual as a human being, not as a quantity or specimen" (85). Although Irmscher has been said to conflate empiricism with positivism (by categorically denying the value of all formal, systematic research) and many scholars have begun to ferret out differences between empirical and positivistic research (e.g., Berkenkotter; Flower; Flynn, "Composing 'Composing as a Woman' "), he speaks for composition scholars who have become disillusioned with the narrow focus of many experimental studies. Irmscher's resistance to experimental research reflects, among other things, his disciplinary training in the humanities and represents a split between scholars who consider themselves primarily composition researchers and those who consider themselves writing teachers or theoreticians.

The call for a single methodology—whether grounded in the humanistic or another tradition—has important social and political consequences. First, it determines what is included in and excluded from the study of composition, thereby potentially limiting rich avenues of research. To set such limitations early in the development of a growing discipline would be premature, even downright foolish, and would limit the study of a complex human phenomenon—writing in its many forms and social contexts. Karen Schriver asserts that "unfortunately, there is a worrisome trend in our field of asserting that some perspectives and methods are better than others. . . . This sort of talk implies that a single approach is best for all questions in our field. . . . Because any one window can provide only a partial view on what we want to know, an empirical inquiry into rhetoric and composition must be pluralistic" (284–85). Second, to declare one methodology most suitable for composition studies is to declare other methodologies less suitable, less valuable, and less intellectually worthwhile, thereby undermining important contributions made by many researchers. Such arguments can take on an immediate political dimension because they enter the institutional reward and merit system, affecting the well-being of instructors, scholars, and researchers as well as the quality of writing instruction, as Susan Miller and Lisa Ede suggest in their chapters in this volume.[3] The call for a single methodology poses the danger of reasserting the same kind of hegemony of values (cultural, ethnic, institutional, or gender-based) that many composition scholars want to undo.

One side of the debate about methodological pluralism, then, is represented by scholars who argue that an interdisciplinary field like composition studies is enriched by the use of multiple research methods. They consider different research methodologies as complementary, leading to cumulative knowledge building. On the other side of the debate are scholars who argue for methodological purity. They deem one kind of methodology inherently more appropriate and valuable to the study of writing and do not see continuity in the knowledge that is constructed through the use of various research methods. Stephen North takes up this debate in *The Making of Knowledge in Composition* where he questions methodological pluralism without endorsing any single methodology. North argues that different kinds of research methods used to study composition and rhetoric do not share the same epistemological assumptions and are therefore incompatible. He observes that any research method is embedded in an epistemology—a set of assumptions about the nature of knowledge, truth, and reality. By analyzing studies that use different research methods, North demonstrates that each methodological tradition privileges certain kinds of knowledge over others. Based on these observations, North predicts that composition studies will self-destruct in a "methodological war" (352) because researchers will align themselves according to their preferred methodology, not a common interest in composition studies. North's prediction suggests, for example, that composition researchers using an ethnographic methodology share more interests with fellow ethnographers (and will perhaps join departments of anthropology) than with their colleagues in English studies who subscribe to a different methodology in order to pursue their interests in the nature of writing.

Although North's close study of diverse research methodologies makes an important contribution to current inquiry into the nature of composition research, other scenarios for the future of composition studies are possible. Scholars may engage in a multivocal dialogue, thereby allowing for the possibility of a dynamic tension between multiple research traditions. By articulating their own assumptions and listening to colleagues in the field articulate theirs, researchers may gain a deeper understanding of (and respect for) the working of different methodologies. Researchers who face the epistemological questions that accompany various research methods may discover gaps, fissures, and contradictions—as North would be the first to point out—but such discoveries do not necessarily invalidate or negate the value of any research methodology and its contribution to knowledge making. Rather, discoveries of contradictions and tensions can enrich discussions, stimulate new research, and open up new areas of inquiry. Many researchers now point to gaps and contradictions in their research when they discuss possibilities for future work and the limitations of their studies, but research conventions and publication requirements do not permit a full discussion of these issues. At a time when many academic disciplines are experiencing an "epistemological crisis" (Brodkey 26) and are engaged in critical self-reflection, researchers in composition studies would do well to examine the assumptions underlying their research methods and articulate the principles that inform their understanding of the nature of knowledge produced in composition studies.

Research in composition and rhetoric invites methodological pluralism. The diversity of research questions raised by scholars, the broad territory encompassed by rhetoric and composition, and the multidisciplinary backgrounds of researchers all invite the use of multiple research methods. Methodological pluralism, however, is not unproblematic. Researchers steeped in different research traditions often speak different languages and describe their observations with different sets of vocabulary. Anne Herrington suggests that "embedded in these languages are different views of issues to investigate, ways of defining the phenomena to be studied, and, more generally, valid ways of knowing. These differences make it all the more difficult to appreciate the value of other approaches, especially when one is struggling to authorize one's own approach" (131). At stake in discussions about methodological pluralism are often the disciplinary paradigms that shape scholars' attitudes toward research. Bereiter and Scardamalia, for example, come out of a research orientation based in cognitive psychology. Thus, their discussion highlights the use of experimental and cognitive approaches and describes other methodologies as supplementary to those of their disciplinary orientation. The question, then, is whether scholars are willing to break from a relatively rigid adherence to their disciplinary orientation in order to entertain alternative methodologies.

Embracing Methodological Pluralism: New Research Principles

Continued use of multiple research methods demands a rethinking of *all* methodologies. It becomes necessary to investigate how "the making of knowledge in composition research" works and to require important changes in how researchers design, implement, and report their studies. Specifically, methodological pluralism requires that researchers take into consideration several important principles recently articulated by scholars in women's studies, perhaps most clearly by Sandra Harding. These principles call for an open discussion of (1) the researcher's *relation* to the subject (the researcher's presence and authority are never neutral); (2) the *purpose* of the researcher's questions (they must be *grounded* in the subject's experience and be relevant to the subject); and (3) the researcher's *agenda* (it is never disinterested).

Feminist researchers start with the premise that research methods are never neutral, impartial, or disinterested. They argue that researchers need to confront their biases directly by acknowledging their research agenda and interests and by becoming involved with subjects of research studies.[4] A researcher's self-aware stance can strengthen research studies, feminist scholars contend, because additional insights are gained when researchers and subjects interact. Researchers will be less likely to ignore their own cultural, class, and gender biases; their research designs will include conscious decision making about what methods are used for what purpose and for whose benefit.

For composition studies, this kind of research means opening up the research agenda to subjects, listening to their stories, and allowing them to actively participate, as much as possible, in the design, development, and reporting of research. Such an approach will include interviews, case studies, and retrospective accounts.[5] Qualitative methods become an important part of research—though not the only ones possible—because they acknowledge the diversity of composing activities and writers' histories as shaped by elements of gender, race, class, and ethnicity, among other factors. Qualitative research methods also have the advantage of situating themselves as methods that need interpretation and thereby problematize the interpretive stance of the researcher (rather than disguising it). Ethnographic research, for example, always includes a discussion of researchers' roles as participant-observers because they affect the cultures they study, regardless of their degree of participation in those cultures. Quantitative methods, too, reflect researchers' agendas and the social, cultural, and political contexts of research communities. For example, the use of protocol analysis involves interpretive acts in the development of coding schemes and the classification of writers' comments, as Keith Grant-Davie argues in this volume. Linda Flower has observed that "to understand the role of data in theory-building, we should not ask 'what the data means' but ask 'how it is used to make meaning' within the researcher's interpretive act" (300). That interpretive act, however, is only too rarely discussed in research reports using quantitative methods.

Most important of all, by implementing the principles discussed by Harding, composition researchers will aim to combine roles of observer and participant, teacher and researcher, student and ethnographer. In other words, researchers will make a conscious effort to break down the rigid hierarchy that now exists between the observer and the observed. To do so, researchers will need to confront their own agendas and interpretive stances. If experimental procedures are to be used in composition research, they need to be understood in terms of their social and cultural context. Researchers will need to articulate the assumptions that guide their research questions and acknowledge that research, by definition, is necessarily interested, limited, and partial, no matter the methodology used. Of course, researchers do not automatically validate their work by enunciating what their research interests are and who benefits from the research, but by acknowledging that their interests shape their research agendas, they leave room for new research, for new questions and critical inquiry. Ultimately, scholars cannot transcend their cultural, social, and political situatedness—nor should they want to. Methodological pluralism does not demand that researchers withhold their judgment but, instead, that they articulate the criteria used to arrive at judgments. Flynn suggests one such criterion, that theory and research are meaningful as long as they "can be fruitfully applied to new interpretive problems" ("Composing 'Composing as a Woman' " 87). When a theory fails to explain, for example, why student narratives differ with the gender of writers—the focus of Flynn's research—a new interpretive approach, both in terms of theory and research methods, is called for. Flynn explains: "Research procedures and methods evolve and develop as fields of inquiry evolve and develop. Such procedures and methods are meant to enable discovery, not to impede it. New research questions necessitate new methods" (88–89).

When researchers discuss their data and findings, they need to entertain, even propose, alternative readings and interpretations of their research. Such alternative interpretations will serve to provide additional insights, not to test and eliminate "rival hypotheses," a process that suggests there is one best, correct interpretation of data that researchers can approximate by a process of elimination. As Patricia Sullivan illustrates in her chapter in this volume, for example, the story of North's graduate student who failed her comprehensive exams (described in North's discussion of practice as inquiry) lends itself to several interpretations. North interprets the story by raising questions about institutional demands; Sullivan offers a feminist reading. Other readings, too, are possible. Together, these readings can create layers of narration and interpretation that point to the complexity of human interactions without resolving or oversimplifying diverse issues or reducing them to a single truth. Such an interpretive approach to research, however, does not imply a relativistic stance where one reading is as good as any other. Researchers still need to provide evidence for their findings, develop arguments for their interpretation of data, and convince a community of readers that their interpretations are feasible. What will have changed is that the criteria for selecting research questions and interpreting data will be available to scrutiny, not sanctioned by the invocation of a particular methodology.

Scholars have debated whether or not new research principles, like the ones outlined by Harding, reflect a feminist methodology. Certainly, Harding's principles challenge the (dominantly male) tradition of experimental research that aims to control variables and achieve objectivity. In the process of questioning traditional research, scholars in women's studies have documented ways in which so-called objective and disinterested research in the social sciences has often excluded woman participants or misrepresented women's experiences in studies of human behavior. In an effort to present correctives to such flawed research, feminist researchers have begun to question research methods and findings based on male standards and to argue for more inclusive, context-sensitive research. New research principles, therefore, have sometimes been linked to women's increasing participation in the disciplines and their tendency to emphasize the importance of context, community, and relations with others. For example, Flynn has talked about a "process of feminization" in composition studies ("Composing as a Woman" 424), and Richard Beach has proposed that a contextual approach to research, such as an emphasis on the writing process, might be related to the presence of women in composition studies. "It is no accident that many of the leading researchers on the composing/revision process in the 1970s were women—Shaughnessy, Emig, Sommers, Heath, Bridwell, Lunsford, Bizzell, Cooper, Brandt. Maybe it was due to the fact that they were working in composition programs, but . . . their orientation represented a more process-oriented research approach." However, new approaches to research also reflect the current discussion of the socially constructed nature of knowledge that has been central to poststructuralist debates of the last two decades. Poststructuralist scholars in a variety of disciplines have argued that all research is limited and partial, shaped by the cultural and historical context of the researcher as well as the participants, and that the meaning of research is constructed, not discovered (e.g., Kuhn; Geertz; Rorty). Whether or not the principles discussed by Harding are indicative or typical of a feminist research methodology is a matter of debate and likely to be contested in the future. More important, however, is the challenge these principles pose for composition researchers and the new avenues for research to which they point. That challenge is beginning to be met by some composition researchers.

New Research Principles at Work

The three principles outlined by Harding have begun to inform a variety of research studies recently published in composition journals. Researchers have begun to examine their relationships with subjects, grounded their research questions in subjects' experiences, and acknowledged their research interests and agendas. Although explicit discussions of new approaches to methodology are still rare, a number of changes are visible in current research studies (for example, studies by Glynda Hull and Mike Rose and by Anderson et al.).

In their study "Rethinking Remediation," which focused on remedial writers and their understanding of writing tasks and goals, Hull and Rose approached the researcher-subject relationship in a new way. In addition to using a variety of ethnographic and cognitive process tracing methods (observing writers in the classroom setting, collecting writing samples, listening to student-teacher interactions), Hull and Rose got actively involved with participants by tutoring them for four months. The researcher-subject relationship was transformed into a tutor-student relationship, allowing the researchers to learn in greater depth about students' thinking and writing processes than observation and writing samples alone would allow. Through their close interactions with students, the researchers learned how students' career goals contributed to their perceptions of writing tasks. The result of the interaction between researchers and students is an insightful study. Hull and Rose examine the "procedural rules" that interfere with one particular student's writing process and look at the social and cultural conditions that have led this student to develop a fearful attitude toward schooling. What appears at first glance as a case of plagiarism in the student's text turns out to be a serious but misguided effort to avoid plagiarism on the student's part. Hull and Rose's stated research goal was to study "what it is that cognitively and socially defines an underprepared student as underprepared" (143). They realized their goal by allowing themselves to get to know the students closely, thereby taking advantage of the researcher-subject relationship and contributing to a research methodology that implements a more interactive, collaborative approach between researchers and subjects.

The researcher-subject relationship is an issue that cuts across all research methodologies but has received little attention in composition studies. In fact, most discussions that address the researcher-participant relationship are designed to document the researcher's lack of interest in and interaction with research participants. North criticizes several researchers for failing to discuss the kinds of relationships they had with their subjects (i.e., being teachers, counselors, or even family friends in addition to being researchers) and the possible effects that relationship might have had on research findings. Feminist scholars argue that the researcher-subject relationship does not threaten the validity of research studies but can provide researchers with additional insights. Harding proclaims that "the best feminist analysis . . . insists that the inquirer her/himself be placed in the same critical plane as the overt subject matter, thereby recovering the entire research process for scrutiny in the results of the research. . . . Thus the researcher appears to us not as an invisible, anonymous voice of authority, but as a real, historical individual with concrete, specific desires and interests" (9).

The researcher-participant relationship will become increasingly important as the body of researchers and students diversifies in terms of gender, culture, race, ethnicity, and other factors. Sociolinguists have already described ways in which patterns of talk differ in conversations among same- and mixed-gender groups (e.g., Coates and Cameron; Frank and Anshen; Spender). We can assume that, as researchers increasingly pay attention to their relationships with subjects, they will learn more about the role of participants' culturally diverse backgrounds on the nature and findings of research studies and identify a number of important cultural and social variables. Instead of controlling these variables, however, researchers will highlight them. They will discuss the relations they have with research participants and the insights gained through those relations. The teacher research movement, for example, is built upon just that assumption: that knowledge is to be gained—not lost or distorted—by an active engagement and interactions among teachers, researchers, and students (discussed in this volume by Ruth Ray).

Hull and Rose's study also illustrates the second and third principles at work: that any research needs to be grounded in subjects' experiences and designed to benefit both researchers and subjects. Hull and Rose got an intimate look at basic writers in a remedial English course, and the students received valuable tutoring lessons and a deeper understanding of their writing processes in return. To implement the second and third principles, researchers need to design studies with question like these in mind: Who formulated the research questions and for what purpose? Who is likely to benefit from the outcomes and findings of the research? Are researchers and subjects on the same plane or is the researcher studying "down"?

These questions were part of a recent study reported by Anderson et al. The study, a joint research project conducted by Susan Miller and five of her students, focuses on the "cross-curricular underlife" of a variety of academic courses. The research questions were of relevance and interest to both the researcher and the students involved: they addressed the goals that guide students' choices of college courses, the motivations that determine their level of involvement in these courses, and the studying and writing strategies that lead to success. The research questions and design evolved through the interaction between the researcher-teacher and the students, thereby allowing the participants to become true co-researchers. Furthermore, students became collaborators and coauthors in the writing of the final research report, which is acknowledged in the alphabetical listing of all writer participants involved. In addition to working collaboratively on the research and writing, students were also allowed to express individual perspectives by writing different sections of the final study (indicated by authors' names for separate sections).

The study by Miller and her students illustrates that the researcher-participant relationship can be flexible, cooperative, and mutually beneficial, that the research agenda can be grounded in participants' experiences, and that research findings can be relevant to both participants and researchers. In order to allow for such benefits, researchers like Miller have begun to involve research participants at all stages in the development and reporting of research projects, and their work embodies some of the principles articulated by Harding:

- The research questions were of interest and value to both the researcher and the participants.
- The voices of both participants and researcher were audible.
- The research report was written collaboratively, yet preserves differences in individual perspectives.
- The subjects became true collaborators and coauthors as indicated by the listing of names in alphabetical order on the publication.
- The relationships between researcher and participants were explicit and clear (at least as clear as language and social conventions can make them), not implicit or covert.

Any researcher who uses an innovative methodology like Miller's obviously raises new questions about research designs, collaboration, authorship, and the role and authority of different participants. What does it mean, for example, to juxtapose the observations and opinions of undergraduate students next to the observations and comments of an experienced composition researcher? Clearly these coauthors are not equal in their knowledge, experience, and authority. How does one read an article that is multivocal, presenting distinct views? How much effort should readers and writers make to synthesize different perspectives? Or should such synthesis be resisted? These questions just begin to circumscribe the range of issues that will need to be addressed as composition researchers begin to explore different methodological approaches.

Finally, researchers also need to ask questions about the rhetorical stance—the narrative strategies, for example—they use when reporting research studies because writing research reports is a highly conventionalized and socially constructed process. Scholars in English studies have a long history of studying the rhetorical strategies found in fiction, but there is no parallel history of studying rhetorical strategies in nonfictional prose, particularly of the kind found in disciplinary discourse such as research reports. (A few notable exceptions are recent studies by Charles Bazerman; Susan Peck MacDonald; Carolyn Miller and Jack Selzer.) The rhetorical stance of research reports contributes as much to the making of knowledge in composition research as does the methodology used. In the end, any research report is a form of narration, a story about a selected set of observations. Different forms of narration are grounded in different rhetorical traditions that can bring with them a preferred methodological orientation. Researchers need to question what goals their narrations or stories serve, who is listening to the stories and is affected by them, and what ideological assumptions the stories reflect. Research in composition leads to the formulation of a rhetoric, and as James Berlin reminds us, "a rhetoric is always situated within ideology, not above it, providing a set of rules for deciding, among other things, who can speak, what they can say, how they can say it, who can respond to them, and who will make decisions about all these matters" ("Comment" 771). Research reports reflect researchers' interests and agendas as much as they reflect participants' performances. They need to be read for such reflection, each reading calling for a new reading and interpretation. Such readings create cycles of interpretation, re-searching, re-reading, re-flecting, and re-interpreting, becoming, in the ideal case, an interactive and collaborative process within the research community.

Methodological pluralism is likely to shape future research in composition studies and rhetoric. The diverse disciplinary backgrounds of researchers, the range and complexity of writing processes and written texts, and the new and changing questions developed by each generation of researchers encourage, even demand, the use of multiple methods in composition studies. Continued use of multiple research methods, however, obliges researchers to become critically aware of methodological issues and to change the way they design, conduct, and report research. Changes will be guided by the principles discussed above and many others still to be articulated. As the two studies reviewed above illustrate, such changes are beginning to take place; however, the process is slow and the changes difficult to implement. Herrington suggests in her review of twenty years of composition research that "what the pages of *RTE* reveal is a community constituting itself, characterized at first by a single research paradigm: quantitative 'scientific' studies. Through the years, we have broadened the definition of both what we will study and how we will study it to include qualitative research as well and a variety of theoretical standpoints. Change has been slow, however, and the founding paradigm remains dominant" (118). Change and critical self-awareness are necessary if composition research is to continue to grow and become more sophisticated. Methodological pluralism calls for interactive relations between researchers and participants, between observers and observed. Researchers gain additional insights by interacting with participants; participants learn more about their own writing and the context in which it occurs, and they help researchers formulate their research questions and interpret results. Interactive, cooperative, and coauthored research is, by definition, a provisional and changing enterprise. As researchers begin to fully articulate the socially constructed nature of their inquiry, they will discover that their research questions and findings are as provisional and changing as the communities of writers they study.

Notes

I would like to thank Richard Beach, Charles Cooper, Peter Mortensen, Michael Pemberton, Mike Rose, and Patricia Sullivan for their valuable comments on this manuscript.

1. I use *method* here to mean a specific research technique (e.g.,

protocol analysis) and *methodology* to mean the theory of knowledge making implied in a method or set of methods (e.g., protocol analysis defines cognition as an important part of writing and assumes that some of the cognitive processes involved in writing can be examined in protocols).

2. See also Linda Brodkey for a discussion of narrative strategies used in the writing of ethnographies and Debra Journet for a discussion of narrative strategies used in neurological case histories.

3. See James Berlin ("Rhetoric and Ideology in the Writing Class"), Robert Connors, and Stephen North for further discussions of the historical developments and institutional status of composition research, theory, and instruction.

4. The term *subject* itself is problematic because it relegates participants to the role of specimens rather than portraying them as rich and diverse human beings. In this article, however, I continue to use the term *subject* as part of the research tradition I am discussing.

5. See Marilyn Sternglass for a recent systematic use of retrospective accounts.

Works Cited

Anderson, Worth, Cynthia Best, Alycia Black, John Hurst, Brandt Miller, and Susan Miller. "Cross-Curricular Underlife: A Collaborative Report on Ways with Academic Words." *College Composition and Communication* 41 (1990): 11–36.

Bazerman, Charles. "What Written Knowledge Does: Three Examples of Academic Discourse." *Philosophy of the Social Sciences* 11 (1981): 361–87.

Beach, Richard. Letter to the author. 16 Aug. 1990.

Bereiter, Carl, and Marlene Scardamalia. "Levels of Inquiry in Writing Research." *Research on Writing: Principles and Methods*. Ed. Peter Mosenthal, Lynne Tamor, and Sean Walmsley. New York: Longman, 1983. 3–25.

Berkenkotter, Carol. "The Legacy of Positivism in Empirical Composition Research." *Journal of Advanced Composition* 9 (1989): 69–82.

Berlin, James. "Comment and Response." *College English* 51 (1989): 770–77.

————. "Rhetoric and Ideology in the Writing Class." *College English* 50 (1988): 477–94.

Brodkey, Linda. "Writing Ethnographic Narratives." *Written Communication* 4 (1987): 25–50.

Coates, Jennifer, and Deborah Cameron, eds. *Women in Their Speech Communities: New Perspectives on Language and Sex.* London: Longman, 1988.

Connors, Robert. "Composition Studies and Science." *College English* 45 (1983): 1–20.

Flower, Linda. "Cognition, Context, and Theory Building." *College Composition and Communication* 40 (1989): 282–311.

Flynn, Elizabeth. "Composing as a Woman." *College Composition and Communication* 39 (1988): 423–35.

————. "Composing 'Composing as a Woman.' " *College Composition and Communication* 41 (1990): 83–89.

Frank, Francine, and Frank Anshen. *Language and the Sexes.* Albany: State U of New York P, 1983.

Geertz, Clifford. *Local Knowledge: Further Essays in Interpretive Anthropology.* New York: Basic, 1983.

Harding, Sandra. "Introduction: Is There a Feminist Method?" *Feminism and Methodology: Social Science Issues.* Ed. Sandra Harding. Bloomington: Indiana UP, 1987. 1–14.

Herrington, Anne J. "The First Twenty Years of *Research in the Teaching of English* and the Growth of a Research Community in Composition Studies." *Research in the Teaching of English* 23 (1989): 117–38.

Hull, Glynda, and Mike Rose. "Rethinking Remediation: Toward a Social-Cognitive Understanding of Problematic Reading and Writing." *Written Communication* 6 (1989): 139–54.

Irmscher, William F. "Finding a Comfortable Identity." *College Composition and Communication* 38 (1987): 81–87.

Journet, Debra. "Forms of Discourse and the Sciences of the Mind: Luria, Sacks, and the Role of Narrative in Neurological Case Histories." *Written Communication* 7 (1990): 171–99.

Kuhn, Thomas. *The Structure of Scientific Revolutions.* Chicago: U of Chicago P, 1970.

MacDonald, Susan Peck. "Problem Definition in Academic Writing." *College English* 49 (1987): 315–31.

Miller, Carolyn, and Jack Selzer. "Special Topics of Argument in Engineering Reports. " *Writing in Non-Academic Settings*. Ed. Lee Odell and Dixie Goswami. New York: Guilford, 1985. 309–41.

North, Stephen. *The Making of Knowledge in Composition: Portrait of an Emerging Field*. Portsmouth, NH: Boynton/Cook, 1987.

Pemberton, Michael. Letter to the author. 15 Jan. 1991.

Rorty, Richard. *Philosophy and the Mirror of Nature*. Princeton: Princeton UP, 1979.

Schriver, Karen. "What Are We Doing as a Research Community? Theory Building in Rhetoric and Composition: The Role of Empirical Scholarship." *Rhetoric Review* 7 (1989): 272–88.

Shaughnessy, Mina. *Errors and Expectations: A Guide for the Teacher of Basic Writing*. New York: Oxford UP, 1977.

Spender, Dale. *Man Made Language*. London: Routledge, 1980.

Coding Data

Issues of Validity, Reliability, and Interpretation

IN RESEARCH REPORTS the descriptions of methods tend to be relatively brief and matter-of-fact. The limited discussion is due partly to the restricted length of journal articles and book chapters, and partly, I would suggest, because research reports are arguments, and the main purpose of the methods section is to establish support for the results and conclusions—a purpose that might be thwarted by extensive self-examination of the methods. Researchers like their reports to provoke response from readers, but they generally prefer the debate to rage over the interpretation of the results and their implications rather than over the procedures by which the results were reached. In the ideal or prototypical research report, those procedures are supposed to be valid and reliable, independent of the researcher's subjective viewpoint, and it is part of the rhetoric of research reporting to make them appear so—to make the description of data collection, analysis, reliability tests, and so on seem as straightforward and unproblematic as possible.

In order to interpret any kind of data, some form of coding is necessary (and indeed unavoidable), but the coding process is less determinate than most descriptions of coding systems and reliability tests assert. Unequivocal accounts of methods invariably hide a trail of difficult and questionable decisions. This chapter examines some fundamental questions researchers must face when coding data, and some difficult decisions they must make. What do we mean by data and what does it mean to code?

Why do we code data? What assumptions does coding involve, and what are its limitations? What kind of coding system is most appropriate for the data? Is it possible to code data objectively? How can we tell that the category system is valid (that the categories accurately reflect the data) and reliable (that the system has been applied consistently to the data)? What do measures of validity and reliability mean?

I faced these questions myself in a study in which I coded oral reading protocols, and I will illustrate some of the issues by referring to this study. The study used oral reading protocols to examine when and how readers infer writers' aims, particularly in ironic discourse where the writers imply something other than, or more than, they state. Six graduate students and five freshmen were asked to read five short texts aloud and to comment on their sense of the writer's aim as they read. A coding scheme was developed to analyze the transcripts of their reading protocols.

What Do Data and Coding Mean?

By data I refer broadly to any raw material or information gathered or observed in the course of a research project and considered relevant to the research. The notion of rawness in this definition has problems to which I will return in due course, but it will do for the time being.

For composition researchers these days, data can include written or oral discourse produced in academic situations, in workplaces, or in any other social-rhetorical situations. The data may be collected from many sources or, in case studies, from just one or two individuals. Data may also include background information on readers and writers and their nonverbal behavior if the researcher considers these details to be relevant parts of the discourse context. Data need not take a written form, although oral data still tend to be written down for further analysis. For such oral discourse as think-aloud protocols of readers or writers creating meaning with texts, conversations between collaborating

writers, conversations between students and teachers in conference, or interviews, researchers usually record the raw data on
audio- or videotape and then begin the analysis by transcribing
the recordings into print.

Coding is usually understood to mean the process of identifying units of analysis and classifying each unit according to the
categories in a coding system—either a preexisting system or
one developed for the data in question. Why code data? One
explanation might be that division and classification are strategies
people commonly use to organize their experience of the world.
On the other hand, the impulse to divide and classify is not shared
equally by all cultures. Sondra Perl (*Coding the Composing Process*) argues that using a coding system allows the researcher to
depict what writers are doing from moment to moment as they
write, and coding the composing process in this way avoids
having to rely on the retrospective accounts of the writers themselves, accounts that might be subjective, short, and inaccurate.
This argument is more of a rationale for using protocols than an
argument for the need to develop a system with which to code
them; and as a defense of protocols it is open to a range of
counterarguments. However, my purpose in this chapter is not
to reopen the debate for or against protocols as a valid research
method. That issue has been discussed in detail elsewhere (see,
for example, Cooper and Holzman; Steinberg; Dobrin; Smagorinsky). Instead, I am concerned with more general questions of
how and why we code data—be it gathered by protocols, interviews, observation, writing assignments, or any other method—
and how we cope with the problems inherent in the coding
process.

The main reason for dividing and classifying data is to simplify
the material and impose order on it. Coding organizes data,
allowing researchers to abstract patterns by comparing the relative placement and frequency of categories. It gives them a system
by which to demonstrate these patterns to other readers, and it

provides researchers with a perspective from which to view the data, so that the coding can directly address their research questions.

So far I have defined coding fairly narrowly, in what is perhaps its familiar sense, as the process of dividing and classifying data. I want to broaden this definition, first by making coding loosely equivalent to reading and then by observing that division and classification (the focus of this essay) are just two of the ways in which data may be read or coded. I make these points in order to argue that the term *coding* may be used broadly to include all that a researcher does to the data and to emphasize that division and classification are interpretive acts. That is to say, they involve reader-researchers in the creation of meaning, rather than simply in the extraction and conveyance of meaning that already exists in the data. Researchers construct meaning with the data, identifying patterns and looking for answers to their questions.

What researchers find in the data is influenced by what they look for, and if they find only confirmation of what they expected, they may simply assimilate the data with their existing knowledge or assumptions, reinforcing this knowledge without changing it. More often, however, and more interestingly, researchers do not find exactly what they expected, or they may approach the data without clear expectations or with a range of alternative hypotheses. In these cases, researchers must negotiate with the data, searching their memories for alternative schemas (patterns of relationships into which people organize their knowledge) that might account for the data, revising the schemas they had brought to the analysis, or forming new schemas to account for the evidence. When we classify data into categories, as in any kind of reading, we try to confirm, revise, or add to our understanding of the subject matter, but we learn most through addition and revision—when the knowledge we bring to the data proves inadequate to explain what we find, causing us to accommodate or reconstruct our knowledge.

Preliminary Coding Decisions

In a research study, the process of transacting meaning, described above, begins well before the material is divided and classified. That process is influenced, if not determined, by the researcher's questions and the design of the study. Returning now to my definition of data as raw material, the problem with the idea of rawness should be apparent. If the researcher chooses, collects, and prepares the data, just how raw is that material by the time it is considered ready for the level of coding that involves division and classification? And can data collected by such methods as an oral protocol ever be considered raw? The notion that data can ever be entirely raw or uncoded—that is, free of the researcher's interpretive influence—is problematic because data collection is a selective process and therefore involves interpretation or coding. In effect, then, researchers don't just collect data, they create this material by selecting and defining it, especially if the material is produced under laboratory conditions or in response to the researchers' prompts. Various kinds of coding, including division and classification, occur at all stages in a research study.

Preliminary coding decisions include, for instance, choosing where to set the limits of the data—which parts of the material to include as significant data for further interpretation and which to discard as irrelevant. Theoretically, there is no end to the amount of information about the discourse, its context, or its authors that might be included as data, or at least taken into consideration; but as the kinds and amount of data included in a study increase, the problems of analyzing diverse material multiply, particularly if the analysis involves identifying units within the data, classifying them, and counting them.

In my own study of oral reading protocols, I made a number of preliminary coding decisions as I transcribed the audiotapes. These decisions involved interpretation, but less than my later decisions about how to divide and classify the transcripts. At this stage in the analysis I was trimming and dressing the data, trying to describe what the tape recordings suggested readers were doing (physically, rather than mentally) and how their comments sounded. Most of the coding decisions at this stage concerned the amount of detail I would include in the transcripts and the symbols I would use to record it. I had to decide how to make the transcripts show when subjects were reading, rereading, or commenting on text and what I would include in the transcripts: how accurately to record the pauses and stumblings of the ad lib monologues, how many nonverbal sounds (like sighs, whistling, erasure sounds, and doors opening) to include, and how much prosodic detail I should try to represent. In Ann Matsuhashi's study of pauses in the composing process, the precise timing of pauses was a crucial part of data transcription. For my study, I decided it was sufficient to indicate the relative length of pauses roughly.

The purpose of this preliminary coding was to create a print version of the protocol at roughly the same level of abstraction as the oral version. From here, the main coding began with the task of dividing and classifying the comments readers made while reading. Unlike the preliminary coding, the main coding converted the comments into more abstract forms, involving inferences which were harder to verify.

Identifying Coding Units

After the kinds of preliminary coding decisions described above, researchers typically divide the data into units for subsequent classification into categories. Transcribed protocols have been divided into a variety of units, and the choice of unit has obviously influenced the results. In studies by Fagan and by Flower, Hayes, and Swarts, clauses were used as the coding unit. Other studies have used functional, rather than syntactic units. Perl (*Coding the Composing Process*) describes a system using "units of behavior" (35); Flower and Hayes used "composing episodes," the boundaries between which are signaled by shifts in focus or changes in the writer's train of thought (237); and Hayes and Flower divided their protocols into "a sequence of segments, each containing a simple comment or statement" (14).

For my own data, I saw two problems with using a syntactic unit. First, the syntax of a verbal protocol is often fragmentary, elliptical, stuttering, or revised in midutterance. Second, syntactic units suggest that each unit is a separate instance of the comment category. In other words, if one subject's protocol contains a total of fifty-seven units of a particular kind of comment while another subject's contains only thirty-eight, the implication is that such a comment was more important to the first reader. This may be likely, but it assumes that importance can be measured by quantity. Using the syntactic unit overlooks two things: that verbose subjects will generate many more units of a given kind of comment by repetition than subjects who are more concise; and that speakers may vary the surface structure of their language to say the same thing in one syntactic unit or in several successive units.

Instead of a syntactic unit, I chose what I termed an episodic unit, based on the categories of comment in my coding system. Episodic units vary in length from a single word to a half page or more, lasting for as long as the subject continues to make the same kind of comment. Syntactic units enable researchers to use two separate coding steps; they can first divide the data into units and then classify the units. But episodic units force researchers to treat division and classification as inseparable coding activities; one unit ends and another begins when the reader shifts from one kind of comment to another.

Clearly there are advantages and disadvantages to both syntactic and episodic units. However, with data like transcribed oral protocols, any kind of unit is bound to involve the researcher in some questionable judgment calls about unit boundaries.

Classifying Units into Categories

When researchers organize and interpret data by dividing and classifying, they have to decide how sensitive their taxonomy should be to the range of complex activities that may be found in the data. (I use activities, for want of a better term, to refer generically to the various species of behavior, actions, strategies, or moves that are reflected in the categories of a coding system.) Theoretically, the most sensitive taxonomy would recognize such fine distinctions among the units that no two units could be classified in the same category. Such a taxonomy would contain as many categories as there are units of data, and the data would include only a single example of each category. Therefore, to be both manageable and useful as a means of observing patterns in the data, a taxonomy must be somewhat reductive. It must simplify or ignore the subtlest differences between units of data and, instead, stress similarities, thereby allowing the researcher to sort the data into a limited number of categories and to make generalizations about the data.

However, the more reductive the coding system, the greater the threat to its validity—to its faithfulness to the data. For example, a coding system in which data are divided into units and each unit is classified into a single category seems to assume that people do only one thing at a time—that each unit of data represents only one kind of activity. In fact, one can often find signs of several different activities in a single unit of data, and the coder must decide whether to acknowledge the polysemous quality of the data and design a coding system that reflects it (i.e., one that does not try to pigeonhole each unit of data), or whether to pick out just the dominant activity in each unit and ignore whatever else might be going on in it.

As I developed a coding system for the data in my oral reading protocol study, I had to resolve two such conflicting impulses. One was to focus on the differences between comments and to create a large, complicated category system. Following this impulse, I would let the categories proliferate, adding new ones and subdividing existing ones to reflect the subtler distinctions I noticed between comments. Problems with this liberal approach became apparent when I came across comments that seemed eligible for several categories. The other impulse was to focus less on the differences and more on the general similarities between comments. This impulse led me to combine categories and resulted in a smaller, simpler system, but one in which some comments placed in the same category seemed more different than alike. Of course, neither a large nor a small set of categories is intrinsically more correct or valid; they are just alternative ways of reading the data, each revealing different patterns of similarity at different levels of abstraction from the data. The researcher must decide at which plane of abstraction to float the coding system.

To keep the set of categories manageably small, yet still versatile enough to reflect what I thought were important distinctions between comments in the protocols, I developed a system similar to the subscripts and superscripts used by Perl (*Coding the Composing Process* 36–37) to modify the coding of each unit. In my system, each content statement required three coding decisions. The first was to decide the statement's illocutionary function (e.g., to infer, predict, evaluate). The second was to identify its subject—the material to which it referred (e.g., the text as a whole, the content of the passage just read, the tone of the writing). And the third coding decision was to determine the boundaries of the comment and mark them with parentheses. Below is a relatively clear example of a coded content statement as it appeared in the transcript of a protocol (the underlined passages indicate when the subject was reading from the text): "*It seems that at least half of the 100 finalists in the Bake-It-Easy Bake-Off* O.K., this is whimsical, and ironic—the tone *had brought something with them—their own sausages, their own pie pans, their own apples.*" The comment interrupting the reading passage was coded for its function (an inference) and its subject (the tone of the writing).

Not all comments were as easy to code as the example above, however. While it was usually easy to see a difference between interpretive and evaluative comments, expressions of understanding and criticism are not always mutually exclusive. In the following example, a reader finishes a sentence and offers a cryptic comment on it: "*It would make all our homes and streets safe from crime without ever wrongly convicting anyone or overcrowding our prisons.* It's the candy shop." In one sense, the "candy shop" remark interprets the sentence just read, drawing a conclusion about its meaning, and in fact I did code it as an inference about the passage it follows. Yet I also read it as an evaluative remark, one that implies that the text presents a childish, simplistic view of an ideal society.

For coding systems that assign each unit to a single category, the kind of ambiguity illustrated in the last example raises questions of validity (How well does the category reflect the purpose of the comment?) and reliability (Are such ambiguous comments coded consistently throughout the data?). These kinds of questions are among the most troubling for researchers trying to discover order and meaning in a mass of data. Furthermore, as I will argue in the remainder of this chapter, the concepts of validity and reliability, and the ways we apply them to interpretive coding systems, are themselves problematic.

Validity in Coding Systems

Stephen North, who has himself divided and classified the field of composition in interesting and provocative ways, has criticized the coding methods of the group of researchers he calls the clinicians, particularly the systems developed by Perl ("The Composing Processes") and by Janet Emig. North complains that both researchers appear to have derived their category systems from the data inferentially, with too little explanation and justification for either the kind or the number of categories in their systems and too little attention to the differences between one category and the next. Perl, he argues, offers no evidence for either the validity or the reliability of her system, and, like Emig, she is vague about the collective designation of her categories, calling them behaviors. North argues they would be more accurately defined as inferences about behaviors. The gist of North's complaints is that these coding systems appear too arbitrary, and they lack evidence of validity; however, he does not specify what such evidence might be, and his criticisms raise further questions about the whole notion of validity in coding systems.

What do we mean by validity? Describing systems of measuring writing performance, Janice Lauer and William Asher define the validity of such a system as "its ability to measure whatever it is intended to assess" (140). If we apply this definition to coding systems and define validity as the closeness of fit between the categories and the phenomena they describe, how can that close fit be demonstrated? Do we need some kind of external benchmark against which to measure the accuracy of a coding system objectively, and would such a benchmark be permanent or would it reflect the shifting values of the field? North seems suspicious of coding systems derived inductively from data, but would a system be any more valid if it deductively applied an existing set of categories used as descriptors of human behavior (e.g., modes of discourse, common topoi)? Surely the validity of any such category set is not intrinsic but depends on its relevance to the data to which it is being applied.

North suggests that a more valid alternative to Perl's system would have been one that reflected more of the subjects' individuality and the context in which they were working (224). Such a system would seem to be no less selective or inferential than Perl's (Which background details should be included, and how should they be interpreted?), but it would include and code more data. Whether the addition of more kinds of data make a category system more valid seems doubtful. We need to consider context, and we should discuss the patterns revealed by coding in light of whatever we know about the subject; however, the greater the range of data a category system is required to classify, the more liable the system is to break down. A category system designed to describe and interpret background information about a person, as well as their thoughts and actions on a particular task, would be huge and unwieldy, generating more drag than lift. North is right when he observes that individual clinical techniques are not expected to be particularly valid (220); but the point is, category systems *alone* cannot be fully valid in the sense that they objectively and accurately represent all relevant information about the data they describe and organize. To try to make them fully valid, autonomous instruments of analysis would be futile. Division and classification are part of the process of interpreting data, but the patterns that this kind of coding yields still need to be qualified and interpreted by the researcher. We cannot eliminate the human factor from coding.

Coding is interpretive, and no interpretation can be considered absolutely correct or valid. We can only measure the validity of interpretations relatively, comparing them with the assumptions and practices that define a particular discourse community; and this is what North appears to be attempting in *The Making of Knowledge in Composition*. However, in his critique of the clinicians he seems to treat validity as a kind of absolute standard, a determinable value that can be threatened and lost. I am not suggesting we should disregard questions of validity when we code data, but we should first consider what constitutes validity in a coding system, what levels of validity are possible, and how they might be demonstrated. I would argue that the validity of a coding system should be judged in the context of a particular data base and research purpose; and it should be demonstrated by elaborated definitions of categories and ample examples to illustrate them.

Testing Coding Systems for Reliability

Besides validity, the most important criterion by which coding systems are judged is reliability—the consistency with which the system can be used to code the data. This consistency is usually measured by an interrater reliability test. Swarts, Flower, and Hayes explain the need for such tests:

> It is necessary that reports of what is happening in a protocol
> be more reliable than any one person's reports; without some
> assurance of objectivity, it would be foolish to try to prove a
> proposition through use of protocol analysis. Thus, obtaining
> agreement among investigators is vital. One way to achieve agree-
> ment is to develop a coding scheme for judges to use and then to
> measure their degree of agreement to see whether the categories
> are viable. (68)

English studies involve many kinds of interpretation of data, yet
coding is the only kind for which researchers habitually report
formal reliability ratings and for which readers expect "some
assurance of objectivity." We do not hold literary critics to the
same standards of accountability, demanding, for instance, that
a Marxist or feminist reading of a text be supported by a reliability test.

One reason for this difference in standards is that literary
critics are expected (and encouraged) to read the same text differently. Literary texts are assumed to support many valid readings,
and new readings, if well argued and grounded in currently held
values, are celebrated and rewarded by the reader's peers. Another reason for the difference in standards is that, whereas
readers of literary criticism are usually already familiar with the
texts in question, readers of research reports seldom have access
to the data and are therefore unable to examine all the coding
decisions for themselves. Researchers usually provide only a few
examples of coded data, and readers are expected to trust the
consistency of all the other coding decisions. A reliability test is
designed to win that trust.

I would argue, though, that reliability tests are supposed to
establish not just the researcher's consistency in applying the
coding system, but also the objectivity and replicability—the
impersonality—of the coding, and therein lies a danger. It appears
that, to be credible, a coding system should be shown capable of
working to some extent mechanically and predictably, independent of its creator. If proven reliable, a coding system acquires

added authority, the implication being that it describes, rather than interprets, what is in the data. A high reliability rating thus suppresses the subjective, interpretive nature of coding and endows the system with the appearance of impartiality, making it seem a "truer," more "scientific" instrument of analysis. My point is, we should neither trust nor demand that coding systems be the equivalent of sterile laboratory measuring instruments.

What reliability tests really do when they yield high rates of agreement is show that the researchers have successfully created a small, specialized community of readers who have been "normed," or trained to interpret the data in the same way. This kind of reliability does at least demonstrate that the coding system was applied to the data consistently within that community. However, whether this interpretive consensus within the group assures the objectivity of the system is questionable. As the reliability ratings cited by Flower and Hayes suggest, readers outside the community of trained coders are not likely to achieve comparable agreement when they use the system. And researchers who use an off-the-shelf coding system like the one offered by Perl are likely to interpret its categories in different ways, especially if their data are substantially different from hers. Any claim for objectivity or replicability, then, would seem to require considerable qualification, because a coding system must operate on the assumptions of the community in which it was developed—a community formed both for and by the process of developing the system. The research report becomes an attempt to persuade a broader audience to accept the authority of that small community.

Conclusions

Data are generally thought to be the raw material being studied, and coding is the process of dividing and classifying the data. However, these definitions are deceptively simple because forms of coding actually begin well before the researcher starts sorting the data into categories; and some kinds of data, such as oral protocols, are never really raw in the sense of being entirely free of the researcher's influence.

Division and classification are reductive processes that over-simplify the data. Researchers sacrifice detail when they code in this way, but they do so in order to translate the data into more abstract forms, forms that can reveal patterns that would be lost in the mass and complexity of uncoded data. It is important also to recognize dividing and classifying as ways of reading, and therefore as interpretive processes. The coder negotiates meaning with the data, bringing to the material preconceived ideas, some of which are confirmed when applied to the data, while others must be abandoned or revised to fit the data. Coding systems, then, are never derived entirely from the data but originate in the researcher's prior knowledge and are selected and developed in the context of the data.

To see coding as a kind of reading or interpretation raises difficult questions about the possibility of establishing the validity and reliability of a coding system. The problem with validity is that we have no fixed, external standards by which to prove that certain categories are appropriate for certain data—that a coding system accurately reflects the phenomena it tries to identify. Relia-bility tests are usually conducted on coding systems, and if they result in high rates of agreement between coders they are used to argue that the system is both valid and reliable (i.e., that the same categories can easily be recognized in the same parts of the data by other readers). High reliability ratings do suggest that the coding system is workable and has been used consistently by the researchers, but the lack of standard procedures for measuring reliability makes it hard to compare coding systems in different studies.

Moreover, it is dangerous to assume that the validity of a coding system can be proven according to criteria independent of the context; and it is dangerous to believe that a high rating on a reliability test bestows a kind of blessing on the system, absolving it of all interpretive bias and implying that the system has achieved a state of objectivity. Coding systems are no more objective than any other ways of reading, so we should not expect them to be purged of subjectivity. Reliability tests try to establish the authority of a small community of coders, but rather than asking readers of the research report to place their faith in that authority on the basis of tests alone, researchers should argue the validity and reliability of a coding system by demonstrating it directly to their readers through numerous examples. Inevitably this means that if validity and reliability are to be taken seriously, research involving coding systems cannot be reported briefly. Appendices containing examples must be attached.

Nor should we expect coding systems to reveal all that is interesting or important about the data. They are useful for sorting large amounts of complicated data, but they have a limited ability to convey detail, ambiguity, and contextual information. Examples allow researchers to compensate for these limitations, to explain the patterns suggested by the coding system, and to demonstrate the complexity of the data when the categories are not sensitive enough to reflect it. Coding systems help us read data, but they do not interpret for us.

Works Cited

Cooper, Marilyn, and Michael Holzman. "Talking About Protocols." *College Composition and Communication* 34 (1983): 284–93.

Dobrin, David N. "Protocols Once More." *College English* 48 (1986): 713–26.

Emig, Janet. *The Composing Processes of Twelfth Graders*. Urbana, IL: NCTE, 1971.

Fagan, William T. *Comprehension Categories for Protocol Analysis*. ERIC, 1981. ED 236 664.

———. *The Syntactic Proposition for Protocol Analysis*. ERIC, 1978. ED 236 636.

Flower, Linda S., and John R. Hayes. "The Pregnant Pause: An Inquiry into the Nature of Planning." *Research in the Teaching of English* 15 (1981): 229–43.

Flower, Linda S., John R. Hayes, and Heidi Swarts. Revising Functional Documents: The Scenario Principle. Document Design Project Technical Report 10. Pittsburgh: Carnegie Mellon, 1980.

Grant-Davie, Keith A. "Between Fact and Opinion: Readers' Representations of Writers' Aims in Expository, Persuasive, and Ironic Discourse." *DAI* 46 (1985): 1613A. U of California, San Diego.

———. *Readers' Perceptions of Writers' Aims in Ironic Discourse.* ERIC, 1987. ED 283 154.

Hayes, John R., and Linda S. Flower. *A Cognitive Model of the Writing Process in Adults.* Final Report. ERIC, 1983. ED 240 608.

Lauer, Janice M., and J. William Asher. *Composition Research: Empirical Designs.* New York: Oxford, 1988.

Matsuhashi, Ann M. "Pausing and Planning: The Tempo of Written Discourse Production." *Research in the Teaching of English* 15 (1981): 113–34.

North, Stephen M. *The Making of Knowledge in Composition.* Upper Montclair, NJ: Boynton/Cook, 1987.

Perl, Sondra. *Coding the Composing Process: A Guide for Teachers and Researchers.* ERIC, 1984. ED 240 609.

———. "The Composing Processes of Unskilled College Writers." *Research in the Teaching of English* 13 (1978): 317–36.

Smagorinsky, Peter. "The Reliability and Validity of Protocol Analysis." *Written Communication* 6 (1989): 463–79.

Steinberg, Erwin R. "Protocols, Retrospective Reports, and the Stream of Consciousness." *College English* 48 (1986): 697–704.

Swarts, Heidi, Linda S. Flower, and John R. Hayes. "Designing Protocol Studies of the Writing Process: An Introduction." *New Directions in Composition Research.* Ed. Richard Beach and Lillian S. Bridwell. Perspectives in Writing Research 1. New York: Guilford, 1984. 53–71.

Collaborative Scholarship in Composition

Some Issues

Cultural and intellectual co-operation is the great principle of human life

—S. I. Hayakawa

ONE OF SEVERAL APPROPRIATE starting points for discussing some of the issues surrounding collaborative research is hypocrisy. John Trimbur has recently explained the hypocrisy—and the impossibility—of trying to deny collaborative intellectual effort ("Beyond Cognition"). Trimbur has presented a convincing argument that writers cannot claim sole ownership of ideas that they record on the page. Drawing on the work of Vygotsky in *Thought and Language* and the work of Bakhtin in *The Dialogic Imagination,* Trimbur argues that when any of us write we have others' voices running through our minds. We draw on these voices freely when we write—even though we may not have explicit awareness that we are doing so.

The two of us would argue that this notion is not limited to writing. Instead, we extend it to encompass all text-making activity—including what is usually referred to as research. Further, while some consider research as an activity separate from the writing of a research report, we maintain that such a distinction is artificial. That is, except for some narrow view of what constitutes research and what constitutes writing, the two activities are, themselves, dialogic: they interact; they are catalysts for one another.

Every text probably contains many "intertextual traces" (Reither and Vipond 861), defined by James Porter as "the bits and pieces of Text which writers or speakers borrow and sew together to create new discourse" (34). Clifford Geertz, alluding to a statement by Clyde Kluckhohn, claims that each scholar has an "intellectual poaching license" to appropriate these traces (21). Andrea Lunsford notes that her own composing includes "a lot of reading" (122). She elaborates: "I rarely take notes as I read, but my internal eye is watching for what I call the 'shape' of whatever I want to write" (122). The activities that Kluckhohn and Lunsford describe are both, we wish to note here, applications of collaborative research. The researchers whom we read collaborate with us as we build on their research.

Of course, Trimbur is melding at least two voices—those of Vygotsky and Bakhtin—when he makes his case. That is, he draws on Vygotsky's notion that everything that we humans do is social first and individual later—that "our mental lives . . . are extensions of social experience [directed] inward" (216). Bringing Bakhtin into the equation, Trimbur notes that there is a "polyphony of voices that resonate in the writer's mind" (219) while at work. He notes further that "writers negotiate [these] various languages they hear when they sit down to write" (220). Bakhtin himself referred to these languages or voices as "social heteroglossia" or the "Tower-of-Babel mixing of languages" (278). As the two of us write this paragraph, for example, our polyphony includes the words and thinking of Trimbur, Vygotsky, and Bakhtin, as well as some of our students and colleagues with whom we have discussed the work of Trimbur, Vygotsky, and Bakhtin.

Although Trimbur acknowledges Vygotsky's *Thought and Language,* he does not mention the Russian psychologist's work *Mind in Society.* It is in this later work that Vygotsky defines the now well-known concept of the *zone of proximal development:* "the distance between the actual developmental level as determined by independent problem solving and the level of potential development as determined through problem solving under adult guidance or in collaboration with more capable peers" (86). Vygotsky offered this concept to help argue that we learn more effectively when we work with other people. It is interesting to note that while Vygotsky does define the zone, he explains it fairly vaguely. As a result, readers of *Mind in Society* collaborate with Vygotsky to figure out that central theoretical concept. When readers get together (as the two of us did with twenty or so other people in a seminar taught by Luis Moll, a leading Vygotsky scholar) they are encouraged by the openness of Vygotsky's discussion to collaborate in constructing fuller conceptions of the zone of proximal development. That is, they are forced to work in the zone as they struggle to understand it and its applications to teaching and learning.

Now, based on what we see in Trimbur, in Vygotsky, in Bakhtin—and in the works of others that come to mind as we read Trimbur, Vygotsky, Bakhtin—we would argue that:

- Scholars do not work alone, even when they think they do, because they are always affected by the social heteroglossia.
- Scholars work better when they work, overtly, with others because doing so invokes a zone of proximal development.
- Collaborative work changes the nature of research and knowledge making.
- Despite its many benefits, collaborative scholarship can present considerable problems and risks.

In making these arguments, we are purposefully conflating several processes that are often separated: collaborative writing (indeed, all collaborative text making, including research) and collaborative thinking more generally. This separation may, in fact, account for the irony that many collaborative writing proponents continue to research and publish results alone, and that much collaborative research appears as single-authored publications.

We believe, and we hope that this chapter effectively demonstrates, that to speak of one without the other is to deny the value of both processes.

James Reither and Douglas Vipond explain that

> a primary benefit of . . . collaboration [coauthoring and workshopping] is that writers thereby establish and maintain immediate communities which function within the larger, "disciplinary" communities where their knowledge claims might find a fit. Developing claims cooperatively, collectively, collaboratively, the members of such a community-within-a-community learn from one another, teach one another; they support and sustain one another. (859)

But Reither and Vipond argue that collaboration must go beyond coauthoring and workshopping to include knowledge making—engaging in research and scholarship, if you will. Reither and Vipond note, as Bakhtin does (279), that whenever we make knowledge we "toss [our] thinking into a pool of knowledge" constructed by others before us (860). In this sense, again, we cannot avoid the collaborative construction of knowledge when we do research in composition—or any other field, for that matter.

In Bakhtin's vocabulary, *svoj* refers to one's own word, one's own world view; *cuzoj*, on the other hand, refers to the word or world view of another, the "alien word." According to Bakhtin, we are all *cuzoj* to one another, and it is this phenomenon that makes dialogue between two people or within one person—between an earlier and later self—possible (427). This leads to the dialogic imperative, which suggests that since the appearance of the second human on Earth, monologue has been impossible (Bakhtin 279).

Bakhtin's interesting observation notwithstanding, it is possible to avoid the kind of overt collaborative research that results in two or more names on the by-line. That is, it is possible to have a Flower without a Hayes, an Ede without a Lunsford, a Reither without a Vipond, an Odell without a Goswami, a Gilbert without a Gubar, a Sullivan without a Kirsch, or even a Roen without a Mittan. It happens all the time. We would argue, however, that when there is a Flower with a Hayes, an Ede with a Lunsford, a Reither with a Vipond, an Odell with a Goswami, and so on, the synergistic whole is greater than the sum of the parts. In Bakhtin's terms a John Hayes offers a Linda Flower a very real manifestation of *cuzoj,* another word, another world view, which can stimulate much productive dialogic thinking in the research that Flower and Hayes conduct. Perhaps one of the best examples of *cuzoj* in action is the explicit dialogue that occurs between Paulo Freire and Donaldo Macedo in "Rethinking Literacy: A Dialogue." These two educators discuss literacy in powerfully dialogic ways, and an obvious synergy of knowledge making is the productive result.

In composition terms, collaborators constitute various audiences throughout the research process. For instance, in the preresearch phase, collaborators may discuss topics or general areas they are interested in investigating. We have found—as many others have—that we can't clarify what we think until we hear ourselves say it to someone else. And very often, what others hear in our ideas takes those ideas further than we would on our own. During the research phase, members of collaborative teams offer another kind of audience, one that not only keeps the effort on track, but also helps avoid the biases and narrow or unclear thinking associated with individual work. Much research that uses ethnographic methods, for example, depends upon simultaneous observation from several perspectives—difficult, if not impossible, for individual researchers. Collaborative efforts allow for this broader view as well. Finally, at the reporting phase, collaborators can examine their research as members of their professions and discourse communities, a kind of internal peer review. They can ask, How does this work contribute to our knowledge? What new directions does it suggest for further research? Collectively, the presence of these various audiences shapes, extends, and develops collaborative research in ways less likely to occur in individual research.

In the case of collaborative research teams consisting of senior and junior scholars (for example, faculty members and graduate students),[1] the mentor's alien word (that is, the alternative world view) can serve multiple functions. First, of course, it can lead to the kind of dialogic thinking that Bakhtin has described. Second, it can help the junior member of the team more fully understand and more skillfully produce what Richard Rorty has called the "normal discourse" of a discipline such as composition. Normal discourse, an extension of Thomas Kuhn's concept of normal science, is "that which is conducted within an agreed-upon set of conventions about what counts as a relevant contribution, what counts as answering a question, what counts as having a good argument for that answer or a good criticism of it" (Rorty 320). We see this as akin to what Plato has Socrates do in the dialogues with Phaedrus and Gorgias.

The concrete presence of the two world views can also move both scholars toward abnormal discourse. Rorty identifies two kinds of abnormal discourse, undesirable and desirable. Although we agree that there is a distinction, we prefer to call the two forms "unconscious" and "conscious" because we believe that both can be productive and useful. Undesirable, or unconscious, abnormal discourse is "what happens when someone joins in the discourse who is ignorant of [the] conventions" (Rorty 320), or, as Gerald Graff puts it, when someone doesn't fully understand what constitutes a "good" argument or a "bad" argument in his or her specific scholarly discourse community ("Composition"). In composition studies, this type of abnormal discourse might develop, for example, from one member's unawareness of Maxine Hairston's application of Kuhn's model of revolutionary change to our field. An equally striking example comes from the early research on reading-writing connections. Some of that work—which we will not cite to protect the innocent or the naive—was done solely by composition scholars, some solely by reading scholars. For the most part, that research was amusing to read because the reading scholars were good at showing their expertise in reading and their ignorance or innocence or naivete in composition; the composition scholars were equally good at showing the inverse. Each time we read one of those pieces, we'd sigh, If only these reading scholars and composition scholars would collaborate with one another.

In contrast, Rorty labels as desirable abnormal discourse what occurs when scholars set aside the conventions to create an intellectual revolution. We prefer to call this "conscious" abnormal discourse. Peter Elbow's work, in both *Writing without Teachers* and *Writing with Power,* which presents theory and practice seamlessly blended for an extremely wide set of audiences, is only one of many good examples of this type. Without the concrete presence of the other—whether mentor or mentee—it's all too easy for scholars to forget that not everyone plays by the same rules, with the same deck of cards, for the same reasons.

The mentor need not necessarily be a senior scholar in composition, however. When Linda Flower works with one or more of the many graduate students in composition studies at Carnegie Mellon University, she is clearly the senior composition scholar on the team. However, when Linda Flower and John Hayes work together, Flower is the senior scholar in composition, but Hayes is the senior scholar in cognitive psychology. Flower and Hayes probably don't think of their collaborative work in these terms, though, because theirs is not what Lunsford and Ede call a "hierarchical mode" of collaboration, which is "linearly structured, driven by highly specific goals, and carried out by people who play clearly assigned roles" (235). Rather, theirs seems more like Lunsford and Ede's "dialogic mode" of collaboration, which is "loosely structured, and the roles enacted within it are fluid; one 'person' may occupy multiple and shifting roles as the project progresses" (235). Each possesses the alien word that confronts the other's thinking. And because the alien word of each comes from a different language in Bakhtin's sense of the word, the "interanimation of languages" (296) that occurs when Flower and Hayes collaborate—because they come from different fields—can lead to rich dialogic thinking. The whole (that is, cognitive approaches to composition) is much greater than the sum of parts (that is, composition and cognitive psychology).

The alien word that the junior scholar brings to such endeavors might be *practice* while the senior scholar contributes *theory*. On the surface, this may seem a drastic oversimplification. But it's been our experience that senior scholars, who are often researchers, are also often prevented from practicing what they research; junior scholars, some of whom are researchers-in-the-making, spend such long hours practicing that they have little time to research. Each collaborator can vicariously enjoy—and profit from—standing in the shoes of the other.

Then again, the junior scholar's most valuable contribution might be to say, Explain, please. To return, for a moment, to Vygotsky's notion of the zone of proximal development, what makes collaboration so successful is mutual need: The explainer (the "adult or more capable peer") depends upon the explainee to be a kind of goad to understanding and clarification; the explainee, on the other hand, needs the explainer's push-pull to move just slightly beyond the current level of independent problem solving. As James Wertsch points out, the flavor of the interrelationship between teaching and learning, expressed in Vygotsky's work by the Russian word *obuchenie*, unfortunately cannot be as easily expressed in English: although *instruction* is the favored translation, it often connotes a one-way, one-sided view. The cumbersome English phrase "teaching-learning process" works a little better, Wertsch notes, to capture the relation between learning and teaching, but it pales when compared with *obuchenie* (235, n. 4).

Of course, to be completely pragmatic, there are lots of other contributions that both collaborators can make. Since we've already argued that two heads are better than one, it's worth noting as well that many hands make light work. We know a trio of researchers who generated several conference papers and a book chapter by pooling their resources and energy. One researcher collected students' papers and prepared them for reading by replacing students' names with identification codes; the other two assigned holistic scores. Together, they tabulated, examined, and interpreted the results.

There are also less tangible benefits to collaborative work. As Anne Ruggles Gere has pointed out, the alternative to collaboration is alienation and social isolation (62–63). And Emile Durkheim argues that "when individual minds are not isolated but enter into close relation with and work upon each other, from their synthesis arises a new kind of psychic life" (*Sociology* 91).

We saw this happen a few years ago when we collaborated, along with nine graduate students, on a study of the writing-across-the-curriculum program at the University of Arizona. In addition to producing some fifteen hundred pages of data about the upper-division writing emphasis courses then being offered on campus, as well as a five-hundred-page manuscript, including several coauthored chapters, this collaborative effort established a special sense of community among the participants that continues today. Indeed, some members of that research team credit the project for drawing them into the graduate program now called Rhetoric, Composition, and the Teaching of English, and into composition studies as a profession. As a result of that collaborative project, many participants began to believe that to research, to write, to think alone is to deny not only oneself but also the profession as a whole the new kind of psychic life of which Durkheim speaks.

So far, we've painted a fairly rosy portrait of collaborative work. For the most part, our experiences with collaboration have been successful and productive. But collaborative efforts, like every other type of human relationship, are fraught with potential disaster. Yes, there are times when two "alien words" lead not to dialogue, but to misunderstanding and acrimony.

Collaboration is also vulnerable to conflicts in personality type and work habits. Donald Stewart wisely cautions against assuming that collaborative learning is universally applicable to all students. The same is true for collaborative work among scholars. As Stewart points out, through reference to the work of Isabel Briggs Myers, certain personality types will almost invariably have difficulty working with each other. Some may be opposed to the notion of collaboration at all. Author William Manchester, Stewart notes, "expressed his complete distaste for committee and collaborative efforts which he found time-consuming, time-wasting, and completely frustrating" (78). Such differences may also manifest themselves in time management techniques: eleventh-hour candle burners and radical time budgeters often don't get along. Nor do messy and neat data keepers. Should we enter all the values into tidy columns on ledger paper, or just write them on the backs of photocopied journal articles? Such decisions, although they seem trivial, can easily make or break collaborative work. The best advice we can offer here is that collaborators need to select their partners carefully; get to know someone well before working together on research.

Nor is collaborative scholarship immune from such social and political concerns as gender and status differences. Lunsford and Ede have pointed out the "phallologocentric nature of the academy" in which "power, authority, authenticity, and property" are located in "an autonomous, masculine self" (234). And all of us at one time or another have experienced the kind of collaboration in which one member becomes the authority and others merely instruments of it. The fine distinction between true symbiosis and helotism easily blurs in collaborative relationships, something that must be constantly—and overtly—guarded against. Lunsford and Ede point out many reasons to prefer dialogic collaborations to hierarchical ones. Geoffrey Cross has also recently reported on the disasters that can result from hierarchical work. The problem with such arrangements is that they don't involve minds in the dialogic thinking, the negotiating that can engage minds to mutually grapple with the problems at hand. There tends to be too little real communication in such working arrangements, and they make it too easy for people to push responsibilities aside.

Although these internal difficulties have no doubt ruined a fair number of potentially profitable collaborations, two larger and essentially external factors have prevented many scholars from even attempting collaborative work. The first of these concerns the possibility for methodological or ideological differences among collaborators, especially across disciplines. In earlier chapters in this collection, particularly those in part I, single authors describe many of the differences that distinguish methodologies from one another in composition research. Probably the most obvious difference is terminology, a difference that has recently gained attention through interest in and work on discourse communities. Cheryl Geisler and Susan C. Jarratt, in their observations about the first meeting of the Research Network at the 1988 CCCC in St. Louis, point to the lack of a "common specialized language" as the single greatest barrier separating those composition scholars in attendance. Lacking such an argot, they report, participants "spoke more as nonspecialist to specialist" (290).

But instead of viewing this as a problem, we see it, from a Bakhtinian-Vygotskian perspective, as advantageous. As we've already argued, there is value in such discussions: specialists can learn a lot from explaining themselves to nonspecialists. And while each methodology has its own language in the Bakhtinian sense, "these 'languages' of heteroglossia intersect with each other in a variety of ways forming new socially typifying 'languages' " (Bakhtin 291). As a result, "languages do not exclude each other, but rather intersect with each other in many different ways" (291). Further,

all languages of heteroglossia, whatever the principle underlying them and making each unique, are specific points of view on the world, forms for conceptualizing the world in words, specific world views, each characterized by its own objects, meanings, and values. As such they all may be juxtaposed to one another, mutually supplement one another, contradict one another and be interrelated dialogically. (291–92)

In research in composition, as in any research, explicit collaboration, in which two or more scholars share in the thinking, the writing, the making of knowledge in composition, promotes this kind of dialogic interrelating. This is especially true, and especially productive, when it occurs, as Helene Moglen and Gary Waller suggest, in interdisciplinary ways, following Peter Berger and Thomas Luckmann's observation that "the object of thought becomes progressively clearer with [the] accumulation of different perspectives on it" (10). This accumulation, of course, occurs *across* conference papers and publications in composition, but not very frequently *within* them. Ann Berthoff has suggested that this kind of accumulation can occur within conference presentations if we abandon the common lecture method in favor of more open discussions of ideas, which may follow a very short lecture. She also would include lots of "ink shedding," developed by Russ Hunt and Jim Reither, an activity that has become—in part because of the collaborative insistence of Susan Wyche-Smith and Connie Hale—an integral part of the annual Wyoming Conference on English (Foreword xxi–xxii).[2]

For interdisciplinary research to work, though, we must cast aside what Stanley Fish calls "ideologically frozen divisions of intellectual labor" (16). We must also, as Stephen North warns, eliminate our "squabbling and dissension in Composition . . . [that] arises out of cross-methodological misunderstanding." We must, instead, work toward a "spirit of methodological egalitarianism" (371), which is by no means an easy task. Too often, scholars who do one kind of research (historical, rhetorical, ethnographic, literary, experimental) think, with their minds closed as tightly as a vault at Fort Knox, that other kinds of research have little, if any value. As a result, far too many scholars are unwilling to even read other kinds of research. What we all need to realize is that any given research methodology can answer question X but not question Y. To answer both questions, and perhaps a few others, which differ in kind, an open-minded historian may need to collaborate with an equally open-minded practitioner, an ethnographer with an experimentalist, a literary theorist with a cognitive psychologist. One notable example comes to mind immediately here. That is, in some respects, reader-response theorists such as Stanley Fish, Louise Rosenblatt, David Bleich, and Wolfgang Iser do work that is similar to the work of schema theorists such as Richard Anderson and John Bransford. Unfortunately, in our reading at least, scholars from each group never even acknowledge the work of scholars from the other group.

According to Geisler and Jarratt, this was not a problem for the participants at that first Research Network gathering of composition scholars in St. Louis. Indeed, as they report, "much of the morning talk was given over to expressions of good will and pluralism that initially obscured rather than furthered [the] dialogue" (289). Even if it's not easy—and there will be times when it's not—the potential benefits warrant the effort. Without it, we are doomed to decades of fruitless fighting over territory, similar to the long-raging territorial disputes between literary critics and historical scholars—a dispute that Graff has described so thoroughly.

The second, and by far the profoundest, external deterrent to collaborative scholarship in composition is the way it is viewed, valued, and practiced in the profession as a whole. Unfortunately and ironically, scholars in composition, while often declaiming the virtues of collaborative work, have a history of producing single-authored research and scholarship on the topic (see, for example, Bruffee; Gere; Heath; Karis; LeFevre; Trimbur).[3] And as further evidence that composition scholars in general do not engage in collaborative work as much as members of our profession seem to value it, we point to the 1989 issues of nine of the prominent journals in our field. Excluding reviews, commentaries, and responses, we came up with the following numbers. The highest ratio of collaboratively produced articles (80 percent, or 4 out of a total of 5 articles published in 1989) appeared in *Writing Program Administrator*. Exactly half (12 out of 24) of the articles published by *Written Communication* were collaborative pieces, while *Journal of Basic Writing* (27 percent, 3 out of 11), *Research in the Teaching of English* (25 percent, 4 out of 16), and *College Composition and Communication* (24 percent, 4 out of 17) each devoted approximately one-fourth of their issues to collaborative work. *Rhetoric Review* (12 percent, 2 out of 17), *Journal of Advanced Composition* (7 percent, 1 out of 14), and *College English* (6 percent, 2 out of 31) published substantially fewer collaborative articles, and none of the 10 articles appearing in *Journal of Teaching Writing* during 1989 was collaboratively produced. Overall, of the 145 articles published in these nine journals, only 32, or 22 percent, carried more than one name on the by-line.

Thus, an obvious question: If we value collaborative work, then why don't we produce it? One possible answer: We do, but it's not good enough to warrant publication. Although we don't have access to the data, we suspect that the journals we surveyed publish an equivalent percentage of the collaborative submissions they receive as the single-author submissions. In fact, Theresa Enos, editor of *Rhetoric Review,* has told us that she rarely receives coauthored manuscripts. And she adds that the journal's referees usually give favorable reviews to coauthored work. We think that the problem is not that there isn't very much *good* collaborative work going on in composition, but that there isn't very much collaborative work going on, period. It may be that composition scholars have been trained in classrooms in which too few teachers ever model effective collaboration or ever made collaborative activities explicit—teaching strategies that Mary Ann Janda considers important (313).

Let's also consider some other possible explanations for this situation. Perhaps we have fallen prey to what Lunsford and Ede have called the "phallologocentric nature of the academy" (234). Or it might simply be the capitalistic nature of the academy, in which the written word, as Ede and Lunsford suggest, is considered private property of the author (72–102). Still another possible explanation is that, with an excrutiatingly accurate works cited list and, in many cases, a lengthy acknowledgments note thanking individuals and groups for their contributions, researcher-writers feel they have soothed the sting of irony in their single-author by-line. The problem with such practices, as Lunsford and Ede note, is that they render "the importance of collaboration . . . marginalized by appearing in prefaces or acknowledgements, rather than in the bodies of texts" (240)—especially in by-lines. What we need, they seem to suggest, is a new or revised conception of authorship, one that more realistically captures the polyphony of voices that occurs in any text.

Probably the most credible explanation for the relative paucity of collaborative scholarship is that most composition scholars work in departments of English, populated for the most part by literature scholars. While most literary scholars have a theoretical grasp of Bakhtin's contributions to notions of collaboration, few of them have practical experience with collaborative scholarship. Most of them have never overtly coauthored anything, and most of them, like most other members of departments in the humanities, don't value coauthored scholarship as much as they value single-authored work. Ede and Lunsford provide lots of evidence of this phenomenon when they discuss Ede's tenure case (see Ede; Lunsford; Ede and Lunsford) and other similar scenarios. In one case, a well-known English department withdrew its undergraduate poetry prize when the anonymously written winning poem turned out to have three coauthors (237).

But the situation is beginning to change, however slowly. For example, a promotion and tenure document that comes close to valuing collaboration *fully* was recently drafted by Louise

Wetherbee Phelps and the other Writing Program faculty at Syracuse University. It states:

> Research projects in composition and rhetoric are frequently collaborative ones among teams of scholars from this and related fields. The Writing Program puts jointly conducted research and collaborative writing on a par with individually conducted and authored research. Candidates for tenure and promotion should be prepared to explain and demonstrate their specific contributions to co-authored work. (Phelps et al. 6)

Although this statement goes farther than most in valuing collaborative research, including interdisciplinary work, its last sentence implies that some people still do not view collaboration as a synergistic process in which individual contributions are difficult and sometimes impossible to factor out. This document is a milestone; unfortunately, we still too often face the prospect that promotion and tenure committees, as well as salary committees, hiring committees—even our own colleagues in composition— may not value our collaborative efforts as much as others' single-authored work because, as the American Association of University Professors (AAUP) has recently noted, "Faculty members and administrators making decisions about appointments, promotion and tenure, and salary increases must try to evaluate individual worth and reckon with the significance of authorship" (41). Indeed, when Duane recently extolled the virtues of collaboration at the 1990 Wyoming Conference on English, one of the first questions from the audience—from a scholar who usually does single-authored historical work—was, "Collaborative work may get a scholar promoted, but will it get a new Ph.D. hired?"[4]

Regardless of the extent to which our guild values collaboration, admittedly we are still subject to the political and economic realities of life in academic departments, particularly those in the humanities—especially English departments. Many of us would like to work together as Lisa Ede and Andrea Lunsford, Linda

Flower and John Hayes, or Susan Gilbert and Sandra Gubar do. Each of these twosomes represents a happy, productive, ideally collaborative team. We have pointed out some of those political and economic realities not to discourage others from taking part in collaborative work but rather to encourage it, in hopes that we can begin to change those realities into histories.

Finally, we also suspect, based both on our own experiences and some little observation of our students' forays into it, that collaborative work is unpopular in part because it is frightening, unfamiliar, dangerous even. (The second definition of *collaborate* in *The American Heritage Dictionary* reads: "To cooperate treasonably, as with an enemy occupying one's country" [Morris 260–61].) It's not the way we've all grown up playing the game. Indeed, when we two went to school, *collaboration* was (and, sadly, in many cases still is) a five-syllable word for *cheating*, implying that it's easier than doing the work yourself. We now know that it's not cheating. And collaborative work is, most times, both more challenging and more rewarding than working alone.

So, to help those who wish to enter the frightening, unfamiliar, even dangerous world of collaborative scholarship, we offer the following five suggestions. Call it, if you will, a minihandbook for coconspirators.

1. *Make collaboration a normal part of your work.* It will probably feel strange at first—like the first time you composed at a typewriter or a word processor instead of with pencil and paper. But as most of us have discovered, what once seemed abnormal can quickly become not just normal, but *a necessity.* Yes, there will be times when you'll think, "I'd rather do it myself," just as there are times when it's more expedient to reach for a pen and note pad. But there will also be times when you'll think, "Boy, this is a lot easier than when I worked alone."

For most of us, this means creating opportunities to work collaboratively since they are—unfortunately—as yet unlikely to appear on their own. So start small. For example, we've done textbook reviews collaboratively: the publishers were happy to split the fee, especially since they knew they were getting twice the expertise, and we got the job done in half the time.

2. *Don't be afraid to approach others about collaborating.* This is especially true if you're a graduate student. Perhaps the best way to get involved in collaborative efforts is simply to talk to others, tell them what you're doing, ask them what they're up to. We've heard stories—no doubt apocryphal—about graduate students who discover, after long hours of library research, that a scholar who has published extensively on their topic works just down the hall, in the same department. We know of a graduate student in literature who traveled to a conference devoted to a particular literary figure. After presenting a paper, the student was approached by a sage-looking scholar who remarked, "So, you must know ———. " The student acknowledged that, indeed, he was a faculty member in her department but that she didn't really know him. The scholar remarked how odd it was that the student should not have discussed her paper with such a preeminent authority on the topic who works in her own department. Now, in the world we envision, where collaboration is a normal part of everyone's work, that graduate student would write a note and tuck it in the faculty member's mailbox. And that note might read, "I've been doing some work on ——— and I understand that you also have done some work on it. Could we get together to talk?"

This advice applies equally to faculty members, too. Students, other faculty—especially those in other disciplines, elementary and secondary school teachers: It's all too easy to overlook this wealth of potential collaborators by forgetting to talk with them about your research. And theirs. Pause for a moment and make a list of your closest colleagues; then list the research topics each is currently working on. Don't be too surprised if your list has lots of empty space in it. We recently discovered that each of us has been reading on the same topic for several months. And we consider ourselves avid collaborators.

New technology also makes it feasible to collaborate long distance. By now, most of us have discovered that computer floppy disks allow discussions, conversations, and data to be sent through the mail—or handed back and forth—quite inexpensively. (For more on how this contributes to collaborative thought, see the final section of this chapter.) Users of computer networks, such as BITNET, can even save the cost of floppies and postage. But perhaps the most valuable contribution of such networks is their ability to keep members of a discourse community in touch, much more rapidly and intimately than the usual forums of journals and national conferences. Such networks, which have become absolute necessities among scientists, are still relatively underused by members of our scholarly community. (*Rhetoric Review* has recently begun publishing a BITNET Directory in Rhetoric and Composition, an important contribution to our developing community.)

Whether it's a phone call, a hastily scribbled note, a chance word over coffee, or a transcontinental computer message, collaboration begins when someone reaches out to someone else.

3. *Leave ego out of it.* We've already argued that no one really works alone, no matter whose name goes on the product. Still, we humans have a natural proclivity to label work as though it's a personal possession. Perhaps it's just a linguistic quirk. Then again, maybe there's more to it.

In collaboration, we've found it's absolutely vital to avoid assigning anything to any one individual: there's no such thing as "my hypothesis" or "my results" or "my sentence." But it's not as easy as merely changing the pronouns from singular to plural, although that is important. In addition, every collaborator must genuinely *believe* that everything generated—whether theories, questions to be tested, or words on a page—is collective. Those of us who are avid collaborators wince each time we read or hear about the new rhetoric of Chaim Perelman, for we know that Lucia Olbrechts-Tyteca was there, too, kicking around ideas, asking questions, struggling over the words.

The stakes can be high when egos get in the way. For example, Ede and Lunsford offer the following tragic story:

> A Kinsey Institute sex survey that could help researchers understand how AIDS spreads was delayed for almost a decade because two of its authors fought over whose name should appear first on the title page. . . . Publication was scheduled in 1980, when an intense dispute broke out about whose name should appear on the title page. . . . The survey languished for years, unavailable to most researchers, until [an Institute director] persuaded the authors to settle their differences. (1, quoted from "What Revolution?")

4. *Choose your collaborators carefully.* The experiences of some scholars whom we know suggest that there are some unscrupulous collaborators in the world—indeed, in our own profession. Some of them, we believe, suffer from "Hagar the Horrible syndrome." In one of Dik Browne's recent strips, Hagar says to his two cronies at the bar, "Teamwork is fine—but in the heat of battle, you have to look out for *number one!*" In the next panel he adds, "Incidentally—*I'm* number one." We are familiar with cases in which some members of so-called collaborative teams steal the work of other members of the team. In the worst cases, one person will, without the knowledge or consent of his or her research team, publish individually the fruits of the research and scholarship. In such cases, the unwritten agreement was that all members of the team would have their names on the by-line. To avoid this sort of outrageous exploitation, would-be collaborators should know their teammates well, and they should ask about others' experiences with these people. It is unfortunate that we even need to mention such abuses, but they do exist.

5. *Learn from the example of other successful collaborative teams.* Maximally successful collaborators are those who strive for the kind of working relationship that Susan Gilbert and Sandra Gubar described during a question-and-answer session at the 1990 Wyoming Conference on English. They say that collabora-

tion comes so naturally to them that "describing it would be like describing how we walk." While they used to each write separate sections of their coauthored works, they now almost always draft material together, debating content and style as they proceed.

In their dialogues they manifest the features that Paulo Freire argues are essential for true acts of creation. That is, they exhibit *love* for the world and for other humans; they possess the *humility* necessary to recognize their own ignorance; they have *faith* in each other to make and remake, to create and recreate" (79); they have *hope;* and they engage in *critical thinking* (77–82). (Also see Berthoff, "Reading" 114–26.)

Throughout this chapter we have offered both theoretical and practical perspectives on the nature of collaborative work in composition. But to be truly honest, neither we nor anyone else can fully describe or explain either the activity of collaborative research or its benefits. That would be like describing marriage rather than a particular marriage. We make this confession for two reasons. First, scholars need to experience collaborative research firsthand, for it's different each time it occurs. What any of us see from the outside may not be what we see—or feel— from within the collaboration. Second, because composition scholars are really only beginning to engage in collaborative research, no one yet knows a whole lot about it.

We will close by noting that in our own experience, the dynamics of individual research differ considerably from those of collaborative research. When the two of us sit down together or with other collaborators, we generate many more ideas for orchestrating research than we do alone. When we sit down together to consider relevant theory or to collect, score, analyze, or interpret data, we experience something akin to an adrenalin rush—a burst of energy that makes the sometimes drudgery of research easier to get through. When we sit down to write about what we've discovered in our research, we try out potential wording of sentences and paragraphs on each other and then negotiate compromises that we hope represent more lucid prose. In general, when we sit down together to work, we fuel each other's thoughts and energies. As a result, the task—even though it may take more time—seems less tedious and a whole lot more fun. Even more important is the fact that we finish collaborative projects more often than we finish individual ones; the jobs get done. These feelings, we have discovered, are similar to those of many of our colleagues who have experienced collaborative research. They are also similar to those that we have when we work together on almost any task in which we have engaged: moving furniture, harvesting crops, or building houses.

Notes

We feel compelled to offer thanks to all sorts of people for helping us with this chapter. First, we wish to thank Gesa Kirsch and Patricia Sullivan for their encouragement and their many helpful suggestions for revision. Second, we must acknowledge the assistance of all the people—both living and dead—whom we list in the references. Third, we owe much to Jim Corder, who helped us each—on completely separate occasions—to see that academic papers and personal essays are more alike than we know. Fourth, all our fellow students and fellow teachers, especially Luis Moll and the participants in his seminar, have helped us construct—and reconstruct—our understanding of Vygotsky's zone of proximal development. Finally, we thank all of the colleagues who have collaborated with us on books and articles: Gene L. Piche, Mike Graves, Wayne Slater, Ann Duin, Donna Johnson, Maureen Roen (on Duane's two children, their journals, and a literary map), Patricia Hazeltine, Deborah Grunloh, Stuart Brown, Margaret Fleming, R.J. Willey, Kate Mangelsdorf, Vicki Taylor, Zita Ingham, Mike Rogers, Gesa Kirsch, Diane Clymer, Jan Swearingen, Gerri McNenny, Marvin Diogenes, David Furniss, and Clyde Moneyhun. While we can't include our vitas in an appendix to this article, we will gladly send copies to anyone who wants to know more about how much we should be grateful to our collaborators.

To be safe, we will follow the lead of Maureen Stapleton, who said, upon receiving an Academy Award for her performance in *Reds*, "I'd like to thank everyone I've ever met in my whole life." To do anything less is to run the risk of missing some very important collaborators.

1. We considered several ways to label such teams before settling on these terms. We do not wish to imply that one member is necessarily the "senior" member either in years or in the value of the contribution. Instead, we see such collaborative efforts as *peer* interaction: In Lunsford and Ede's terms, they are in the dialogic rather than the hierarchical mode (235). At the same time, we do wish to draw attention to the value of the members' differential expertise, from a Bakhtinian-Vygotskian perspective.

2. James Reither is the editor of the newsletter *Inkshed*.

3. We wish to note that Duane, thinking it cutely ironic, wrote an earlier paper to appear in this collection. After all, a single-authored chapter—at least on the by-line—on collaborative research could constitute a joke. Duane discovered, though, when he sat down to revise the earlier paper that a feeling of hypocrisy pervaded his thinking. In the end, irony gave way to a sense of hypocrisy—especially after Duane reread Emile Durkheim's observation that "most of our ideas and our tendencies are not developed by ourselves but come to us from without" (*Rules* 4).

4. While Duane was busily, hypocritically drafting the first version of this paper alone, Bob, on the other side of town, was contemplating his own enigma: how to remain an effective, committed classroom composition teacher while completing a Ph.D. in rhetoric, composition, and the teaching of English, *plus* doing all the research necessary for the dissertation. And then, too, there was the irony of the written doctoral exams, the administration of which denies most if not all recent research on when, where, how, and why people engage in text-making activities. Like Duane, Bob discovered, when he sat down to compose his polemic "Why I Can't Join Your Fraternity; or, The Rent's Too High in Your Discourse Community," that irony soon becomes hypocrisy.

As a result of our individual experiences, and a couple of chance phone calls, the two of us, who have collaborated on other projects and who share a theoretical and practical interest in collaboration, decided to work together on this chapter.

Works Cited

American Association of University Professors. "Statement on Multiple Authorship." *Academe* 76.5 (1990): 41.

Bakhtin, Mikhail. "Discourse in the Novel." 1975. *The Dialogic Imagi-

nation. Trans. and ed. Michael Holquist. Austin: U of Texas P, 1981. 259–422.

Berger, Peter L., and Thomas Luckmann. *The Social Construction of Reality: A Treatise on the Sociology of Knowledge.* New York: Anchor, 1967.

Berthoff, Ann E. Foreword. *Literacy: Reading the Word and the World.* By Paulo Freire and Donaldo Macedo. South Hadley, MA: Bergin, 1987. xi–xxiii.

———. " 'Reading the World . . . Reading the Word': Paulo Freire's Pedagogy of Knowing." *The Sense of Learning.* Portsmouth, NH: Boynton/Cook, 1990. 114–26.

Browne, Dik. "Hagar the Horrible." Cartoon. *Tucson Citizen* 17 July 1990: 4B.

Bruffee, Kenneth A. "Collaborative Learning and the 'Conversation of Mankind.' " *College English* 46 (1984): 635–52.

———. "Social Construction, Language, and the Authority of Knowledge: A Bibliographic Essay." *College English* 48 (1986): 773–90.

———. "Writing and Reading as Collaborative or Social Acts." *The Writer's Mind: Writing as a Mode of Thinking.* Ed. Janice N. Hays, Phyllis A. Roth, Jon R. Ramsey, and Robert D. Foulke. Urbana: NCTE, 1983. 159–69.

Cross, Geoffrey A. "A Bakhtinian Exploration of Factors Affecting the Collaborative Writing of an Executive Letter of an Annual Report." *Research in the Teaching of English* 24 (1990): 173–203.

Durkheim, Emile. *The Rules of Sociological Method.* Trans. Sarah A. Solovay and John H. Mueller. Ed. George E. G. Catlin. 8th ed. New York: Free Press, 1964.

———. *Sociology and Philosophy.* Trans. D. F. Pocock. London: Cohen, 1953.

Ede, Lisa. "Studies in Collaborative Writing." Southern Arizona Writing Project. Tucson, 15 June 1989.

Ede, Lisa, and Andrea Lunsford. *Singular Texts/Plural Authors: Perspectives on Collaborative Writing.* Carbondale: Southern Illinois UP, 1990.

Elbow, Peter. *Writing Without Teachers.* New York: Oxford UP, 1973.

———. *Writing With Power.* New York: Oxford UP, 1981.

Fish, Stanley. "Being Interdisciplinary Is So Very Hard To Do." *Profession* (1989): 15–22.

Freire, Paulo. *Pedagogy of the Oppressed*. Trans. Myra Bergman Ramos. New York: Seabury, 1970.

Freire, Paulo, and Donaldo Macedo. "Rethinking Literacy: Dialogue." *Literacy: Reading the Word and the World*. South Hadley, MA: Bergin, 1987. 47–62.

Geertz, Clifford. *Local Knowledge: Further Essays in Interpretive Anthropology*. New York: Basic, 1983.

Geisler, Cheryl, and Susan C. Jarratt. "The Research Network 1988: Impressions from the Floor." In "What Are We Doing as a Research Community?" *Rhetoric Review* 7 (1989): 289–93.

Gere, Anne Ruggles. *Writing Groups: History, Theory, and Implications*. Carbondale: Southern Illinois UP, 1987.

Gilbert, Susan, and Sandra Gubar. "The Further Adventures of Snow White: Feminism, Modernism, and the Family Plot." Wyoming Conference on English. Laramie, 28 June 1990.

Graff, Gerald. "Composition and Controversiality." Wyoming Conference on English. Laramie, 26 June 1990.

———. *Professing Literature: An Institutional History*. Chicago: U of Chicago P, 1987.

Hairston, Maxine. "The Winds of Change: Thomas Kuhn and the Revolution in the Teaching of Writing." *College Composition and Communication* 33 (1982): 76–88.

Hayakawa, S. I. *Language in Thought and Action*. In consultation with Basil H. Pillard. New York: Harcourt, Brace, 1940.

Heath, Shirley Brice. *Ways with Words: Language, Life, and Work in Communities and Classrooms*. New York: Cambridge UP, 1983.

Janda, Mary Ann. "Collaboration in a Traditional Classroom." *Written Communication* 7 (1990): 291–315.

Karis, Bill. (1989). "Conflict in Collaboration: A Burkean Perspective." *Rhetoric Review* 8 (1989): 113–26.

Kuhn, Thomas S. *The Essential Tension: Selected Studies in Scientific Tradition and Change*. Chicago: U of Chicago P, 1977.

———. *The Structure of Scientific Revolutions*. 2nd ed. Chicago: U of Chicago P, 1970.

LeFevre, Karen Burke. *Invention as a Social Act*. Carbondale: Southern Illinois UP, 1987.

Lunsford, Andrea. Panel discussion. Wyoming Conference on English. Laramie, 26 June 1986.

Lunsford, Andrea A., and Lisa Ede. "Rhetoric in a New Key: Women and Collaboration." *Rhetoric Review* 8 (1990): 234–41.

Moglen, Helene. "Crossing the Boundaries: Interdisciplinary Education at the Graduate Level." *The Future of Doctoral Studies in English.* Ed. Andrea Lunsford, Helene Moglen, and James F. Slevin. New York: MLA, 1989. 84–90.

Morris, William, ed. *The American Heritage Dictionary of the English Language.* Boston: Houghton, 1980.

Myers, Isabel Briggs, with Peter B. Meyers. *Gifts Differing.* Palo Alto: Consulting Psychologist's P, 1980.

North, Stephen M. *The Making of Knowledge in Composition.* Upper Montclair, NJ: Boynton/Cook, 1987.

Perelman, Chaim, and Lucia Olbrechts-Tyteca. *The New Rhetoric: A Treatise on Argumentation.* 1958. Trans. John Wilkinson and Purcell Weaver. Notre Dame, IN: U of Notre Dame P, 1969.

Phelps, Louise Wetherbee, Patricia L. Stock, Catherine F. Smith, Margaret Himley, Carol Lipson, and James Zebroski. "Writing Program Promotion and Tenure Guidelines." Unpublished document, 14 Dec. 1989.

Plato. *Gorgias.* Trans W. C. Hembold. Indianapolis: Library of Liberal Arts, 1952.

———. *Phaedrus.* Trans W. C. Hembold and W. G. Rabinowitz. Indianapolis: Library of Liberal Arts, 1956.

Porter, James E. "Intertextuality and the Discourse Community." *Rhetoric Review* 5 (1986): 34–47.

Reither, James A., and Douglas Vipond. "Writing as Collaboration." *College English* 51 (1989): 855–67.

Rorty, Richard. *Philosophy and the Mirror of Nature.* Princeton, NJ: Princeton UP, 1979.

Stewart, Donald C. "Collaborative Learning: Boon or Bane?" *Rhetoric Review* 7 (1988): 58–83.

Trimbur, John. "Beyond Cognition: The Voices of Inner Speech." *Rhetoric Review* 5 (1987): 211–21.

———. "Collaborative Learning and Teaching Writing." *Perspectives on Research and Scholarship in Composition.* Ed. Ben W. McClelland and Timothy R. Donovan. New York: MLA, 1985. 87–109.

Vygotsky, Lev S. *Mind in Society.* Ed. Michael Cole, Vera John Steiner,

Sylvia Scribner, and Ellen Souberman. Cambridge, MA: Harvard UP, 1978.

———. *Thought and Language*. 1934. Trans. Eugenia Hanfmann and Gertrude Vakar. Cambridge, MA: MIT P, 1962.

Waller, Gary. "Polylogue: Reading, Writing, and the Structure of Doctoral Study." *The Future of Doctoral Studies in English*. Ed. Andrea Lunsford, Helene Moglen, and James F. Slevin. New York: MLA, 1989. 111–20.

Wertsch, James V. *Vygotsky and the Social Formation of Mind*. Cambridge, MA: Harvard UP, 1985.

"What Revolution?" *Corvallis Gazette-Times* 27 June 1981: 1.

14   Lisa Ede

Methods, Methodologies, and the Politics of Knowledge

Reflections and Speculations

THINK OF THIS CHAPTER as a counterpoint to those you have already read. For rather than reflecting upon a specific kind of research or a specific approach to research, I will be considering a number of broader issues and questions. What, for instance, is at stake in discussions of method and methodology? How should we conceive of—and enact—the relationship between theory and practice, between our multidisciplinary discipline's two related goals: the production of knowledge and the advancement of literacy? Similarly, how should we view the relationship between our experience (and the narratives we construct to make sense of this experience) and the work we produce?

These are difficult questions. My goal in this chapter is not to answer these questions but to emphasize their heuristic importance. As is perhaps appropriate for the final chapter in a collection such as this, I hope to challenge, provoke, complicate: hence the word speculations in my subtitle. The other term in my subtitle, reflections, highlights another characteristic of this chapter. For reasons that I hope will become clearer as I proceed, I will emphasize, rather than ignore, the ways in which the points I wish to make grow out of my own experience.

I am aware that some readers may question the insertion of my experience into this discussion. By embedding my argument in my own experience am I naively assuming that experience is somehow outside language, outside ideology? Am I attempting, in effect, to reintroduce the humanist subject, the coherent, stable self that since the Enlightenment has been the authority for knowledge? Postmodern challenges to the subject and skepticism about the possibility of knowledge and of truth necessarily problematize the nature and significance of experience. They also, as Jane Flax notes in *Thinking Fragments: Psychoanalysis, Feminism, and Postmodernism in the Contemporary West,* raise other crucial questions for those whose work involves the production of scholarly texts: "How is it possible to write? What meanings can writing have when every proposition and theory seems questionable, one's own identity is uncertain, and the status of the intellectual is conceived alternately as hopelessly enmeshed in oppressive knowledge/power relations or utterly irrelevant to the workings of the technical-rational bureaucratic state?" (5). And yet how can one *not* write?

I have written this chapter in the only way that seems possible at this moment. My research, like my life, is situated, contingent. My research, like my life, constitutes an enactment of my current commitments and beliefs. This chapter, then, represents an acting out of my current (inevitably limited and partial) reflections on methods, methodologies, and the politics of knowledge. It also represents both an engagement with and a response to the work of other scholars—particularly Stephen North and Louise Wetherbee Phelps—whose thoughts have stimulated my own. In the future, rereading this chapter, rereading my life, I will inevitably see things differently.

Fifteen years ago, for instance, the issues that now seem so pressing did not exist for me. If someone had written me then asking me to "reflect on the issues, questions, and problems associated with the research methods [I] typically employ," as Gesa Kirsch and Pat Sullivan did some months ago, I would not have known how to respond. As an undergraduate English major in the mid-1960s, and then as a graduate student in the early 1970s, I was part of what I now realize (thanks to the efforts of

Gerald Graff and others) was one of the few generations of students of English studies who could, if they were so inclined, remain innocent of theoretical and methodological issues. For though by the late sixties new criticism was already beginning to be challenged, "organic unity or bust" (Graff 232) was still the motto in many English departments.

My undergraduate training focused entirely on the explication of texts. I didn't question why this was so, just as I never consciously articulated the interpretive conventions that Graff in *Professing Literature* describes as having "the ritualized character of a competitive sport" (232). Although I took a course in literary criticism, I don't recall ever discussing either how to do literary criticism or what might be at stake in literary critical endeavors. Rather, the reigning assumption seemed to be, as Graff again observes, that *"literature teaches itself"* (9–10), and thus that the best way to become adept at literary criticism was to do it. So I did.

Although as a graduate student specializing in Victorian literature I was aware of faint rumblings of theoretical ferment, my absorption in my dissertation and my growing interest in the teaching of writing encouraged me to keep my distance. By the time it was becoming clear that graduate students in English ignored discussions of theory and methodology only at their peril, I had already decided (spurred on by genuine interest and a disastrous job market) to redirect my energies toward composition studies.

Thus at a time when my peers were studying reader response and feminist criticism, deconstruction, and semiotics, I was reading basic texts in composition and rhetoric—struggling to learn my new field even as I directed an undergraduate writing program at a state college in upstate New York. Furthermore, in the mid-seventies I simply wasn't very interested in critical theory. As a self-defined composition specialist, I more or less consciously rejected critical theory as irrelevant—perhaps even hostile—to my concerns. This rejection did not include, however, an analysis of research methods or assumptions. As I attempted to understand, and then to participate in, ongoing conversations in composition studies, I continued to hold the assumptions and apply the methods I learned as a student of literature.

When I first began doing research in composition, then, the only methodological issue I recognized as potentially relevant to my research involved the distinction between quantitative and traditional humanistic research. My training had prepared me to do, and to value, the latter. I was willing to recognize that others might reasonably wish to undertake quantitative research and to accept its results—particularly when they confirmed my own biases. If pressed, I might have noted that quantitative research didn't seem to engage important issues and questions in ways that struck me as compelling or helpful. But I lacked a vocabulary and approach that would enable me to address the theoretical and methodological issues that my unexamined reservations could have generated.

Like many at that time, I pragmatically drew upon whatever research seemed helpful, no matter what the discipline. In my struggle to make sense of the research that I was reading, to find strategies that worked in my classroom, I never stopped to consider whether there might be problems in jumbling together insights developed in competing methodological contexts. I was happily and naively eclectic in theory and practice, never questioning whether the relationship between theory and practice might itself warrant scrutiny or just what made my "new" discipline of composition studies a discipline.

I was hardly alone in these assumptions and practices. In *The Making of Knowledge in Composition: Portrait of An Emerging Field*, Stephen North describes his own "excitement, the enthusiasm of the new recruit, that blinded [him] . . . to any problems in [his] . . . new object of loyalty" (preface, n. pag.), composition studies. North describes how the exigencies of his situation as an advisor to and initiator of graduate students led to "a kind of crisis point," one which caused him to fear that "the field didn't have a core or a center" (preface, n. pag.). The fruit of this crisis was, of course, North's influential study, which, while granting that individuals can "belong to— . . . be fluent knowledge-makers in—more than one [methodological] community" (2), nevertheless categorizes scholarly efforts in terms of eight different "modes of inquiry" (6).

Throughout his analysis, North demonstrates a concern with methodological integrity that calls to mind Mary Daly's caustic references to "methodolatry" (11). In his discussion of "The Philosophers," for instance, North is shocked that the discourse of those he calls the philosophers "often seem[s] more zealous than reasonable, fervent than curious, converted than, in the best sense of the word, disinterested" (92). Philosophers' "scholarly reformism," North worries, "risk[s] the demise of methodological integrity" (115). Finally, the picture that North paints of composition studies is deeply pessimistic. Those in the field have been engaged in a ruthless "methodological land rush: a scramble to stake out territory" (317). Furthermore, North claims that "composition as a knowledge-making society is gradually pulling itself apart" (364). Thus, North apocalyptically concludes his study by predicting "that either (a) Composition as we know it will essentially disappear, reverting to something much like its pre-1963 form; or that (b) it might survive, but probably only by breaking its institutional ties with literary studies and, hence, English departments" (373).

The Making of Knowledge in Composition represents North's attempt to come to terms with a situation that he and many other "member[s] of the first generation of English teaching professionals whose primary allegiance is to the teaching of writing" (preface, n. pag.), including myself, shared. North's study also highlights what's at stake in discussions of methods and methodologies: the politics of knowledge itself. In his concern for methodological integrity, his insistence that to be a valid discipline composition studies must have "a core or a center" (preface, n. pag.), North both draws on and reflects almost twenty-five centuries of anxiety in the West about method and methodology and their relation to epistemology.

It is interesting, for example, to read North's work in the context of Plato's *Gorgias* and *Phaedrus*. North's chagrin at the failure of those he calls "The Philosophers" to remain "disinterested" (92) and his charge that researchers and scholars in composition studies have been involved in "a methodological land rush" (317) are reminiscent of Socrates' assertion in the *Gorgias* that oratory requires not wisdom but practitioners with "a shrewd and bold spirit together with a natural aptitude for dealing with men" (44). And just as Plato finds rhetoric to be "a knack and not an art because it has no rational account to give of the nature of the various things which it offers" (*Gorgias* 46), so too does North—who shares Plato's love of "methods of division and collection as instruments which enable me to speak and to think" (*Phaedrus* 82)—find composition studies to have "an accumulated knowledge of a relatively impressive size, but one that lacks any clear coherence or methodological integrity" (preface, n. pag.). North's analysis is thus essentially conservative; he neither challenges nor deconstructs the assumptions and categories undergirding his discussion.

Do alternatives to North's pessimistic vision of composition studies exist? My reading of the rhetorical tradition leads me to believe that they do. North is discouraged that his review of research in composition reveals participants to be engaged in "an inter-methodological struggle for power" (321). Except during periods when it has been reduced to stylistic display, rhetoric has generally understood that as a human activity language is, in Kenneth Burke's terms, "intrinsically hortatory" (20). Burke argues, in fact, that when language is viewed as symbolic action, as he believes it should be, "the necessarily *suasive* nature of even the most unemotional scientific nomenclatures" (45) becomes clear. A rhetorical or, in Burke's terms, "dramatistic" (44) approach to the methodological and epistemological issues raised in *The Making of Knowledge in Composition* would take for granted, rather than be alarmed by, the fact that when researchers and scholars argue in support of or opposition to a particular thesis they are also implicitly arguing for the preeminence of their own "terministic screens" (45).

Connected with North's discussion of "inter-methodological struggle[s] for power" (321) in composition studies is another issue, that of the appropriate relationship not only between theory and practice but between theoreticians and practitioners. North's position is that practice constitutes "a distinguishable mode of inquiry" (22), one that ought to be valued equally with such other modes as historical, experimental, and ethnographic research. Practitioners thus ideally should be on a par with scholars and researchers. However, North argues, practitioners are viewed as needing either conversion or remediation.

North is right to challenge the conventional relationship between theory and practice and between theoreticians and practitioners in our field. But his argument for the authority of practitioner knowledge, which he terms "lore" (23), proves ironically limiting. Consider North's description of lore, which he defines as having three characteristics: (1) "literally anything can become a part of lore" (24); (2) "while anything can become a part of lore, nothing can ever be dropped from it, either" (24); (3) "because lore is fundamentally pragmatic, contributions to it have to be framed in practical terms, as knowledge about what to do; if they aren't, they will be changed" (25). This depiction of lore works against North's own argument that lore should be valued equally with the results of research and scholarship. For if anything can become part of lore and nothing can ever be dropped from it, how can lore constitute inquiry? Confronting this problem, North is forced to admit that most of what practitioners do must be viewed as craft, not inquiry. North estimates, for instance, that "for a full-load classroom teacher at the college level, handling something in the range of 120 students in three meetings per week, practice qualifies as inquiry less than ten percent of the time" (34).

North cites other factors, such as impatience with "complicated causal analyses" (40) and "practical inertia" (43), that make it difficult for practitioners to contribute to inquiry on the teaching of writing. And when practitioners do attempt to engage in inquiry, they are often unsuccessful in communicating the results of their effort with their colleagues: "Partly because of the medium, and partly because of pressure from institutions and other communities, when Practitioners report on their inquiry in writing, they tend to misrepresent both its nature and authority, moving farther and farther from their pragmatic and experiential power base. And the harder they try, it seems to me, the worse things get" (54).

I applaud North for his defense of practitioner knowledge and for his foregrounding of the conflict between theory and practice in composition studies, and I am grateful to him for so clearly and provocatively articulating these issues. My lengthy response indicates, I hope, my respect for his study and the challenges it poses to those in our field. Nevertheless, North's argument in favor of practitioner lore does not adequately resolve the methodological and theoretical issues he poses. More helpful, in my view, is Louise Phelps's discussion in "Toward a Human Science Disciplined by Practical Wisdom," the final essay in *Composition As a Human Science: Contributions to the Self-Understanding of a Discipline*. Here Phelps addresses many of the issues North raises. At the start of her essay she urges, for instance, that it is time to "candidly expose and assess the conflictual relation between theory and practice in composition" (206). Phelps notes that theorists have tended to share certain assumptions about the relationship of theory and practice: "(1) there is inherently a relationship between formal theory and practice; (2) this relationship is well defined and fixed, that is, 'good' theory would inform or govern practice in exactly the same (rule-governed) way in any concrete situation; and (3) within such a relationship, theory is automatically the privileged term" (207). Like North, Phelps emphasizes the disadvantaged position of practitioners in this situation. Since according to Phelps most theorists take the above assumptions so completely for granted that they are not subject to argument, practitioners can do little other than simply resist or deny the value of theory—a response that places them in the same position as students who resist teachers. In fact, Phelps notes, drawing on Freire, "between the teacher and Theory exist the same possibilities for oppression or freedom that Freire discovers in the teacher-student relation" (213).

Like teachers applying the banking model of education, theorists have failed, Phelps argues, to recognize that the relationship between theory and practice, theorists and practitioners, must itself be dialogic. The practitioner must be "not the object of Theory, but a Subject who mediates between the systematic knowledge-creation of disciplinary communities and the reflection of learners" (214). Phelps goes so far as to suggest, following Gadamer, that "theory, at least theory as defined by the natural sciences, cannot govern daily teaching practices, but that conceivably it might work the other way around" (205).

Central to her argument is Phelps' assertion that conventional assumptions and practices fail adequately to recognize that composition studies involves more than the production of knowledge. Rather it is, in Phelps's terms, an "engaged and committed activity" (56)—one that requires the exercise of *phronesis,* or practical wisdom. Unlike North, who presents practitioner inquiry as one of eight possible modes of inquiry, Phelps elevates practice so that theory and practice are not only equal but equally essential: "Theory and praxis mutually discipline each other" (238). What determines their relationship then? Teachers' and students' rhetorical situations: "Each specific case of practice raises anew the question of what theory, if any, is relevant, and how in particular it applies, and with what changes, caveats, and consequences" (207–8). Phelps's comments emphasize the radical situatedness of research in composition studies; they also encourage a view of knowledge not as a search for truth but as practice.

"Theory is autobiography" (vii), Phelps comments in the preface to *Composition as a Human Science*. "Theory is a way to make sense out of life" (vii). When I look back at my own life as a scholar, I recognize that my awareness of the need to confront theoretical and methodological issues, to rethink the relationship between theory and practice in composition studies, has developed haltingly, gropingly. Rereading some of my early essays, I am struck by how theoretical and methodological issues are obscured or downplayed, rather than directly addressed. My 1984 review of research on audience, for example, asserts that quantitative and theoretical studies contribute equally to a sophisticated understanding of the nature and role of audience in written discourse. But the essay itself subtly privileges theoretical research, undermining my assertion that theoretical and quantitative research are equally valuable. The objective tone and pluralistic stance of this essay now seems an evasion, an accommodation, an unwillingness to confront hard questions and to recognize that I was not and could not be a neutral evaluator of the studies that I reviewed.

How is it that discussions of theory and methodology now seem of crucial importance to me? I could construct two narratives to describe what has led me to my present concern with these issues. One narrative would emphasize the intertextual: it would focus on my reading in composition studies, rhetoric, philosophy, critical theory, and feminism and the ways in which works in these areas taught me the importance of the issues with which I am now engaged. The other narrative would be experiential: it would focus on the ways in which my involvement with these issues grows out of personal interests and motives.

Both narratives seem true to me, though each tells a different story. The form and method of this essay, with its discussion of the work of Stephen North and other scholars, demonstrates how important intertextual conversations with others have been for me. (And to the extent that this essay depends on a reading or interpretation of these theorists, it of course represents a traditional humanistic approach to my subject.) Other conversations have, however, played a crucial role in catalyzing my current involvement with theory and methodology.

Andrea Lunsford's and my research on collaborative writing, for instance, not only grew directly out of our experience as friends and coauthors but was motivated, situated—not disinterested. As we note in *Singular Texts/Plural Authors: Perspectives on Collaborative Writing,* we began our study hoping to persuade those in our field that writing is not inherently and necessarily a solitary act. Originally, we assumed that surveys of and interviews with members of seven professional associations would provide the data necessary to convince our colleagues. We soon realized, however, that resistance to collaborative writing stems from more than ignorance of contemporary collaborative writing practices; rather, it reflects deeply held assumptions about truth, knowledge, and subjectivity—assumptions we needed to address in order to persuade our readers.

Our study of the concept of authorship taught me concretely how much is at stake in discussions of theoretical and methodological issues. I am also aware of another influence: the desire more strongly to connect my research and teaching with the feminism that was an important part of my experience in graduate school and that has remained a central force in my personal (though not always my professional) life. Reading the work of feminists such as Linda Alcoff, Sandra Harding, and Jane Flax— reading to see how I might more directly situate myself in my research and professional life as a feminist—I experience in a different way the importance of discussions of theory and methodology.

Jane Flax, for instance, calls for a theory and methodology that allows for resistance to oppressive social systems and for a concept of subjectivity that recognizes the possibility of individual agency. There must be an alternative, Flax believes, to the current apparently limited options of commitment to the "Enlightenment story" (30) or the endless deconstruction and relativism characteristic of postmodernism. Flax's alternative—one she represents as transitional, exploratory—is to resist closure. Thus in her study, she notes: "I will not attempt to resolve conflicts within or between the theories discussed here [psychoanalysis, feminism, and postmodernism], nor will the conversations among them result in any new, grand synthesis. Instead of a conclusion I will raise further questions about this conversational mode of writing and the adequacy of all its voices, including my own" (4). This approach requires, Flax observes, that scholars be "self-reflective about . . . [their] methods and the limitations of knowing" (42). It also requires readers to tolerate considerable ambiguity, for the resulting discussion has—as Flax insists via the title of her last chapter—"No Conclusions," or at least no traditional conclusions.

I read Flax's book six months after Andrea Lunsford's and my study of collaborative writing was published. Yet our answer to Flax's question, "How is it possible to write?" (5), mentioned at the start of this essay, though responding to different concerns and drawing upon different justifications, is similar. Like Flax we recognized that we needed to draw upon theoretical and methodological differences as a means of complicating or problematizing our subject:

> Any attempt neatly to resolve the paradoxes and ambiguities that multiplied as our research progressed would radically oversimplify the phenomenon we were studying. Rather than attempting to dissolve or minimize these paradoxes and ambiguities, we have endeavored to heighten them in an effort to set into play a mutual interrogation of research methods and of the discourses through which this book has been constituted (130–31).

Drawing upon Burke, we chose to look at collaborative writing "from the vantage point of shifting terministic screens, striving to achieve a series of perspectives by incongruity" (131). Like Flax, we also attempted to resist the temptation to "speak as a disembodied, impersonal truth teller or critic" (Flax 43). Instinctively unwilling to erase the connection between our personal lives and our study of collaborative writing, we found theoretical support for this resistance in the work of feminists.

Finally, in *Singular Texts/Plural Authors* Andrea and I address more directly than I have in the past the difficult but essential question of the relationship between theory and practice—an issue that Flax discusses when she insists that feminists must develop theories that allow for an "agentic subjectivity" (220) and political action, but that she does not explicitly connect to pedagogy. As we note in our discussion on the pedagogy of collaboration, "When we began our research on collaborative writing, we envisioned developing detailed, specific guidelines for teachers—guidelines that would address such issues as the characteristics of effective collaborative writing assignments and the most efficient ways to organize and evaluate group efforts" (121–22). We resisted what was for us a strong impulse toward such pedagogical closure. This decision developed in part as a result of "our growing appreciation of the complexity of our rhetorical situation as teachers and our awareness of the profound ways that explorations of collaborative writing challenge not only many traditional classroom practices in English studies but our entire curriculum" (123).

Andrea's and my study does *not* represent, I wish to emphasize, the culmination of a narrative charting my progress from theoretical and methodological ignorance to experience. (As a coauthored work, *Singular Texts/Plural Authors* also emphasizes that "my" is never really *my*, even when writing alone.) Many issues and questions that motivated me to write both this essay and Andrea's and my study remain unresolved. I find myself wondering, for instance, what my current preoccupation with theory and method (inevitably) prevents me from seeing, from understanding. I also have been unable to resolve my ambivalence about the dangers—and benefits—of theoretical and methodological pluralism. Although increasingly I feel, as does Patricia Bizzell, that scholars in composition studies must be "forthright in avowing the ideologies that motivate our teaching and research" (Bizzell 672), my urge to argue against certain theoretical and methodological approaches is moderated by Flax's reminder that different "conceptions of a practice may capture an aspect of a very complex and contradictory set of social relations" (179).

At this particular time and place I see "No Conclusions" (Flax 222) to the major theoretical and methodological issues that face scholars and researchers in composition studies—and I am not troubled by this situation. In *Thinking Fragments,* Flax observes that rather than attempting a "neat integration, new synthesis" she instead wishes to offer "a possible approach to the practice of postmodern philosophy, one that is self-reflective about its methods and the limitations of knowing and of reason as the basis for knowledge and about knowledge as a source of power" (42). I cannot claim to have accomplished similar purposes in this essay. I hope that I have persuaded you, however, that those in composition studies might fruitfully set similar goals.

Though I do not wish to argue for conclusions or solutions, I do hold a number of what I might best describe as provisional intellectual commitments. With Louise Phelps, I believe it is important for those of us in composition studies to remember that we are taking part not simply in the production of knowledge but in an "engaged and committed activity" (Phelps 56), the teaching of writing. We also need to establish a nonoppressive, dialogical relationship between theory and practice, theoreticians and practitioners—a relationship that enables, rather than hinders, political action and that encourages self-reflection and critique. Additionally, in order to study and teach literacy we must, as Andrea Lunsford observes in "The Nature of Composition Study," resist the temptation "to focus centripedally on a static center or to hedge round a sure or certain 'nature' of our field." Instead, we more fruitfully might envision composition studies as an "intellectual space" (Lunsford) within which to study certain questions—and to engage in public and private action.

Finally, as I teach and read and write and talk with others, I increasingly find myself looking for ways to connect, rather than to separate, what I experience as my "personal" self with my scholarly and pedagogical work. In so doing, I do not envision myself as expressing some unitary or essentialist self; postmodernists are right to critique this limited concept of the subject. We need, as Flax argues, to construct "concepts of self that do justice to the full complexity of subjectivity and the spaces in which it is likely to find itself" (219), just as we need to construct—and enact—conceptions of literacy that are both theoretically sophisticated and politically empowered and empowering.

Works Cited

Alcoff, Linda. "Cultural Feminism Versus Post-Structuralism: The Identity Crisis in Feminist Theory." *Signs* 13 (1988): 405–36.

Bizzell, Patricia. "Beyond Anti-Foundationalism to Rhetorical Authority: Problems Defining 'Cultural Literacy.'" *College English* 52 (1990): 661–75.

Burke, Kenneth. *Language as Symbolic Action: Essays on Life, Literature, and Method.* Berkeley: U of California P, 1966.

Daly, Mary. *Beyond God the Father: Toward a Philosophy of Women's Liberation.* Boston: Beacon, 1973.

Ede, Lisa. "Audience: An Introduction to Research." *College Composition and Communication* 35 (1984): 140–54.

Flax, Jane. *Thinking Fragments: Psychoanalysis, Feminism, and Postmodernism in the Contemporary West.* Berkeley: U of California P, 1990.

Graff, Gerald. *Professing Literature: An Institutional History.* Chicago: U of Chicago P, 1987.

Harding, Sandra. "The Method Question." *Hypatia* 2 (1987): 19–33.

Lunsford, Andrea A. "The Nature of Composition Study." *An Introduction to Composition Studies.* Ed. Erika Lindemann and Gary Tate. New York: Oxford UP, 1991.

Lunsford, Andrea A., and Lisa Ede. *Singular Texts/Plural Authors: Perspectives on Collaborative Writing.* Carbondale, Il.: Southern Illinois UP, 1990.

North, Stephen. *The Making of Knowledge in Composition: Portrait of An Emerging Field.* Portsmouth, NH: Boynton/Cook, 1987.

Phelps, Louise Wetherbee. *Composition as a Human Science: Contributions to the Self-Understanding of a Discipline.* New York: Oxford UP, 1988.

Plato. *Gorgias.* Trans. Walter Hamilton. New York: Penguin, 1960.

———. *Phaedrus and Letters VII and VIII.* Trans. Walter Hamilton. New York: Penguin, 1973.

Tompkins, Jane. "Me and My Shadow." *New Literary History* 19 (1987): 169–78.

Notes on Contributors
Index

Notes on Contributors

RICHARD BEACH is professor of English education at the University of Minnesota. He is coeditor of *New Directions in Composition Research* (Guilford) and *Developing Discourse Practices in Adolescence and Adulthood* (Ablex) and coauthor of *Teaching Literature in the Secondary School* (Harcourt, Brace, Jovanovich) and *Literature and the Reader* (NCTE). He has published research on composition and literary response. He is chair of the board of trustees of the NCTE Research Foundations (1990–91) and president of the National Conference of Research in English (1991–92).

ROBERT J. CONNORS is associate professor of English at the University of New Hampshire. He is author of a number of articles on rhetorical history and theory, published in *College English, College Composition and Communication, Rhetoric Review, Rhetoric Society Quarterly,* and other journals. With Lisa Ede and Andrea Lunsford, he coedited *Essays on Classical Rhetoric and Modern Discourse* (winner of the MLA Mina P. Shaughnessy Award). He coauthored *The St. Martin's Handbook* with Andrea Lunsford and *The St. Martin's Guide to Teaching* with Cheryl Glenn and edited the *Selected Essays of Edward P. J. Corbett*. In 1982 he was given the Richard Braddock Award by the CCCC for the article "The Rise and Fall of Modern Discourse." His current projects include research on genre in student writing, a study of student spelling patterns, and a long essay on the feminization of rhetoric.

LISA EDE is associate professor of English and director of the Center for Writing and Learning at Oregon State University. Her publications include *Essays on Classical Rhetoric and Modern Discourse,* with Robert Connors and Andrea A. Lunsford (winner of the MLA Mina P. Shaughnessy award), *Work in Progress: A Guide to Writing and Revising*, and *Singular Texts/ Plural Authors: Perspectives on Collaborative Writing*, with Andrea A. Lunsford.

KEITH GRANT-DAVIE is assistant professor of English at Utah State University where he teaches advanced composition, technical writing, and reading theory. His work has appeared in *Reader: Essays in Reader-Oriented Theory, Criticism, and Pedagogy, Literary Research Newsletter*, and the *Maryland English Journal*. Currently, he is working on a book that explores interdisciplinary perspectives on reading and their relevance in the writing classroom, tentatively titled *Reading Theory for Writing Teachers*.

THOMAS N. HUCKIN directs the University of Utah writing program and is an associate professor in the Department of English. He teaches courses in discourse analysis, stylistics, and technical and professional writing. He has written many articles on these topics and has recently coauthored, with Leslie Olsen, a new textbook, *Technical Writing and Professional Communication* (McGraw-Hill, 1991).

GESA KIRSCH is assistant professor of English at Wayne State University. Her research interests include theories of audience, gender and discourse, social contexts for writing, and epistemological issues in research methodologies. She is coeditor of *A Sense of Audience in Written Communication* (with Duane Roen) and has published articles in *Research in the Teaching of English, Journal of Basic Writing, Reader*, and *WPA: Writing Program Administration*. Currently, she is writing a book on gender and academic writing.

SUSAN MILLER is the author of *Writing: Process and Product, The Written World: Reading and Writing in the Social Contexts, Rescuing the Subject: A Critical Introduction to Rhetoric and the Writer, Textual Carnivals: The Politics of Composition*, and numerous historical and theoretical articles about composition, rhetoric, and academic culture. She teaches composition theory, writing, and cultural studies at the University of Utah, where she is professor of English and a faculty member in the university writing program and in educational studies (adjunct). In 1990–91, she was University Bennion Public Service Professor.

ROBERT K. MITTAN is coordinator for outreach for Academic Learning Support Services at the University of Arizona where he completed his M.A. in ESL. He has taught a variety of writing courses and workshops to both native and nonnative English speakers. His publications include work on peer interaction in writing classrooms and a textbook, coauthored with Duane Roen and Stuart Brown, for writing-intensive courses across the curriculum (*Becoming Expert: Writing and Learning in the Disciplines*). Currently, he is studying writing classrooms as discourse communities.

PETER L. MORTENSEN is assistant professor of English at the University of Kentucky. He has published a number of essays and chapters on authority in written discourse; his work has appeared in *Reader* and *A Sense of Audience in Written Communication*. He is currently studying representations of literacy in nineteenth- and twentieth-century writing about southern Appalachia.

BEVERLY J. MOSS is assistant professor of English at Ohio State University where she teaches courses in writing, rhetoric, and composition studies. Her research interests include literacy in community settings, particularly literacy in the black church, and the nature of ethnographic and qualitative research. Currently, she is editing a book on literacy in nonacademic settings.

THOMAS NEWKIRK is a professor of English at the University of New Hampshire where he has directed the freshman English program and the New Hampshire Writing Program, a summer institute for teachers. His work has appeared in *College English, College Composition and Communication, Research in the Teaching of English,* and other journals. His most recent book is

More than Stories: The Range of Children's Writing (Heinemann), and he is currently completing a book on children's discussions of literature.

RUTH RAY is assistant professor of English and director of composition at Wayne State University in Detroit. Her areas of interest, besides the teacher-research movement, include studies of diversity in writing (she has written about basic writers, bicultural students, and women writers); computers and composition; and the ethics of teaching. She is currently writing a book entitled *Teacher Research: The Practice of Theory* in which she argues that teacher research can significantly change our concepts of knowledge in the field of composition and teachers' roles in making that knowledge.

DUANE H. ROEN, associate professor of English, directs the graduate program in rhetoric, composition, and the teaching of English at the University of Arizona. He also serves as the coordinator of graduate studies in the department of English. He teaches courses in composition theory, research, and practice; writing across the curriculum; and discourse analysis. His research interests include audience awareness, composing processes, writing across the curriculum, collaborative writing, and gender differences in writing. In addition to numerous articles and conference papers, he has coauthored (with Robert Mittan and Stuart Brown) *Becoming Expert: Writing and Learning in the Disciplines.* He has coedited (with Donna Johnson) *Richness in Writing: Empowering ESL Students* and (with Gesa Kirsch) *A Sense of Audience in Written Communication.*

KAREN A. SCHRIVER is assistant professor of rhetoric and document design at Carnegie Mellon University. She has published in *College Composition and Communication, Rhetoric Review, Technical Communication,* and *IEEE Transactions in Professional Communication.* She is interested in the cognitive and cultural dimensions of writing and document design. She has been studying various aspects of planning and revising visual and verbal text. She is currently working on a large study in which she is interviewing professors in rhetoric, composition, and literature about their representations of the role of theory in English studies.

PATRICIA A. SULLIVAN is assistant professor of English and associate director of composition at the University of New Hampshire. She has published articles and chapters on composition theory and pedagogy in *Research in Basic Writing, Reader, National Women's Studies Association Journal,* and *Journal of Advanced Composition.* She is currently engaged in a study of the psychopolitical contexts of academic discourse, focusing on issues of authorship and authority in the writing of minority students, women students, graduate students, and junior faculty.

Index